TRAILS
OF THE
IRON HORSE

TRAILS OF THE IRON HORSE

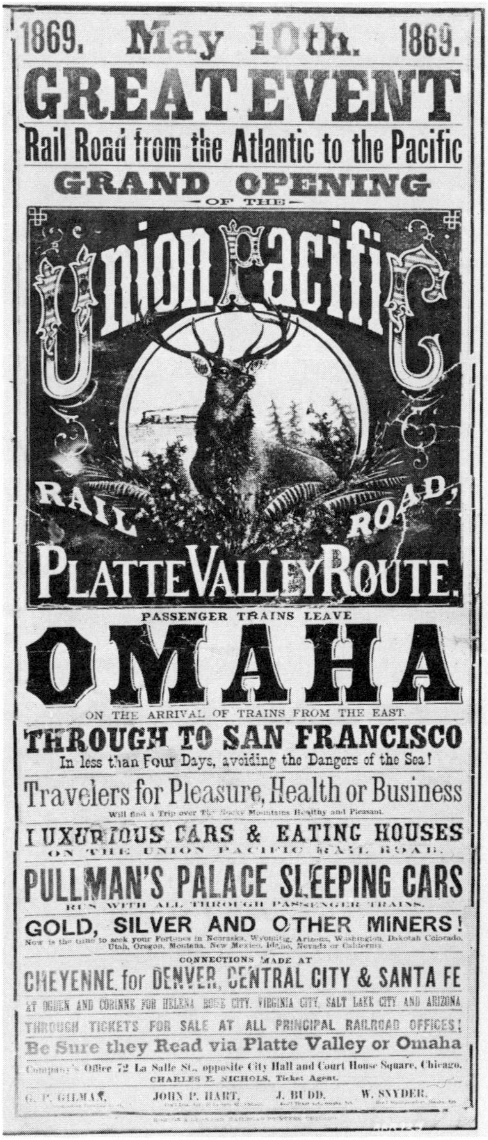

An Informal History by The Western Writers of America

EDITED BY DON RUSSELL

Doubleday & Company, Inc.   Garden City, New York   1975

Library of Congress Cataloging in Publication Data

Western Writers of America.
Trails of the iron horse.

Includes index.
1. Railroads—The West—History. 2. The West—History. I. Russell, Don, 1899– ed.
II. Title.
HE2763.W47 1975 385'.0978
ISBN 0-385-02123-2
Library of Congress Catalog Card Number 74–18887

Printed in the United States of America
9 8 7 6 5 4 3 2

Acknowledgment

Western Writers of America is an organization of professional writers whose aims are to promote their common interests, encourage the writing of quality Westerns, and bring them more effectively to the attention of the reading public.

One part of WWA's program has been the publication of collections of the best short stories and novelettes by its members; there have been thirty WWA anthologies published in the United States since 1953. Many of these have also appeared in British editions and have been translated into Spanish, Portuguese, Norwegian, German, and other foreign languages. These all consisted of fiction, most of it previously published in magazines, some expressly written for a particular anthology, contributed by members of WWA and selected by member editors.

Trails of the Iron Horse is *not* an anthology. It is a group project of original writing, each of the chapters researched and especially written for this book by a qualified member to whom it was assigned. It does not pretend to be a history, but rather an informal, factual portrayal in text and pictures, of how the railroads contributed to the development of the American West. It represents nearly five years of unique fraternal effort.

As an organization, Western Writers of America owes thanks to many of its members as well as non-members who generously gave of their time and effort in its creation:

To Don Russell, our editor, and to all the WWA member-contributors listed on the contents page

To Harold Kuebler, our Doubleday editor, for his patient advice, suggestions and help

To Donald Duke for reviewing and advising us on every chapter, and particularly for his generous contribution of many illustrations

To Other Members of WWA who contributed material, research information and valuable suggestions: Henry W. Allen, Elsa and S. Omar Barker, Ron Bishop, Everett L. de Goyer Jr., Allan Vaughn Elston, Mildred Fielder, Ken Fowler, Giles A. Lutz, Dudley Dean McGaughey, Wayne D. Overholser, Lewis B. Patten, Marie Richardson, Glenn Shirley, and Ruby Wilson

And to Non-members who graciously helped with source material and in obtaining pictures: Kerry Ross Boren, Lawrence L. Dodd, Frederick T. Oltmann, John K. Payne, Martin Schmitt, P. W. Stafford, and John J. Stewart.

Undoubtedly there must be a name or two more that should have been listed above, and which I've missed among the nearly four hundred letters in my file on *Trails of the Iron Horse.* To you, too, our thanks—with apologies!

AUGUST LENNIGER
Anthology Chairman
Western Writers of America

October 1974

Contents

Introduction

DON RUSSELL

Had the railroad not been invented, the Westward movement of the United States might have continued at the leisurely pace that brought the first permanent settlement more than a century after Columbus, and the Alleghenies barely crossed three centuries after the New World was known. From another point of view, it was inevitable that the railroad should appear at a certain stage in human progress, and that the 400th anniversary of the discovery of America should be celebrated at the mid-continent railroad center, Chicago. It was not entirely coincidental that at that same Chicago exposition Frederick Jackson Turner should note that there no longer was a frontier and call attention to the significance of its passing.

It is more accurate to say that the railroad appeared than that it was invented. The railroad first of all was merely a road of rails. Paved roads were non-existent in colonial America and many an idea was advanced to get wheels out of the mud. One of these ideas was a corduroy road, made by laying logs crossways on the right-of-way. It was a bumpy solution. A rail for the wheel to roll on was an improvement and a strip of strap iron would make it more durable. It was such a railroad that the Baltimore & Ohio started in 1828 for horse-drawn vehicles. It was assumed that any farmer living along the line could drive his wagon on the track and go to town.

The locomotive changed all that. The railroad ceased to be a highway and eventually became an incorporated octopus. It was the steam locomotive that opened the West, despite its mechanical inefficiency, made all too evident when the internal combustion engine took over in the twentieth century. Had anyone remembered that the railroad was essentially a highway, a road of rails, much of its latter-day troubles might have been averted.

The locomotive was not exactly invented. It was derived from the steam engine of Thomas Newcomen, improved by James Watt, and set on wheels by Richard Trevithick, George Stephenson, Edward Cartwright, Oliver Evans, John Stevens, Peter Cooper, Horatio Allen, Matthias W. Baldwin, and others who experimented with it and improved it, but never perfected it. After a hundred miles or so, the locomotive was out of water and out of coal, and was taken into a roundhouse for minor or major repair, while another engine took over. That is why railroads established division points at hundred-mile intervals. Around these division points, cities grew, for they were homes for hostlers, mechanics, blacksmiths, inspectors, carpenters, switchmen, engineers, firemen, brakemen, conductors, track workers; the hundreds of employees needed to keep the railroad operating. Even in the closing days of steam, half these division points were eliminated, and the diesels took away more, leaving behind them declining or dying cities.

This was only one of the railroad's contributions to the settling and unsettling of America. Even passenger locomotives had to make occasional stops for water, and the freight train had to do a lot of stopping, sidetracking, switching, and backing on its daily rounds. Water tanks were built for their convenience every few miles, and around them grew many "tank towns."

With all of this tail to drag behind, it is surprising how rapidly railroads were built. Most of the lines were quite short to begin with. Some kept extending their tracks, as did the Baltimore & Ohio. Others achieved trunk line status by combining a number of companies, as did the New York Central and the Pennsylvania. The trend was generally westward. By 1850 there were 9,021 miles of railroad in the United States, but not a mile of it was beyond the Mississippi. Yet there were already proposals for a transcontinental railroad. As early as 1838 John Plumbe, Jr. of Sinipee, Iowa, petitioned Congress for an appropriation to start a railroad to Oregon—and got it—but as the sum was only $2,000 his road did not get very far. Asa Whitney came along with a more extravagant scheme, and in 1850 Congress authorized a series of Pacific Railroad surveys, carried out by the Army's Corps of Topographical Engineers. North and South squabbled over the various routes proposed, and it was not until the Civil War eliminated the Southern routes from consideration that the Pacific Railroad Act was approved in 1862.

The building of connecting lines by the Union Pacific and the Central

Pacific was one of the great dramas of the West, some part of which is reflected in these pages. But the many competing lines that almost simultaneously started for the Pacific Coast again persuades us of the inevitability of even the driving of the Golden Spike. The Kansas Pacific, originally Union Pacific, Eastern Division, when it had hopes of becoming the main line, never quite made it, but when it got as far as Abilene there started the great cattle drives that made the cowboy the outstanding figure of American folklore and tradition. The Santa Fe took over a road with the ambitious name Atlantic & Pacific, but became famed in Western annals when its end-of-track was Dodge City, the "Beautiful Bibulous Babylon of the Frontier."

The Great Northern and the Northern Pacific penetrated into unsettled territory. The Southern Pacific, in devious role both as The Octopus and benevolent benefactor, absorbed the Central Pacific. In latter days the Chicago, Rock Island & Pacific and the Chicago, Milwaukee, St. Paul & Pacific added Pacific to their names when they *made* it. For others it was a goal—Texas & Pacific, Missouri Pacific, Western Pacific.

East of the Mississippi, railroads generally followed settlement. There was someone to welcome the first train into town with a brass band and a parade. West of the Mississippi there was nobody for hundreds of miles. Most of the railroads west received grants of land, alternate sections on each side of the right-of-way. This has often been denounced as too generous a subsidy, but it seemed no princely gift when much of it was dubbed the Great American Desert. In selling it the railroads competed with much larger amounts of government land, open to settlement under the Homestead Act. Actually the railroads were less interested in making profit from the land sale than in getting someone to live along the right-of-way who would have something to ship, and perhaps take a trip to town a few times a year.

Traditionally settlers moved West by covered wagon, and that continued long after railroads were built. The covered wagon was a migratory farm, with a plow slung underneath and a cow roped behind, and it became a farm wagon when it reached a destination. But the railroads became colonizers, recruiting parties in the Eastern states, and also sending agents to Europe to sell Germans, Scandinavians, Bohemians, and groups of many other nationalities on the possibility of owning a farm on the Western Plains. Railroads moved entire communities from their homes in Europe to farms along the right-of-way. That much of this was oversell was not entirely the fault of the railroads. Scientists and pseudoscientists, publicists and boosters had agreed in abolishing the Great American Desert and replacing it with the Garden of the World. It worked. By 1912 the mishmash of territories with ever-changing boundaries was replaced by a solid band of states stretching from sea to sea. Until that time everything was progress, onward and upward. It was not until the twentieth century was well along that the statistical graphs began sloping downward, and some states moved backward in population and production.

While the railroad not only contributed, but was also essential, to Westward expansion, it also had a large part in that other West, the West of film and folklore, the Wild West of fiction and fable, of tradition and television, that has almost obscured the West of history—which must have been quite dull at times. It was the railroad that made the cowboy necessary, and that in itself is a great contribution to legendry. It was the railroad that primarily forced Indians onto reservations, although generously allowing them to ride free as passengers (but not in passenger coaches) under many treaty stipulations. Without the railroad of course there could have been no train robber, to the gain of society but to the loss of a vast array of literature and subliterature.

The railroad also developed a folklore and legendry of its own. There are few occupations, such as the sailor in the days of sailing ships, or the stagecoach driver, that have had a more romantic appeal for those actually working at it, than has railroading. There is a vast literature to prove it. All of us are aware of model railroad clubs, of railroad museums and railroad clubs that seek out steam locomotives to ride behind, of tourist trap trains, reclaimed or rebuilt in miniature, and of the collectors of locomotive pictures and of timetables, tickets, and trivia. If railroading were not an industry it might be a hobby—and sometimes is.

This book is not offered as a history of railroads and railroading, but rather it is an attempt to recapture some of the fascination surrounding that transportation medium. It has been compiled by the Western Writers of America, an organization of professional writers of the West, both of fact and fiction. In these chapters they have striven mightily to stick to the facts—no easy task when history has become overladen with a century and a half of legendry and fable. There are tales of the great trunk lines that built the West, and also of smaller railroads that rate high in storytelling. And there are pictures that are worth more than a thousand words.

TRAILS OF THE IRON HORSE

1

The Pathfinders

TOM CURRY

The railroad did not miraculously materialize out of nowhere in the nineteenth century. Methods of moving heavy objects on rails date back to the dawn of history, though steam and steel were unknown.

In 427 B.C., ships were transferred from the Aegean to the Ionian Sea on *diolkos,* parallel stone blocks into which grooves had been cut. The Venetians hauled galleys from shore to shore on tracks by means of windlasses and oxen, while in 1453, the invader Soleiman Pasha, one dark night, bypassed a chain blocking the Hellespont by dragging his fleet overland on a tramway, an unpleasant surprise to the sleeping enemy.

There were numerous experiments abroad and in the United States before our vast transportation system was developed. Its magnitude is taken for granted, but it is what welded us into one mighty nation.

In 1753, Governor Robert Dinwiddie of Virginia sent a young surveyor named George Washington across the Alleghenies to order the French out of disputed Ohio regions. Though his hosts treated the legate with Gallic politeness, they sent back word to the governor telling him just where he might go. This resulted in the French and Indian War.

This same Washington was aide-de-camp to General Edward Braddock, who blundered into an ambush set by the French and their savage allies. Braddock was mortally wounded, but Colonel Washington, several horses shot from under him and his uniform riddled by bullets, rallied the shattered force and led the survivors to safety.

Washington's travels west of the Alleghenies made him aware of persistent separationist movements in the region, cut off as it was from the Atlantic seaboard by the mountain wall. When he became our first President, he said, "It is necessary to find a cement to bind all parts of this Union by indissoluble bonds."

The railroad became this binder.

Washington owned large tracts of land in western Pennsylvania and Ohio. While inspecting these in 1784, he traced a National Road to the Ohio and Mississippi valleys. Later he was appointed chief of the Potomac Canal Company, and he disposed of the holdings in his will.

Thomas Jefferson brought off one of the grandest real estate deals in history with the Louisiana Purchase. After many dark threats had flown back and forth across the Atlantic, Napoleon I sold the vast, vaguely defined empire to the upstart new nation, for he realized it would otherwise be grabbed by Britain or Spain, then at war with France, even if the United States didn't seize it.

Lewis and Clark were sent out in 1803 to survey and explore the new lands, even before the Purchase was finalized. Among other objectives, they were to seek a route to the Pacific which might prove a shortcut to Asia. The rich trade with the Orient was a prime motive for many great explorations in our history. Columbus discovered America as he groped for a shortcut to India, while Henry Hudson and Sebastian Cabot, among others, hunted for a Northwest Passage for the same reason.

Lewis and Clark started up the Missouri in four keel boats. The Mandan Indians proved friendly, and they were assisted by a young Shoshone squaw, Sacajawea. She was a chief's daughter, captured by raiders and carried far eastward, where she was sold, according to Indian custom, to a French-Canadian, Toussaint Charbonneau, hired by Lewis and Clark as guide and interpreter.

Though the Shoshones, or Snakes, ranged in what now is Idaho, Sacajawea recalled landmarks noted years before, when she had been kidnaped. She gathered roots and berries for the larder, and she knew the universal sign language, so the explorers could communicate with Indian tribes they encountered, among these the brawling, warlike Dakotas or Sioux. To indicate Sioux by sign, the forefinger was drawn under the chin from ear to ear—cutthroat.

They reached Great Falls and marched through Nez Percé Pass. But they might never have penetrated beyond the headwaters of the Salmon River had it not been for Sacajawea. When they saw the whites coming, the Shoshones

The first locomotive, The Catch-Me-Who-Can, *invented by Richard Trevithick in 1804.* New York Public Library.

hid, but she was one of them and spoke their tongue. So the Shoshones furnished horses, food, and guides, enabling Lewis and Clark to reach the Snake, cross the Columbia and finally gaze on the Pacific, November 7, 1805. This expedition was the basis for our claim to the Northwest Territories.

Meanwhile Daniel Boone had pierced that dark and bloody ground which became Kentucky and Tennessee, hunting as far west as the Missouri, while to the north, George Rogers Clark battled British and Indians, opening Illinois and Indiana to our western push.

In 1805, Zebulon Pike explored the upper Mississippi, then swung southwest to explore Spanish lands where most of our western rivers rise. He hunted for the source of the Red River, and while he did not find it, he penetrated to Colorado, where he built a fort. Captured by a Spanish patrol, he was taken to Santa Fe, then to Chihuahua. After a long detention, he was released; he had kept careful notes, and the data he brought back proved valuable.

In 1821 the Mexicans revolted against Spain. The new Mexican government was too weak to protect the distant reaches of its northern territories, offering juicy opportunities to the bold, belligerent Anglo-Saxons inexorably pushing west.

The Oregon Trail had been broken. The Mountain Men, hunting pelts and other wealth, threaded through the vast hinterland, as did explorers and surveyors. They followed trails made by Indians. The savages avoided most natural obstacles such as mountains and deserts, usually staying near rivers, where the going was easier and there was water and game for food available. White men enlarged the traces for horses, then for wheeled vehicles, and in due time, these routes proved the most practicable for the Iron Horse. As a famed railroad pioneer put it: "Where a river can go, a railroad can go!"

In 1812, Colonel John Stevens of Hoboken urged Congress to consider the idea of railroads as the only satisfactory solution to growing transportation problems as the population expanded westward. He envisioned joining the Atlantic and Pacific oceans, a fantasy to be laughed at till tears sprang to sensible people's eyes. Stevens spent most of his life in futile attempts to have his idea adopted; he was ridiculed when he proposed a railroad, with wooden rails, be constructed from Albany, the end of ship transport on the Hudson, to the Great Lakes, insisting that railways and steam carriages were superior to canals, which were all the rage at the moment. To the further amusement of the nation, he claimed steam carriages could travel 100 mph, though in practice, 20 to 30 would be safe.

In 1818 the brash boy editor of the St. Louis *Enquirer,* Thomas Hart Benton, dreamed up another one: a canal system up the Missouri to Great Falls, then a portage road over the mountains to the Snake River Valley and on to the Pacific, the ocean route to India. "This will make St. Louis the Queen City of the West!" he proclaimed.

Oliver Evans of Pennsylvania invented the high-pressure steam engine, and predicted people would travel from one city to another by rail. Another prophet who ruined himself and was considered soft in the head was Henry Meigs of the New York Legislature when he said that horseless steam carriages could somehow be successfully operated.

"Hare-brained visionaries!"

The whole passel of them.

In 1826, overland ship transport began in England, utilizing small iron wheels on the vessels running along rails. In 1811, John Blenkinship had made an engine equipped with pinions engaging teeth along the track, for it was believed impossible for a locomotive with smooth wheels to draw cars along a smooth metal track. The British experimented with racks, cable-worked lines and other devices, chiefly to move mine cars. For steep gradients, funiculars were built, cable types of railroads where the weight of the ascending car partly or wholly counter-balances the weight of the descending car. Cog railroads were constructed for use on mountainsides, and are still functioning.

There was no end to the novel schemes dreamed up by fertile minds. One atmospheric railway was patented in 1811, in which carriages laden with freight would be driven through airtight tunnels on iron rails. In 1838, a guide-rail system was built, with the track of iron plates secured to longitudinal timbers and wheels running free on the axles, and a strong projecting arm from the carriage center equipped with guides. In time, overhead railways and monorails would be constructed.

It was the canals which were envisioned as the solid wave of the future. In 1825 the Erie Canal, 363 miles long, was completed, linking the Atlantic with the Great Lakes, thus making New York City the nation's greatest seaport. Philadelphia and Baltimore, heretofore supreme, now panicked as more and more traffic deserted them.

In 1829, Congress issued a solemn report unfavorable to railroads of any type, ignoring the facts that in 1827 Horatio Allen had laid a tramway from Quincy, Massachusetts, to tidewater three miles distant to carry granite for the Bunker Hill Monument, that the Mauch Chunk was hauling coal from Pennsylvania's Carbondale mines, that the Delaware & Hudson, first to operate a steam locomotive, was a success, that in the South a railroad-canal system was moving cotton bales from interior stations to the port of Savannah.

A powerful canal lobby in Congress, backed by magnates who had invested heavily in canals, defeated all attempts to gain money grants for railroads.

Thus each state had to finance its own railroads. Costs were skyhigh, and myriad problems had to be solved, locomotives, cars, rails and ties, brakes, gauges, ballast, signals, no end to it. Bridges must be built, tunnels driven, and since the state owned its railroad, one refused to permit another's rails to cross its boundaries, thus making hookups impossible.

To counter New York's Erie Canal, the remarkable Pennsylvania System was built, consisting of railways, portage railroads, and canals. Special vessels were fashioned that could quickly be separated into two sections for easier handling. Horses drew the boats through canals; then they were taken apart and pulled on trolley rails to the Columbia terminus. Reassembled, they moved by canal to Hollidaysburg at the foot of the Alleghenies, where a portage railroad drew them over the mountain wall to Johnstown. The Allegheny Portage Railroad included inclined planes worked by ropes, while locomotives were used on level stretches. Rolled iron-edge rails on stone sleepers formed the roadbed, and stationary steam engines furnished power on grades. Passengers and freight completed the journey to Pittsburgh by another canal.

So Philadelphia had a direct connection with the West. Charles Dickens made the trip, enthusiastically describing it in his *American Notes.* When it eventually became obsolete, the System's route was taken over by the Pennsylvania Railroad.

Not to be left behind in the rush, Maryland incorporated its own Baltimore & Ohio, and started work, although the railroad was not completed for many years.

The first four locomotives used in America were imported from England, where George Stephenson and his fellow engineers had been perfecting them, but the British machines proved unsatisfactory here and were used very little.

Peter Cooper built his *Tom Thumb,* which performed well, while Matthias Baldwin's *Old Ironsides* was a lusty success. The pace grew frenzied as Yankee mechanics and blacksmiths turned out hundreds of homemade engines of various size and shape. The single perpendicular boiler soon gave way to the horizontal one.

Other early shops were Hinckley & Drury, Breeze Knowland, William Mason, Richard Norris, Portland Company, West Point Foundry, and Lawrence Machine Shop. The first tracks were giddy contraptions, stone blocks three to five feet apart on which planks were laid a foot above ground. L-shaped iron strips were bolted to the planks, the high side of the "L" forming the outer edge of the track.

As practical men strove to perfect the Great Machine of the nineteenth century, the locomotive and all its accompanying requisites, they began to

The first train imported to America, the Stourbridge Lion. New York Public Library.

typify the Spirit of the nation. The railroad was the technological symbol of an era and, by the 1840s Americans had come to believe that they could accomplish just about anything.

Manifest Destiny! "To overspread and possess the whole of the continent for development of our great experiment in liberty and self-government!"

This had been envisioned by early Presidents such as George Washington, Thomas Jefferson, James Madison, and Andrew Jackson. The puny new nation brought forth on this continent by our forefathers was hemmed in by territories belonging to powerful, threatening giants, masters of the world, England, France, and Spain, struggling with one another for spoils of conquest.

Andrew Jackson, President from 1828–36, had defeated the British at New Orleans, but the War of 1812 had proved indecisive. Spain held the Southwest plus California and Florida. The Spanish inflicted the last thorn

Peter Cooper's Tom Thumb, *1829*. New York Public Library.

in our nation's foot, when they armed and incited the Indians to raid south Georgia. The fiery Jackson wouldn't stand for this and sent a punitive expedition into north Florida to retaliate, and rather than lose Florida by war, as seemed inevitable, Spain sold the peninsula to the United States.

Sam Houston was a pupil and disciple of Jackson, who was his mentor and idol. Secretly, Jackson sent the young giant to Texas, with acquisition in mind. Houston defeated Mexican General Santa Ana and formed the Republic of Texas, which in due time joined the United States, as Jackson had hoped.

Surely a transcontinental railroad would further Manifest Destiny! What's more, the mouths of our Eastern capitalists watered at the prospect of tapping Asia's riches by such a shortcut to the Orient. Almost without exception, early promoters of the railroads based their argument on the Asiatic trade.

In 1844, a Yankee merchant, Asa Whitney, born in Groton, Connecticut, and apprenticed in his youth to a New York City businessman, made his voice heard in the Wilderness. He presented Congress with a remarkable proposition: he asked the United States to deed to him, at 16 cents per acre, a strip of land 60 miles wide from Wisconsin to the Pacific Ocean on which he would build a railroad. He would finance his railroad by laying a few miles of track, which would increase the land's value. He would sell the completed stretch of track at a large profit, using the proceeds to pay for further construction, on and on until he reached the mouth of the Columbia River. In twenty-five years, declared Whitney, the United States would have a railroad over which the treasures of the Orient would flow! But the time was not yet ripe. A young Congressman from Illinois, Stephen A. Douglas, said, "By all means, build a railroad, but begin it at Chicago!" "Not so," cried out in print the editor of the influential *Police Gazette,* based in Independence, Missouri, "*this* should be the starting place!" And the ubiquitous John C. Calhoun led a Memphis convention to champion a Southern city.

Nobody believed more than one transcontinental railroad would ever be laid. So the city or section from which it started would gain overwhelming supremacy. In a journalist's flowery language, "It would rival Carthage in her power into which would pour the commerce of the world!"

In 1847, to escape persecution in the States, Brigham Young led his Mormon Saints westward. From Council Bluffs they marched along the Platte, "a mile wide and an inch deep," which handily flows west to east for a long distance. At Fort Bridger they swung southwest into the Rockies to Salt Lake, which their Leader declared was The Place. Here they built their marvelous metropolis, with canny foresight laying out wide avenues, numerous parks and setbacks for structures.

But hardly had they settled in what was Mexican territory than they found themselves back at the old stand. For President James K. Polk was a continentalist who not only believed in Manifest Destiny, but in 1848 he did something about it. He went to war with Mexico, and the treaty of Guadeloupe Hidalgo ceded to the victor our great Southwest and California. Polk, another of Andrew Jackson's pupils, had learned his lessons well.

The stagecoach-like Atlantic, operated by the Baltimore & Ohio Railroad. New York Public Library.

Now the United States spread from ocean to ocean. But the East was separated from the West by 2,000 miles of terra incognita, "The Great American Desert," as our fertile wheat and livestock heartland had been named, and by "impassable mountains," the Rockies and Sierras.

Addressing the Senate in 1845, the eloquent Daniel Webster boomed in his mighty, persuasive voice: "What do we want with this region of savages and wild beasts, of deserts and shifting sands and whirlwinds of dust, of cactus and prairie dogs? To what use could we ever put those endless mountain ranges, impenetrable and covered to their bases with eternal snows? What could we do with a western coastline three thousand miles away, rockbound, cheerless, and uninviting!"

When Webster sounded off there were less than four hundred Americans in California.

Thaddeus Stevens, omnipotent in the Pennsylvania Legislature and in Congress following the Civil War, when he so usurped Presidential powers that he virtually governed the nation, was at first against railroads, but he soon realized his error and backed construction. As is so often the case, once a great idea proves practical, men grow enthusiastic: everybody wanted to get into the railroad act. Tracks began lacing the East and South.

Monopoly was a bugbear to the sturdy, tobacco-chewing, whiskey-drinking freemen of the young republic. So railroad rights-of-way had to be open to public use, like any other highway. A farmer in a wagon could meander along a track, stopping as he pleased to rest his team or admire the view, cursing a train behind which could not pass and was frightening his horses. The absurdity of this soon grew apparent and the rails were reserved for trains.

Peter Cooper has been mentioned. He was an ex-foundry owner who had invested heavily in Baltimore real estate and so had a strong interest in railroads which would increase the value of his holdings. He built the *Tom Thumb* for the Baltimore & Ohio, a tiny, one-cylinder engine with a forced draft in a crude but effective multi-tubular boiler, and it was a pronounced success.

Pennsylvania incorporated the Pennsylvania Railroad to replace its outmoded System, and while New York had the Erie Canal, the Empire State realized railroads must be built if she was to maintain New York City as the foremost Eastern seaport. The Mohawk & Hudson had been incorporated in 1826, and the *DeWitt Clinton,* turned out by West Point Foundry, was the first locomotive to travel its rails. This road became a link in the mighty New York Central in 1853, when Cornelius Vanderbilt merged ten small lines.

The Erie was first to run from New York City to Lake Erie, through Binghamton, Corning, and on to the Great Lakes at Dunkirk, near Buffalo.

Then, in 1848—GOLD! Gold to the grassroots in California, lying around, waiting to be picked up!

Covered wagons began moving endlessly over the dry, rolling plains, clawing over the western mountains. Other hopefuls sailed from the East Coast around Cape Horn, or shortcut from ship to ship over the Isthmus of Panama, disease-ridden and perilous. Many never reached Golconda, but died en route, in shipwrecks, from fever or whims of cruel Nature. Yet despite all these obstacles, California soon had a population of 100,000 eager souls.

And the immigrants poured in, 300,000 land-hungry folk a year. The great heartland could not be properly settled until faster, more economical transportation than ox-drawn wagons could be furnished. The railroad was a vital need, to carry in people and their goods, to bring in the Army to protect the settlers from Indians, and to transport their produce to market.

Steamboat service on navigable rivers was a tremendous enterprise, but as the westward migration increased, it could not handle the traffic.

In 1849 Stephen A. Douglas finally prevailed over the canal lobby and a bill was pushed through, giving land grants to railroads in Illinois, Mississippi, and Alabama. Basic Federal aid finally was available.

Douglas was primarily promoting his own state's Illinois Central. This was the first time land grants were offered to inspire and help finance railroads. The bill was debated by such stalwarts as Thomas Hart Benton, Hannibal Hamlin, and John C. Calhoun, while Daniel Webster, who had changed his tune, shaped its final form. President Millard Fillmore signed it into the law of the land.

General George B. McClellan was appointed Chief Engineer, while on the legal staff was a young Illinois attorney by the name of Abraham Lincoln. Grenville M. Dodge, who was destined to be Chief Engineer of the Union Pacific, figured in the building and operation of the Illinois Central, gaining valuable experience needed in construction of the transcontinental line.

The bill stipulated that in order to gain the grants, the Illinois Central's main roadbed must be completed by 1854. Unforeseen obstacles were encountered between Chicago and Cairo, and it was a photo finish as the line was completed December 28, 1854, only three days before the deadline.

After the experiment with the Illinois Central, land grants to spur railroad building became common practice.

The American Geographical Society, founded in 1851, was involved from its inception with the grand scheme of a Pacific railroad. The first paper presented to the Society was by the irrepressible Asa Whitney. While he still had his eye on that luscious Asiatic trade, he came up with further arguments. The two halves of the nation were separated by the Great American Desert plus the Rockies and the even more insurmountable Sierras. In case of war, which then seemed likely with England or Spain, how could California with all its riches be defended? How could the increasing pressure generated by floods of land-hungry immigrants be eased? Why, all this could be accomplished by a transcontinental railroad!

Now myriad petitions rained on Congress to construct the Pacific Railroad as it was then generally called. Apparently the only problem was to locate the best route to link the populous East with the burgeoning young West.

But legislation was repeatedly introduced, only to be defeated. Selection of the route proved impossible, due to sectional ambitions and jealousies. For the cancerous slavery problem preoccupied the nation. Abolitionists feared that, with the railroad in the South, the advocates of slavery would soon populate the nine new territories seized in the Mexican War, while the South believed that if the line started in the North, Yankees would pour in.

In 1853, Congress stepped aside, deciding to let Mother Nature determine the best route. Five surveys were ordered, to be made by the Army's Corps of Topographical Engineers. Jefferson Davis, a Mississippian by choice, was

Secretary of War, so as head of the Army was in command of the undertaking. Five wagon trains, guarded by Army units, set forth to explore. Among the personnel were not only engineers, surveyors, and cartographers, but geologists, botanists, zoologists, and artists.

Two years later, in 1855, a preliminary report was issued. Two more years passed when the finished masterpiece, *Exploration & Surveys, Railroad Route From the Mississippi River to the Pacific Ocean,* was presented. This was a stunningly handsome 12-volume opus, filled with picturesque, confused data and expensive engravings of the world's most gorgeous scenery and the flora and fauna of the continent. It cost hundreds of thousands of dollars, but failed to give surveys, elevations, profiles, grades or reliable cost estimates, along with profits that might be realized from the stupendous undertaking.

But it did prove there were several practicable routes.

Beginning in the north, the first survey followed the 47th and 48th parallels, along the Missouri to the Columbia River, from St. Paul to Vancouver. This was based on Lewis and Clark's trail and Thomas Hart Benton's plan for a Missouri-Columbia canal road. Cost was estimated at $130,781,000. (Later, the Northern Pacific built along this.)

The 41st and 42nd parallels line ran from Council Bluffs, Iowa, following the Mormon Trail in the Platte Valley, through South Pass to Benicia, California, cost estimate $116,085,000.

The 38th and 39th parallels, Westport, Missouri, to San Francisco, was given no cost estimate, since it was considered impracticable, as there was no pass under 10,000 feet. While no transcontinental railroad was ever built along this, the Denver & Rio Grande later crossed the Rockies close to the 38th parallel. (The Denver & Rio Grande was cleverly engineered, using a three-foot gauge which was ideal for negotiating steep mountain gradients as it industriously plied from settlement to settlement, carrying in mining tools, supplies and mail, freighting out ores from the fabulous mines. It was first financed by citizens of Denver, who feared they would be isolated by construction of the Santa Fe, farther south. Its saga, including the tiny company's race for a vital pass, is a fascinating one.)

The 35th parallel route, via Fort Smith, Arkansas, and on along the famous Santa Fe Trail, through Raton Pass to Santa Fe, and following Spanish trails used by the Army of the West in 1846, had a cost estimate of $169,210,000, the most expensive given, and it was believed it would be impassable six months out of the year due to snowdrifts, northers, and spring floods.

Fifth and last was the 32nd parallel, Fulton, Arkansas, to San Pedro,

California. The cost was only $68,970,000, lowest of all. This route was also known as the South-Oxbow, from the Red River Valley, via El Paso and Gadsden Purchase land. (The Southern Pacific eventually built along this.)

As Secretary of War in charge of the surveys, Jefferson Davis had the inside track as he made the presentation to Congress. He dealt at length with the five routes, stressing the disadvantages of the first four and extolling the Oxbow line. He pointed out this had only occasional snows, cost far less than any of the others, and he strongly recommended it. The "South & Pacific Railway," he called it, could be constructed for under $70,000,000.

But no Northern congressman hopeful of re-election could possibly support an all-Southern route. Nor would the Southerners vote for a Northern railroad. Quibblings, bickerings, delays stalled the matter, and as late as 1860, legislation for a Pacific railroad was defeated. Sectional lines were hardening.

The first train to cross a bridge over the Mississippi ran from Illinois to Iowa in 1856, the beginning of the Rock Island, its road completed to Council Bluffs at a later date. Wisconsin laid rails from Lake Michigan's west shore to La Crosse, while Chicago and Iowa City were linked, as were Hannibal and St. Louis. Surveys began for the Texas & Pacific.

Locomotives were undergoing numerous improvements, with larger cylinders and the steam injector. Steel replaced iron in the construction of fireboxes, while firebrick arches were installed as coal replaced wood as fuel. But until 1868 brakes had to be set by hand, when Westinghouse invented the air brake and automatic coupler. Rails had evolved from stone or wood to malleable and wrought iron, finally steel.

Railroad construction was going on throughout the East and Midwest and yet there was still no agreement on the Pacific Railroad.

In 1858 a private plan was worked out to connect two obscure Kansas towns, Atchison and Topeka, 40 miles apart, because except for the busy Pacific Coast, not one mile of track had been laid west of Kansas. A year later, in 1859, what would become one of our greatest railroads, the Atchison, Topeka & Santa Fe, was incorporated, but no work was done, due to financial problems and the outbreak of the Civil War. In 1863, new capital took over and land grants were bestowed on the project.

The sectional squabbles continued to harass Congress. Just before the war, rails connected Richmond and Memphis, through Bristol and Knoxville, and the North linked to the South through Baltimore. The Iron Horse puffed from New Orleans to Cairo, Illinois, while but a few gaps remained in an east-west line from Savannah to Texas.

And *still* no route was picked for the Pacific Railroad!

California was financing her railroads through state and private interests. Among the adventurers who made the difficult trek west after the discovery of gold were a number of men who figured largely in railroad promotion and construction. Four were merchants: Collis P. Huntington, Leland Stanford, Mark Hopkins, and Charles Crocker. A fifth was a young Yankee, Theodore Dehone Judah, an engineer who had built railroads in the East and Midwest.

With financial backing, Judah constructed the first railroad in California, the Sacramento Valley line, from the capital city to Alder Creek, and in time extended to Folsom.

Judah's obsession, however, was the Pacific Railroad. In 1856 he traveled to Washington to push for it, with no success. In 1857 he again was in the nation's capital after a careful study of the 1853–55 surveys. He wrote a pamphlet, pointing out that private money, which was needed along with Federal aid, could never be drawn in by such fanciful reports.

"When a Boston capitalist," wrote Judah, "is invited to invest in a railroad it isn't sufficient to tell him someone rode over the route on horseback and pronounced it practicable. He doesn't care to be told there are 999 varieties and species of plants and herbs, or that grass is abundant here and buffalo scarce there. He wishes to know the exact length of the railroad. He says, 'Let's see your map and profile so I may judge alignments and grades, how many cubic yards of excavation and embankment are required, tunnels, bridges, masonry, foundations, timbers, and fuels. Estimate of cost in detail. What effect will the road have on trade and travel, how much business, freight, and travel revenue will it produce?' "

Judah demanded preliminary data along these lines, believing the railroad stock would find ready buyers if so presented.

But Congress was hamstrung by the slavery problem.

The Sacramento *Union,* January 29, 1859, reported: "A Californian, Judah, writes from Washington City, 'There is no chance this session of Congress will do anything toward developing a railroad over the central route. The President [James Buchanan] will veto any bill for the Pacific Railway over any other.' "

Judah said the solution was to authorize two transcontinental railroads, one in the North, the second in the South, making the same appropriations of land and bonds for both.

The California Legislature voted for a Pacific Railway Convention, which formally requested Congress to lend aid by granting lands in the state, to guarantee bonds through the territories, and to remit duties on railroad iron.

In 1859 Horace Greeley made his famed trip West to publicize the Pacific

Railroad. On his return, he wrote of his overland journey to California: "The Railroad will add more strength and wealth to our country than acquisition of a dozen Cubas. My long, fatiguing journey was undertaken in the hope I might do something toward early construction of the Pacific Railroad."

On December 6, 1860, Judah saw President Buchanan, who declared he was generally in favor of the railway. Congressman J. C. Burch sponsored legislation again in the House, but again the dreary sectionalism reared its ugly head, and the bill was put over until the next session in December 1860. Senator William Gwin of California then presented a compromise bill, but couldn't even get it called up for consideration, although it was in many respects a forerunner of the 1862 Pacific Railroad Act.

A typical newspaper comment of the time: "Over it the trip will be made from London to Hong Kong in 40 days, over a route with every comfort and attraction . . ."

The indefatigable Judah kept exploring for a practical route across the Sierras. The 1860–61 House passed a bill providing for *two* railroads, as Judah had suggested, but the Senate amended this, calling for *three*. The House sulked, refusing to act.

On December 20, 1860, South Carolina seceded, and the other Southern states soon followed. On April 1, 1861, Fort Sumter was fired on. All Congressional opposition to a northern route for the Pacific Railroad magically evaporated, as there were no Southern legislators left in that august body to put up a fight.

What's more, the old arguments were reinforced by the need of binding California more closely to the Union, since there were strong Confederate sympathies in that wealthy, distant state. And protection of the Pacific Coast from foreign enemies suddenly assumed real rather than theoretical importance as Maximilian conquered Mexico with a French army lent him by his uncle Napoleon III.

Against such an array, the assertion that building the railroad might distract from the war effort carried little weight. However, a wrangle of local interests still made a decision most difficult, until the exasperated delegate from New Mexico Territory complained that advocates of the Pacific Railroad would not support any bill, "unless the railroad starts from the corner of every man's farm and runs through all his neighbors' plantations!"

But at long last, the first Pacific Railroad Act passed in 1862. The tremendous cost would require Federal aid, yet when members of Congress tried to persuade President Lincoln the United States should build the line, he replied, "All the Government can do is assist." This meant that a private company must be formed.

There were critics of the Grand Scheme. Said one, as the act gave away vast public domain along the right-of-way: "While fighting a war to retain eleven refractory states, the nation lets itself be cozened out of territory sufficient to form twelve new republics!" Economist Henry George warned, "Let us not imagine ourselves in a fool's paradise where golden apples will drop into our mouths!"

Nobody listened. The East felt it needed a railroad to the Pacific, while the West needed one to the commercial and political centers in the East.

The 1862 Act provided for formation of the Union Pacific Company to build the main line to the California border. The Central Pacific would lay track from Sacramento to meet this, with land grants of ten sections per mile, and a first-mortgage loan from the Government of $48,000 per mile through the Sierras and Rockies, $32,000 per mile across the Great Basin between the mountain ranges.

This proved insufficient to lure much private capital. The first stock offering was a miserable fiasco, despite the magnificent pyrotechnical gyrations and displays of that promoter of promoters, Thomas C. Durant. The U. P. Company raked in about $2,000,000, just enough money required for incorporation. A fraction of the amount was spent to start construction for publicity's sake, but most of it was used attempting to gain more favorable terms from Washington.

Ground was broken, a little grading done, and a few miles of track laid, although labor and materials were scarce due to the war.

By 1864 it was obvious the original Federal grants were not going to sucker hardheaded magnates into building the railroad, so that year more substantial subsidies were offered, while the Government's claim was reduced from a first to a second mortgage.

The more liberal terms did the trick and big private money was attracted. Durant was everywhere, publicizing the Pacific Railroad with startling schemes to sell stock and maintain keen public interest.

Omaha, Nebraska, had been picked as a starting point for the Union Pacific, a compromise grudgingly agreed to by several rival cities, among them Chicago and St. Louis.

Grenville M. Dodge, then a general in the Union Army, was appointed Chief Engineer of the Union Pacific. Dodge and Durant never came to understand or like one another. Durant was a promotive genius, Dodge a splendid, practical engineer; they had to work together, but it was like trying to mix oil and water.

Gauge was a festering sore; there were many different track widths, so transfer of rolling stock, without adaptation, wasn't possible. Some states had deliberately used a different gauge from a neighboring commonwealth chiefly from jealousy or spite. The Railroad Acts gave the President authority to fix the gauge for the Pacific Railroad. Finally, Lincoln ordered that the width be four-feet-eight-and-one-half-inches, and so it was.

One day in 1863, President Lincoln sent for General Dodge to discuss the railroad. Lincoln told Dodge that he had tentatively approved a five-foot gauge. But the New York & Hudson River (later the New York Central), the Burlington and Missouri River Railroad, the Michigan Central and Lake Shore & Southern all had built with the four-foot-eight-and-one-half-inch gauge. Their representatives had wailed that if he decreed a five-foot width, they would be forced to adjust the wheel trucks of all their cars, or else make a financially ruinous realignment of their roadbeds, enlarging bridges and tunnels from the Atlantic Coast to Iowa. Lincoln said to Dodge that he had bowed to this powerful pressure, though he knew a five-foot standard gauge would have been better.

The terrible war raged on, the nation too preoccupied with the bloody conflict to spend much time on railroads or anything else.

But the Civil War proved the railroad's value, for it was a war of logistics. Troop and supply movements, even over the unsophisticated roadbeds of the era, proved a vital factor. The North had the better of it, as it hemmed in the Confederacy and commanded much more wealth and manpower.

Tearing up enemy trackage was great sport for hard-riding cavalry units of both sides as they managed to get behind the foe's lines. There are many stories of daring raids on the enemy's railroads. One true tale is familiarly known as the Great Locomotive Chase, and has been written about and re-enacted on film. A band of daring Union spies, in civilian garb, boarded the Confederates' wood-burning locomotive, *The General,* near Kennesaw, Georgia, while its crew was away, enjoying breakfast.

The raiders meant to destroy bridges and trestles behind them as they rode the rails to Chattanooga. As the engine started off, manned by the Union men, *The General*'s crew ran out and sped on foot after their charge. They soon found a handcar on which they reached Etowah, where they commandeered an ancient locomotive, the *Wm. R. Smith.* The track was blocked by the fleeing Union crew at Adairsvile, but standing clear on a siding past the block was *The Texas,* a new, fast engine.

The Texas gained on *The General* so rapidly the desperate Union spies had no time to blow up the bridges and trestles as planned. At Ringgold, they ran out of wood to feed the boiler. They jumped for it and took to the forest, but were captured. Six were hanged as spies; the rest escaped or eventually were exchanged.

The General had been built in 1855 by Rogers, Ketchum & Grosvenor of Paterson, New Jersey, for the Western & Atlantic, and ran on the five-foot

Southern gauge, between Atlanta and Chattanooga. After the war, the engine served well on the W&A, throughout the 1880s. In 1891, it was found on a siding, rusting away and ready for the scrap heap after 200,000 miles of use. Put on display in 1893 at Union Station, Chattanooga, it was refurbished in 1961 for a Civil War memorial tour through seventeen states and two hundred cities. In 1962 the engine ran over the old Chase route, one hundred years to the day after the event.

Tennessee claimed *The General,* refusing to surrender the famous relic to Georgia. But after a five-year court battle, *The General* went home to Kennesaw, Georgia, early in 1972, acclaimed in triumph by the newspapers of the Peach Tree State. A special building has been prepared to house the historic locomotive.

The war ended on April 12, 1865, at Appomattox.

Construction of the Pacific Railroad now became paramount. The Union Pacific rushed westward while the Central Pacific pushed east at a feverish pace, in a thrilling drama without equal in the history of railroading.

2

The Union Pacific

NELLIE SNYDER YOST

Work on the Union Pacific roadbed, west of Omaha, began in earnest in July 1865, with 30 miles of grade thrown up and rails laid beforc the ground froze that winter. Real progress was made the next year, and by fall the line was completed to the banks of the North Platte River, nearly 300 miles west of the Missouri River. Crude though that first track was, by today's standards at least, the laying of so many miles of it in so short a time seems incredible in view of the many obstacles to be overcome.

One of the greatest drawbacks was the shortage of timber for ties—2,400 to the mile. From the Missouri to the Rocky Mountains stretched an almost treeless expanse of country across which the roadbed had to be built. Good timber was available only as the contractors approached the comparatively short stretch of rugged canyons that make up the divide between the Republican and Platte rivers, some 250 miles west of Omaha. Here hundreds of thousands of ties were cut from stands of magnificent red cedar that at that time covered the 30-mile stretch of hills. Until the road reached the foothills of the Rockies, in Wyoming, all other ties, as well as the rails, spikes, tools and all other necessities, had to be brought along or shipped in later.

Hostile Indians, however, were the greatest hazard. As General Grenville

General John S. Casement, UP contractor, stands beside his boarding and supply train in Wyoming. Golden West Collection

Dodge stated, "Every mile had to be run within range of musket and there was not a moment's security. In making surveys, numbers of our men, some of them the ablest and most promising, were killed; and during the construction our stock was run off by the . . . thousand. As one difficulty after another was overcome in the engineering, running and construction departments, a new era in railroading was inaugurated. Each day taught us a lesson by which we profited the next." The statement that a man died for every mile of track laid was no exaggeration.

The surveyors led the way, working well out ahead of all the rest in the most exposed and dangerous position. The actual building of the road was done by brawny, hard-working gangs of men, most of them Irishmen, many of them Civil War veterans. First in line were the bridge builders, then the graders, throwing up the shallow grade and scooping cuts through the hills with shovels and horse drawn slips or "scrapers." Next came the tie men, laying the rough logs that served as ties, and finally the track layers. These last were the men who drew the plaudits of a nation.

Capable engineers had laid the involved plans for the entire project before ever a spike was driven. Since none of the Iowa railroads had yet reached the Missouri River, all supplies had to be shipped from the industrial east to St. Louis and there transferred to steamboats for the haul upriver to Omaha where they were put upon the rails for the west. To speed the work, each car of the construction train was loaded in St. Louis with its complement of rails and the exact number of spikes to lay them, then hauled by river and rail to the far away end-of-track. There the iron was thrown off, loaded onto smaller horse-drawn cars and pulled up onto the last rails, laid down only minutes before.

There a dozen husky men grasped a rail for each side of the track and ran it down on the already laid ties. As the supply car was pulled ahead, a man gauged the last laid rails while others dropped the spikes and still others drove them, even as another pair of rails were carried forward. The moment the car was empty men seized and flipped it off the track as a loaded car was hauled up to replace it.

These hard working, hard fighting, hard drinking men who laid the Union Pacific tracks soon came to be known as "gandy dancers," because, so it is said, a man by the name of Gandy bossed one of the fastest of the track-laying gangs and, due to the peculiar shuffle or "dance" they did while tamping ties, the descriptive name was given them. At any rate, these crews could lay two miles or more of trackage a day. Not bad at all considering their crude equipment *and* the fact that only one eye could be kept on the job, the other being peeled for Indians.

The trainmen were responsible for their own protection because the United States Government simply did not have enough soldiers in the area to patrol

Track crew laying track. Photographed at 100th meridian by Carbutt. Union Pacific Railroad Photo

the right-of-way across the plains and effectively protect the track layers at their work west of Fort Kearny. The latter was only an infantry post, not too effective in pursuing mounted Indians, and Fort McPherson, 80 miles west, though a cavalry post, was almost always understaffed. It was difficult for Washington to conceive of the vast distances these troops had to patrol in attempting to control the wily hit-and-run red men, then engaged in the desperate struggle for possession of their homelands. With troops also needed to protect settlers on the Republican to the south and the Loup rivers to the northeast, there were often not enough left to effectively scout the forward reaches of the Union Pacific tracks, where bands of fighting Sioux and Cheyenne frequently rode down upon the track gangs, running off stock, killing workmen and certainly disrupting the work.

During the spring of 1867 few rails were laid west of North Platte because of the ferocity of these attacks, which also stopped all horse and wagon traffic on this stretch for a time. The reports from Fort McPherson show how often cavalry details were sent out during this time, and how thin the lines were stretched. As one writer put it, "The resistance of the Indians to the building of the railroad was continuous, with never a moment's let-up."

The first locomotive to run on the new rails was the *Major General Sherman*. Built in Paterson, New Jersey, by Danforth and Cooke at a cost of $14,450, it was described as a thing of wonder and beauty. Under the watchful eye of its engineer, Thomas Jordan, it was shipped, knocked down, to St. Louis, then up the Missouri to Omaha. There Jordan unloaded and put it together on the UP rails and ran it west to the end-of-track, in the fall of 1865.

The *Major General McPherson,* in charge of Luther O. Farrington, arrived by the same route shortly after the *Sherman*. Soon at work on three UP rails

The General Sherman, *UP's first locomotive*. Union Pacific Railroad Photo

were other sturdy little steamers: the *Major General Sheridan, Vice-Admiral Farragut, Idaho, Omaha, Osceola, Denver,* and *Colorado,* among them. All were wood burners and had four driving wheels preceded by a four-wheel truck, the popular 4-4-0 engine of that period. It was the *Osceola* that pulled the first construction train into Grand Island, a division point, on July 8, 1866.

Although Gerald M. Best, well known railroad historian, gives the full names of the engines, as listed above, all local references to the little locomotives use only the familiar and friendly titles of *General* or *Admiral,* never the formal prefixes of *Major* or *Vice.* Thus a North Platte newspaper noted that by 1875 the proud *General McPherson* had been demoted to switching duty in the yards at North Platte.

As the rails were laid, depots or stations were located alongside them at ten- or twelve-mile intervals. Rubbing elbows with each depot (and spaced between them in the far reaches of the Nebraska Panhandle) stood the water tanks, big wooden tubs perched on stubby legs and enclosed in pine jackets with a stove in the lower part to keep the water from freezing in winter. The tanks were filled by handpumps until windmills could be erected, and afterward, too, when the mills broke down or the wind didn't blow.

Some modern authorities claim that the volume of water in these tanks was enough to keep them from freezing, but this was not always so. The dry, bitter cold of the Nebraska and Wyoming winters, sometimes hovering from 20 to 35° below zero for four or five days at a time, could freeze the tanks solid, especially if they were not full, as occasionally happened when the wind did not blow for several days at a time. During such cold spells men pumped little handcars up and down the tracks, tending and fueling the heating apparatuses in the tank houses.

The little engines gulped enormous amounts of wood and extensive wood yards were maintained at many of the stations. At McPherson Station (now Maxwell), handy to the wooded canyons, a 40-acre yard was set up. Here, big John Burke kept more than two hundred loggers and teamsters busy in the hills for many months, cutting and delivering one hundred cords of cedar per day to the big yard.

And so the rails stretched westward into the raw and savage wilderness, and with them went an equally wild and savage conglomeration known as the "Hell-on-Wheels." Offloaded at each temporary end-of-track, the lurid collection of hell's offscourings flourished for a few weeks, then moved on with the ever lengthening road. Made up mostly of tent saloons, gambling joints, and dance halls that never closed, this canvas city knew no law except that which each man chose to lay down for himself—and enforce if he could.

Groceries, liquor, furniture, fuel, *everything* had to be brought along with

The Union Pacific roundhouse and shops at Laramie, Wyoming, under construction during May 1868. Donald Duke Collection

the portable town. At that, it was quite complete, even to a newspaper, the *Frontier Index.* This rough little sheet, known also as the *Pioneer on Wheels* and the *Press on Wheels,* was put out by Leigh and Richmond Freeman from a boxcar pressroom-office and published whenever and wherever the brothers could set enough type to fill a page or two. When the town moved on the paper rolled on over the rails with it.

In the fall of 1866 the tracks reached North Platte, the next division point west of Grand Island, located at the forks of the Platte River. A few log shacks made up the town that awaited the coming of the rails. And there, where buffalo, elk and deer had grazed between the broad shining ribbons of water that spring, the year's end saw a reported 3,000 men and women competing for such shelter and supplies as the raw new town afforded.

A. J. Miller, a partner in the town's first store which opened its doors for business on November 9, 1866, with goods brought in on the first commercial freight to cross the river, in later years told of the mammoth tent, just east of his place, which housed a saloon, billiard tables, and numerous gambling devices.

Because of hostile Indian activity on the plains to the west, track laying was not resumed with any regularity until late the next spring. And while the boisterous town was pinned down in the valley between the rivers, one Henry M. Stanley who, on the shores of Lake Tanganyika in Africa, was later to utter the immortal words, "Dr. Livingston, I presume?" alighted from the train in North Platte on May 25, 1867. A correspondent for the *Missouri Democrat* of St. Louis, he had been sent to the end of the Union Pacific track to gather data on Indian depredations, the killing of settlers and burning of ranches.

The trip, he wrote, "was made from Omaha on a fast passenger train in fifteen hours, at the speed of nineteen miles per hour. The country as seen from the train appears to offer meager opportunities to the agriculturist . . . The whole region is a vast pasture trod over by buffalo and ranged by hostile Indians."

He described North Platte as "a gay frontier hamlet, with the days of Pike's Peak and the California Gold Rush revived. Its citizens are a motley crowd of construction camp denizens, roughs, toughs, gamblers and emigrants but a few months from the countries of the Old World. Women from the dance halls, bullwhackers and teamsters line the tracks to see the train come in. Timid passengers, fearing to face so desperate appearing a multitude, were glad to follow hotel runners to a hastily constructed hostelry that charged a lot but gave little in the way of comfort. A gambling establishment was conducted in a large tent where games of chance seemed never to stop."

Stanley estimated there were 15,000 tons of piled-up government freight awaiting transportation by oxteam to Military Posts beyond the railhead, and camped in the vicinity were 1,236 wagons of Mormons, Utah bound; each train of twenty-seven wagons officered by twenty-nine men and a superintendent. He mentioned the *Pioneer on Wheels* and predicted that, except for the railroad men, the whole place would move on, as the location was "wholly unsuited for a townsite, being intersected by numerous sloughs and populated by swarms of mosquitoes."

The construction delay at North Platte resulted in the establishment of a government military barracks at that point, staffed with cavalry troops. These, in addition to the mounted troops from Fort McPherson, 18 miles east, were able to mount a slightly more effective patrol on the finished road as well as to supply a few more men to help chase Indians off the open area to the west.

When the rails began to stretch toward the mountains once more, the town picked up and moved on and, true to Stanley's prediction, only a skeleton force remained at North Platte, barely enough men to staff the ten-stall roundhouse and the machine shops built there that summer. As the aggregation known as Hell-on-Wheels moved westward it grew in size and hellishness. The working crews would hit town each evening at dusk, ready for a roaring all-night spree in the saloons, gambling dens and floozie shacks. By dawn some had been robbed outright, others left behind the shacks with their throats cut, and the rest in no condition to turn off much of a day's work.

By the time the road made its brief dip into Colorado at Julesburg, before curving back to Sidney and on across the Panhandle into Wyoming, the all-night roistering had slowed progress so much that it endangered the Casement brothers' contract with the Union Pacific Company. The Casements, princes of construction though they were, were little men, "about the size of twelve-year-old boys but wearing larger hats." And at this point they took matters into their own hands, descending on the burg one evening ahead of the workmen. With pick handles and guns they cleaned out the gamblers and floozies, who fled in terror to the sagebrush. The crews then went back to laying track with speed and dispatch. A bit later when General Dodge heard rumors of a "slow down" out west and asked Jack Casement about it, the little man replied, "Oh, it's all right. We took care of it."

By the time the tracks reached Cheyenne in mid-November the lawlessness had gotten out of hand again; so much so that General Dodge called on General J. E. Stevenson, commander at nearby Fort D. A. Russell, for help. General Stevenson came in with enough troops to run the entire bad element out of town a mile or so, where he held a parley and made arrangements for more orderly conduct in the future.

According to General Dodge, however, an Indian raid was responsible for starting the graveyard at Cheyenne, when two members of a Mormon grading crew were killed by raiding braves and buried there. For even with constant patrolling by the hard riding troops, deaths from Indian guns and arrows were frequent. There just were not enough soldiers to protect the workers at every point, and while the Indians always knew where the soldiers were, the soldiers as a rule could only know where the Indians had been.

By this time upward of 10,000 animals and from 8,000 to 10,000 men were employed on the construction, and General Dodge wrote, "Our Indian troubles . . . lasted until the tracks joined at Promontory. We lost most of our men and stock while building from Fort Kearny to Bitter Creek, Wyoming Territory. I remember one occasion when Indians swooped down on a grading outfit in sight of the end of the track. The graders had their arms stacked in the cut. The Indians leaped from the ravines and, springing on the workmen before they could reach their arms, cut loose the stock and caused a panic."

As the mileage westward from the wooded Missouri valley increased, so did the trainmen's difficulties due to fuel and water. At some of the yards out on the Nebraska prairie the only wood obtainable was green cottonwood, a fuel that tried the souls of enginemen. They swore that it actually sprouted after it was fed into the firebox and that it was all but impossible to get up enough steam with it to pull a train.

In the fall of '66 a traveler over the first completed section of the road recorded that the train left Omaha at seven in the evening but didn't reach

The "Hell-on-Wheels" settlement at Bear River City, near the Utah-Wyoming border. Bear River City vanished as soon as the train crew moved on. Union Pacific Railroad Photo

Fremont, 46 miles west, until the next morning. There had been no delays, he said, other than stopping to take on water and to "wood up," or just standing still with the blower on, trying to get up enough steam to go on.

Even more frustrating were the trials of the crew that put the first commercial train over the line from Omaha to Cheyenne late in 1867. The engine had no blower, and at a station well out on the plains there was no wood. With only a small supply of cedar left, the crew was forced to take on some Iowa coal which, because of the lack of a blower to force a draft, gave them plenty of trouble.

West of Sidney sparks from the smokestack set fire to two carloads of hay. In trying to ditch the burning cars before they set fire to the rest of the train, the crew inadvertently pulled the trucks from under one of the cars. At that point they cut the engine loose and ran it on to Potter, where the section crew had already seen the fire's reflection against the night sky and, supposing Indians had attacked the train, were piling onto a handcar to ride to the rescue.

With the help of the section men the trainmen cleared the track, coupled up the train and started on. But by then a snowstorm was whistling out of the north and they were low on water. With visibility cut almost to zero, they missed the first water tank. They saw the second in time to stop, but found it empty. Their need too urgent to go on, they sidetracked the train by the empty tank and backed the engine to the first tank. And by that time the

One of series of six paintings done by J. Gogolin, famous German artist, in 1931, depicting events from life of Adolph Roenigk, member of a section crew working on the UP. This painting illustrates a band of Cheyenne Indians led by Tall Bull tearing up railroad tracks near Fossil Creek (now Russell), Kansas, about 1 P.M.*, May 28, 1869, following the attack upon the section crew.* Union Pacific Railroad Photo

coal had made such a heavy clinker in the firebox that they could no longer get up enough fire to make steam. So the bedeviled engineer had to go into the firebox with a pick to loosen the clinker and shovel it out. He burned up a new pair of boots doing it, but he took his train on through to Cheyenne.

The bizarre Turkey Leg raid near Plum Creek (now Lexington), Nebraska, had occurred in August of that same year. There the Cheyenne chief and a large band of his warriors piled some ties on the tracks crossing a one-span bridge about 3 miles west of the station, and cut lengths of wire from the telegraph line to fasten them down. Most accounts agree with the above, but one source, Gerald M. Best, in his book *Iron Horses to Promontory,* adds that they rolled "a large boulder" onto the tracks. This seems unlikely in view of the fact there were no native boulders even as big as a fist within one hundred miles in any direction of the site of the wreck, central Nebraska being singularly free of any rocks larger than pebbles.

At any rate, when the Plum Creek operator found the line to the west dead, he sent William Thompson and four helpers to find and repair the trouble. The men pumped a handcar to the obstruction. While his helpers set about clearing the tracks, Thompson climbed the pole to begin repairs to the wire. At this moment Turkey Leg and his braves rushed out of hiding, killed the trackmen and shot Thompson off the pole. He fell at the foot of it and was scalped by an Indian just as an approaching train whistled, far down the track. The Indians at once went into hiding again.

Engineer W. F. Murphy of Grand Island, who just missed being one of the principals in the scene that followed, has left one of the best accounts of what happened next. He and his running mate had been called to take the freight west from Grand Island, that trip, he said, but they were too tired to make the run as they had just finished a "long trip from the front to Omaha and back to Grand Island." Another engineer, "Bully" Brooks, and a fireman were called and the train headed out. Murphy says the engine was No. 53, a Dick and Norris type, one of only two on the UP. Best states that it was No. 22 but does not name the crew.

"Of course he [Bully] saw nothing of the Indians or the obstruction until he was into it," says Murphy. The engine overturned and two flatcars and three boxcars piled up on top of it. The Indians shot the engineer and fireman but the conductor, Billy Kinney, and the brakeman got away and carried the alarm to Plum Creek. Nichols, the operator, received the news about midnight and wired Grand Island. A relief train under Hank Makely was immediately made up and sent to the scene of the wreck. Murphy was one of the rescue crew, which was armed with all the guns they could lay hands on, and with pitchforks and old cavalry sabers as well.

Best says there were four men in the caboose, the conductor, brakeman and two passengers, and that one of the latter, Charles A. Radcliffe, managed to work his way forward to the overturned engine, where he tried to extricate the wounded engineer. The fireman was already dead. Failing, he returned to the caboose, under which the other three men were hiding. Radcliffe then ran back along the line and stopped a following freight train. The four quickly boarded the freight, which then backed 6 miles to Plum Creek Station. There a telegram was sent to Grand Island, resulting in an order to back the train to Elm Creek, 20 miles east, and to take all the families living at Plum Creek to safety there.

Murphy says the rescue train reached the wreck the next forenoon and that the Indians were still there, having the time of their lives with the merchandise they had found in the cars before they set them afire. "Plunder was scattered all over the prairie for half a mile. It looked as if a big cyclone had picked up a general merchandise store and sifted its contents over half the country. They [the Indians] cut the tops out of hats and the seats out of trousers and cut the arms off of coats. They cut the feet off the boots, threw them away and wore the legs. They wanted plenty of ventilation. They had tied the end of a bolt of cloth to a horse's tail and rode around with it streaming behind them. When we arrived they drew off to the edge of the hills, apparently in no hurry to go, and made signs to us to come out and fight. We knew the soldiers were coming shortly from Fort McPherson, 50 miles away. They had got word to them by the government telegraph across the river." (This was the line John Creighton built in 1860–61, which ended the Pony Express.)

Best says the freight returned to the wreck the next morning, where it stopped a safe distance away while its crew watched the Indians through field glasses. "They were all very drunk from liquor found in one of the cars, were dancing around the burning train, looting it of all manner of merchandise, while twelve Indian lookouts were seen on top of the bluffs overlooking the scene. (The bluffs here are about 5 miles south of the tracks.) Toward evening a company of soldiers arrived by train from Lone Tree, 112 miles west, and quickly drove the Indians away." This last may have been a typographical error, as Lone Tree is approximately a hundred miles *east* of Plum Creek.

In any case, Fort McPherson was the logical place from which to send troops to Plum Creek, being 50 miles nearer than Lone Tree, which was only a road ranch, not a military post. Captain James Murie, with troops and a detail of the Pawnee scouts, followed Turkey Leg and his band into the hills and a few days later caught up with them, killed several braves, captured a woman and a boy and recovered some of the goods from the wrecked train.

While the Indians were plundering the train, scattering flour and other goods to the four winds and staging the most macabre scarf dance in history with the calico streaming from their horses' tails, William Thompson, bleeding from an arm wound and the wide slash on his head where his hair had grown that morning, lay at the foot of the telegraph pole playing dead. Whether he lay there all night, or whether he managed to crawl to a place of concealment under cover of darkness when the light of the burning cars died down, is not known. It is generally believed that when the whistling relief train finally drove the Indians to the hills Thompson got to his feet and saw, nearby, the bloody wad of hair that had been his handsome locks, accidently dropped there by the brave who scalped him. He picked up the scalp and was taken, as soon as possible, to a doctor in Omaha. The hair piece, carried along in a bucket of water, could not be reattached to its former location, as its owner had hoped, so he lived out his normal life span without it. As a grisly memento to the dangers attendant on railroad building on the plains, the scalp, encased in glass, can still be seen in the Omaha Public Library.

Another band of Indians, using the same derailing tactics near Ogallala a little later, toppled another engine from the tracks. The engineer was thrown clear as the engine rolled on its side but the fireman was pinned inside, where steam and boiling water cooked him alive. The dying man begged his trainmate to shoot him and end his torture, and three times the engineer put the pistol to his friend's head but could not pull the trigger. Then, flinging away the gun, he ran screaming up and down beside the train. The watching Indians, wanting nothing to do with a crazy man, rode away in a hurry. The demented man, still running and screaming when the relief train arrived, was ill for many weeks but finally recovered and went back to work.

By the spring of 1868 the Casement construction crews were encamped west of Cheyenne, near Sherman Pass. The entire camp, of course, was housed in tents, which were also used for food storage and cook and mess halls. Since dogs couldn't very well be kept out of tents, and because food supplies were expensive on account of the long haul from the Missouri, all dogs were strictly banned from camp.

The cook for one of the crews was a Mrs. Bictoll, a large woman weighing well over 200 pounds. One evening when supper was about ready Mrs. Bictoll went to a storage tent for sugar, leaving her little daughter Emma to watch the kitchen. While she was gone she heard Emma scream. She rushed back to find Emma flown and what she took to be a big black dog in the kitchen. The animal had upset several pans of biscuits, overturned the slop bucket on the floor and was trying to gobble up a hot roast it had pawed out of the oven.

Mrs. Bictoll grabbed up an ax, slammed the dog over the head with the flat side of it and ran him out of the kitchen. A minute later the men began coming in for supper. "You'll be in luck if you get anything to eat here," she told them. "A big black dog just about finished up everything." The camp hunter, James Daugherty, hired to keep the outfit supplied with wild game, came in in time to hear her announcement. "Which way did he go?" he asked. "I'll have to kill him before he damages any more grub." Mrs. Bictoll said the dog had gone off up the mountain and Daugherty grabbed his rifle and went after him, following the trail left in a light covering of snow. Back at the mess tent they soon heard a shot. "I might as well've killed him in the first place," the cook observed, "for Jim never misses."

A few minutes later Daugherty came in and asked Mrs. Bictoll to come out and see if he had her dog. Everybody followed her outside, where she took a quick look and said that was the dog, all right. "Well," Daugherty told her, "that happens to be a grizzly bear." Whereupon the poor woman fainted and fell back into the arms of a small man, the crew's walking boss.

In the spring of 1869 the rails reached Echo City, Utah. While a station, water tower and sidetrack were put in, the crews pushed rapidly on toward the upcoming wedding of the rails. And there, above Echo, one sunny morning, occurred the wild ride of Paddy Miles. Paddy, a Casement foreman, had started down Echo Canyon with sixteen flatcars loaded with ties, rails and workmen bound for the end-of-track below. From the top of the divide down to the mouth of the canyon the grade was "heavy," with no level stretches where the train might slacken its speed. The hitch had gone but a few miles down the canyon, traveling at a lively rate, when Paddy discovered his train had parted, leaving four loaded cars behind.

Where the cars had come apart was the only "easy" section of the grade, which had allowed the fore part of the train to gain about a half-mile on the lost cars. By the time Paddy became aware of his loss they were again on heavy grade and the runaway cars were coming down on them with lightning speed. This put him in a bind. He dared not stop to pick up the cars for, at the rate they were coming, the collision would shiver both sections and kill all on board.

Then Paddy remembered that he had seen two Dutchmen on the loose cars, both asleep behind a pile of ties. If he could waken them they could put on the handbrakes and stop the runaway section. He blew a mighty

During construction of the Summit Tunnel near Echo Summit, Utah, a bypass line was built to keep construction moving west. Donald Duke Collection

whistle blast, and then another and another, but the men slept on and the cars did not slacken their frightful speed. On they came, bounding from the rough tracks at every bump; and on shot the locomotive, around curves and over bridges, past rocky points and bold headlands, on with the speed of the wind, but no faster than came the hurtling cars behind.

"Let on the steam," yelled Paddy. With the throttle wide open and with wild and terrible screams of the whistle, the locomotive plunged on through the gorge, the mighty rock walls sending back the screams in a thousand ringing echoes. "Off with the ties," shouted Paddy, as the whistle shrilled its warning to the station men ahead to keep the track open and free, for there was no time to pause. The speeding cars were now close upon them and if they collided the canyon would have another fearful tale to add to its history. On went the train, the frantic men hurling off the ties, hoping some might lodge on the rails and throw the runaway cars from the tracks, thus saving the forward section. On down the gorge they tore, the terror close behind them, leaping along, almost flying, while the engine strained every iron nerve to gain on its dreadful follower.

Again the wild scream of "switches open" wailed out on the morning air. And below in Echo City, although the reason for it was unknown, the signal was heard, its wild cry understood and the switches opened, the track cleared. If the fleeing train could be granted that needed instant of time, those few desperate yards of leeway, the death cars might yet be switched off the main-line, to spend their uncontrolled force against the mountainside. On shot the locomotive like an arrow from the bow, the white-faced men hurling the last of the ties from the flatbeds. Now they were almost upon the last curve, the one on which trains rolled into Echo. If only the wheels of the thundering train could cling to the rails, if only they had headway enough to clear the switch before the pursuing cars reached the spot. And at that moment the runaway cars leaped into the air and plunged down the embankment to the little valley and creek, fifteen feet below.

"Down brakes," shrilled the whistle, and the reprieved train rolled on into the station where the whole town, totally alarmed by the prolonged screams of the whistle, was gathered in great excitement. Upon learning the cause of the commotion everybody dashed off up the track to the scene of the disaster to bring in the crushed and torn bodies of the unfortunate Dutchmen. But they were spared the trouble, for the pair was sitting philosophically on the creek bank, smoking their pipes and surveying the twisted mass of car frames, wheels and ties in the stream below them. They had, it seemed, awakened only at the instant when, unharmed, they were pitched from the sommersaulting cars onto the greensward beside the stream.

All that winter and spring the Casement crews had labored at top speed to close the gap between their own railhead and that of the Central Pacific, moving eastward at a speed paralleling their own. For Congress had, as yet, set no point for the joining of the rails when the Union Pacific, late in January 1869, reached a spot one mile west of Weber Quarry, exactly 1,000 miles from Omaha. There a tall tree beside the tracks at once became famous as the "1,000 Mile Tree."

To the builders of both roads the delay in setting the junction point was an open invitation to capture territory *and* government bonds before the other fellow did it. Consequently Leland Stanford, president of the Central Pacific, hired Mormon grading crews to build a grade west from Ogden until they met the CP graders working east around the west end of Great Salt Lake. At the same time he set crews to grading *east* from Ogden to Echo Summit. Equally desirous of claiming more territory, the Union Pacific at the same time staked out and partially graded a line to Humboldt Wells, over 200 miles *west* of Ogden. This meant that the two companies were throwing up a useless duplication of grades totaling 258 miles.

On April 9 Huntington of the Central Pacific and Durant of the Union Pacific agreed on Promontory, Utah, 53 miles west of Ogden, as the meeting place and Congress ratified the agreement the next day. On May 1 the Chinese laid their last rails at the designated spot. On May 7 the Irish laid down their mauls and shovels, two rail lengths short of the Central's end-of-track.

The continent had been spanned and a national celebration was in order.

3

"Everywhere West": The Burlington

EDITH THOMPSON HALL

Twelve miles of track.

That was the start of the Burlington.* Incorporated by grain millers at Aurora, Illinois, in 1849, the Aurora Branch, as it was then called, seemed to have one purpose: connecting the flow of merchandise from the East Coast to Chicago. The company directors, however, had a more ambitious goal, a vision far beyond their modest beginning. Their dream would only be fulfilled when the line reached the Pacific.

But there were many difficulties confronting the growth of the Burlington, or of any railroad; problems too numerous for a single chapter. Our intent is to look at some of the highlights of the Burlington's history, events which were typical of the achievements of many railroads. One of the more vital problems, luckily, was also one of the more colorful—bridges!

The railroads needed them, but they were a threat to the ferries and steamboats; the ferries were especially in danger. Once the railroads spanned the rivers, the ferries were doomed. Nor could steamship companies continue to rely on the ever-expanding railroads as a major source of traffic. The rivermen had ample cause for worry from the moment they knew the trans-

* Like most major railroads, the Burlington is an amalgamation of feeder lines and previously existing roads. For purposes of clarification, we'll refer to the company as the Burlington throughout this chapter.

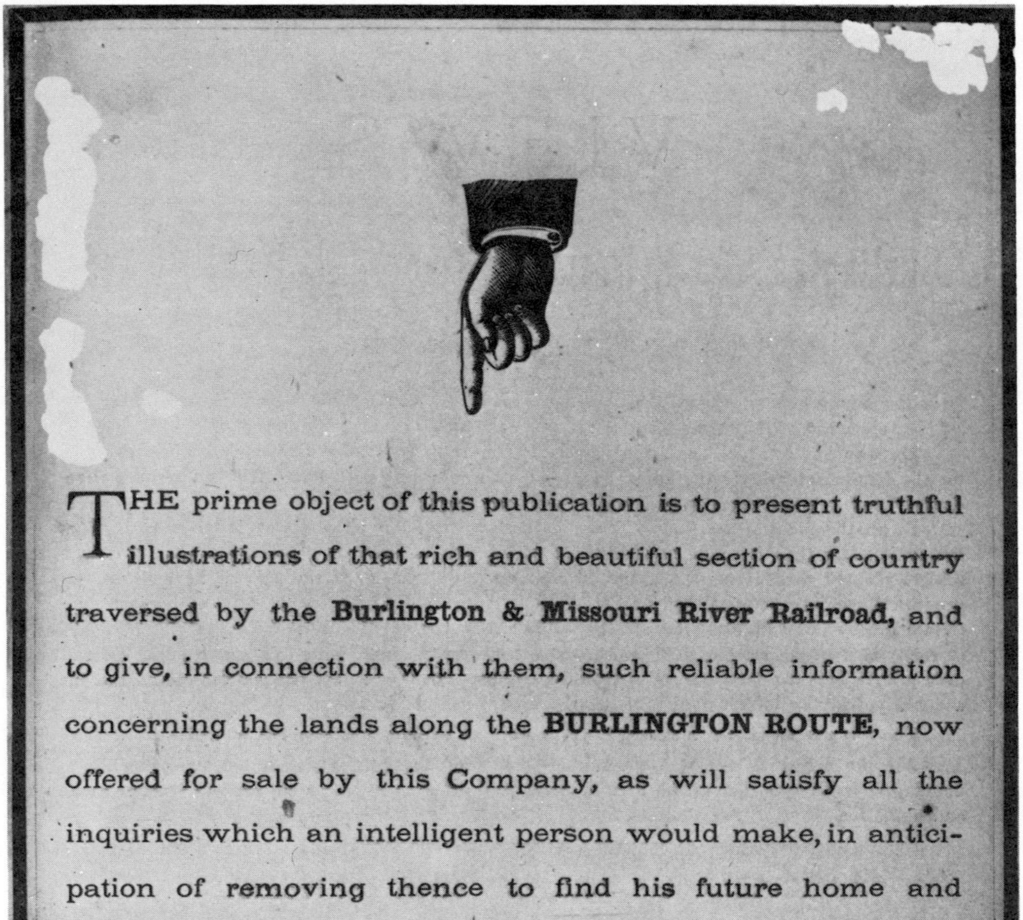

THE prime object of this publication is to present truthful illustrations of that rich and beautiful section of country traversed by the **Burlington & Missouri River Railroad,** and to give, in connection with them, such reliable information concerning the lands along the **BURLINGTON ROUTE,** now offered for sale by this Company, as will satisfy all the inquiries which an intelligent person would make, in anticipation of removing thence to find his future home and fortune.

It will be found worthy of careful examination.

"I hear the tread of pioneers
Of nations yet to be;
The first low wash of waves where soon
Shall roll a human sea.

The rudiments of empire here
Are plastic yet and warm;
The chaos of a mighty world
Is rounding into form.
[WHITTIER.

Burlington & Missouri River Railroad pamphlet cover. Nebraska State Historical Society continental road was coming. The rivermen were afraid, angry. In a way, they considered the rivers their private property and were determined to protect their rights. For a time, it was felt the railroads had no right to bridge the rivers and that no one could grant them this authority. It was too soon to know that the railroads would bring a new and greater prosperity.

No wonder the Burlington was shocked when it discovered that its tenacious competitor in Illinois, the Rock Island, had also received permission to bridge the Mississippi in its Iowa charter. The Burlington was deeply concerned, since the rivalry between the two companies was a carryover from earlier competition. Both lines had wanted to reach the Mississippi and the profitable western trade; the young Burlington snatched up several short lines in Illinois, just beating out the Rock Island from buying the longest, most strategic line in Illinois, the Central Military Tract.

Bridging the Mississippi was of significance to all. But to the Burlington, it was a setback that this project had gone to the Rock Island. Along with another competing railroad, the North Western, the Burlington awaited the outcome.

The Rock Island began constructing piers in 1853, while the river people watched with trepidation. The future, with all its uncertainty, was here.

The bridge was in trouble even before construction began. There had never been a bridge, railroad or any other kind, over the Mississippi. The long overdue confrontation festering between steamboat interests and railroaders was coming to a head with the projected Rock Island bridge. Public opinion leaned toward the steamboats; they were efficient, reliable and, of course, they had been there first.

But work went on inexorably. Gradually, the wood and iron structure arose from granite piers. The wooden structure was 1,582 feet long, the spans 250 feet with the drawbridge span 285. When opened, the channel for river traffic on both sides of the pier was 120 feet wide.

Work was officially completed April 21, 1856. The first train crossed the following day. Traffic immediately flowed regularly across the stream linking Iowa and Illinois by rail for the first time.

Spectators were amazed and disappointed. The bridge was a novelty for its time and place and they had expected it to collapse under the first train.

The Rock Island's triumph lasted only two weeks.

A steamboat, the *Effie Afton,* came upriver. It was dusk and the bridge tender did not see her at first. The low-muffled blast of her whistle alerted him. He peered through the growing darkness, saw the boat coming nearer, and opened the draw as quickly as the mechanism would allow.

The steamboat moved carefully through the draw and proceeded some 200 feet before something went wrong. She suddenly veered even though there was no wind. Then she heeled hard to the right. Her starboard engine stopped, the port engine quickened. The boat slammed into the span next to the open draw. There was an explosion from the depths and the *Effie Afton* burst into flames. The new bridge was blazing, a pier badly damaged, the draw pivot jammed.

Rock Island Railroad's bridge between Rock Island, Illinois, and Davenport, Iowa, the first bridge across the Mississippi River. Courtesy Chicago, Rock Island and Pacific Railroad Company

Volunteer firemen from both states saved all but one span. But before repair could be made a high wind swept downriver against the crippled bridge, lifted the draw span and threw it on its side.

Undaunted, the Rock Island began repairs in the face of a lawsuit from the steamship company. Long court battles ensued. Abraham Lincoln, appointed the railroad's principal attorney, defended the railroad's right to bridge the river. "People have as much right to travel east and west as north and south," he remarked.

Already known for his simple, direct approach, Lincoln and a boy helper measured the river's flow. There was no current at point of impact. It was in keeping with a report on the river in the bridge area made earlier by Robert E. Lee, then an Army engineer. With no current at point of impact, the cause of the crash lay either with the steamboat captain or the *Effie Afton*'s defective machinery.

Sympathy for the steamboat interests held greater sway than Lincoln's simple, logical explanation and he lost the first two trials. However, the groundwork he laid for the defense became known in the courts, in Congress, and throughout the nation. The case finally ended in the Supreme Court in 1862 and the railroads won. It was the last time they had to defend the right to bridge a navigable stream.

While Burlington officials were impatiently absorbing the results of the bridge battle, the road moved into northern Missouri. Beginning to lay rails in 1856, the Burlington was able to operate the first passenger train ever to travel from the Mississippi to the Missouri River on February 14, 1859. A train ferry carried the train from Quincy, Illinois, to Hannibal, Missouri. Later a celebration was held in St. Joseph when the waters of the two rivers were married by dumping a jug of Mississippi water into the muddy Missouri. Traffic across the state of Missouri soon grew in size and importance.

But progress was not only helped along by the powers behind the railroads and the skills of their legal advisers. Many an average workman also pitched in, using native ingenuity to help the advance of the railroads. A favorite anecdote about the railroad workers' imaginative solution to problems involves the Hannibal Railroad, one of the feeder lines to be absorbed by the Burlington.

The Hannibal ended at St. Joseph, Missouri, and since there was no line farther west, this city became the principal embarkation point to western trails. Ferries operated from the east bank of the Missouri River into Kansas. With business steadily increasing, St. Joseph men decided to replace some of the trails on the other side of the river with a railroad terminating in central Nebraska.

Getting the first locomotive to the other side was a challenge, and a search was made for the smallest locomotive available.

The locomotive was in Missouri. The tracks were in Kansas—carried there by ferry and dragged to the railhead by mule-powered handcars.

It was late in the year when the locomotive was brought to St. Joseph, adding to the problem of getting it over to the other side. It was too late in the year to get a large steamboat upriver to carry it across, and the ferries weren't sturdy enough to take it. Waiting until spring was out of the question. So they pinned their plans on a hard freeze. Then, as was the custom, regular highways for loaded wagons were established across the river ice.

They graded on the higher east bank in Missouri—down to the river's edge. Some grading was also necessary on the Kansas bank. Then they waited. And hoped.

In January 1860 the temperature dropped and the ice froze to over 18 inches thick. They laid long telegraph poles on the ice, spiking the rails to them. Stripping the locomotive of everything that *could* be taken off, they fired the engine and it started across.

Slowly the locomotive approached the ice. At the very edge of it, the engineer jumped off. Crowds on both sides of the river watched as the engine rumbled on alone over groaning, cracking ice, leaving some open water in its wake. Another engineer waited near the west bank and as the locomotive approached, he leaped aboard, accelerating the engine and as the onlookers cheered, guided it safely up the bank.

Kansas had its first locomotive.

Know-how, imagination, and a flair for publicity; these were some of the Burlington's assets. When the company received the honor of carrying on its Missouri line the first Pony Express messenger, its publicity experts made the most of the occasion. On April 4, 1860, the man reached Quincy, Illinois, crossed the river to Missouri on the Quincy ferry, where a locomotive and one car waited. The engineer, his hand on the throttle, was under orders to establish a record.

He did.

Swaying and bumping, barely rounding the sharp curves on too light rails on an untried roadbed, he covered the route from river to river, 192 miles, in 4 hours and 51 minutes.

The record held for fifty years.

At St. Joseph, the waiting Pony Express rider grabbed the mail sack and was off to the St. Joseph steam ferry—and Kansas.

The feat brought national attention to the far west railroad.

Proud of being the first to carry a Pony Express messenger, the Burlington sought after "firsts." The attempt was successful and, in July 1862, the Burlington was authorized to convert a car to sort and bag mail while in transit from Quincy to St. Joseph. This was the first railway post office in the United States.

The Civil War brought new problems to the railroads. Trade patterns were affected, and attention was focused on the war. The Burlington, like many other railroads, was destitute. The final blow came when the Mississippi was closed to New Orleans, ruining Iowa's corn market.

In desperation, the Burlington turned from corn to hog shipments, which delighted the company with their financial success. By 1862, this market had increased so much the Burlington had to build their own line into Chicago. They bought seventy-five acres with 200 feet of river frontage to serve as their Chicago terminus. In two more years the Burlington had moved so many cattle and hogs over their rails the directors purchased forty more acres just inside Chicago's city limits. Here they planned to construct a stockyard.

The Chicago Pork Packers' Association pressured the Burlington to consolidate their facilities with other railroads. They did not want a separate yard for each railroad entering the city. Consolidation appealed to the company's backers and the directors yielded.

The Stock Yards opened the day after Christmas 1865. Still proud of their tradition of "firsts" and mindful of the publicity to be gained, the Burlington made sure of operating the first trainload of meat animals to enter. The Burlington's train of fifteen cars carried 761 hogs. The Burlington reaped publicity.

And Chicago took on a new identity.

The Burlington's next strategic move was to reach Kansas City. Action began in November 1867. Until a bridge could be built, they shared the Missouri River ferry with another railroad.

Bridge crossing the Mississippi at Burlington pictured in 1873, five years after completion. Courtesy Burlington Northern, Public Relations and Advertising Department, Chicago

Near Kansas City, the Missouri veers east traveling in a direct line to St. Louis. The Burlington constructed their bridge at this point from north to south, after the river's right angle turn, to reach North Kansas City, Missouri.

If it was not the best place to bridge the river, perhaps the right place did not exist. The river was shallow, too shallow for the draft of steamboats from east of the Mississippi. It continually changed its course, seemingly overnight, leaving sand bars and islands where there had been water the day before. It was a river boat pilot's nightmare.

Construction of the railroad span took two and a half years to complete and on Independence Day, 1869, the Kansas City bridge was opened for traffic. The Burlington enjoyed the publicity that it had another "first"—they had built the first permanent bridge across the Missouri.

In the meantime, the Burlington had also put up two bridges across the Mississippi in 1868. One was at Burlington, Iowa, the other at Quincy, Illinois.

With the arrival of the railroads at the Missouri, competition in Iowa over connecting Union Pacific business became so heated that the three rivals, the Burlington, the Rock Island, and the North Western met in the summer of 1870. They formed the Iowa Pool, a loose organization, and agreed to certain percentages and rules; this agreement lasted fourteen years.

The three lines had a long history of intense rivalry. All three roads had started near Chicago at about the same time, wanting the same thing—the transcontinental route—and going in the same direction, toward the Mississippi. Of necessity they all jockeyed for the many short lines built, or about to be built, in Illinois. The continuing rivalry was unavoidable. All roads wanted the advantage of the large, portal cities. One followed where the other led.

The Burlington expanded into Nebraska, building ahead of its needs. To recover their investment, they took an idea from the Union Pacific, and advertised the advantages Nebraska offered. The advertising was placed nationally and overseas, increasing the flood of emigrants from Europe, as well as revenue and business for the Burlington.

The competitive spirit between the Burlington and the Union Pacific exploded west of the Missouri. The Union Pacific permitted the Burlington little access to the gateway at Kearney Junction although it had been set by law. The Burlington wanted to reach Denver and formalized a plan. They organized the Republican Valley Railroad Company—and worked west.

On May 29, 1882, the Burlington rolled into Denver on the first steel rails produced in Colorado. Some 247 miles of track had been laid in 229 working days.

Prior to this, Denver was serviced by the Union Pacific and the Santa Fe & Rio Grande. The Union Pacific was not enthusiastic about sharing this business with a third railroad, particularly the aggressive Burlington.

Continuing to flourish on publicity gained by its tradition of "firsts," the Burlington in 1884 ran its first solid mail train from Chicago to Council Bluffs. A baggage car held Chicago newsmen, the train averaged 32 miles an hour and made the run in 16 hours. The train, the *Fast Mail,* had picked up New York's mail car, delivering it to a train heading for California. The express continued until the airlines took over in recent years.

December 1884 saw the Burlington pushing northwest across Nebraska into Wyoming. Ten miles of track were put down every two days while maps were read the third day for the company to buy the right-of-way.

Branch lines were run to Deadwood and Hot Springs, South Dakota, in 1891–92 to tap the mineral resources of the Black Hills. Two years later the Burlington was approaching Billings, Montana, the terminus of the Northern Pacific. Both roads wanted to exchange business so traffic immediately began flowing through the portal—east and west.

Through mergers, acquisitions, and aggressive construction, the dream was realized: the Burlington had reached the Pacific.

From the Aurora Branch near Chicago in 1849 to the Pacific meant the merger of many roads. The list resembles the litanies of railroad names

B&M in Nebraska No. 7, the Wahoo, *built at Manchester, New Hampshire, 1870.* Courtesy Burlington Northern, Public Relations and Advertising Department, Chicago

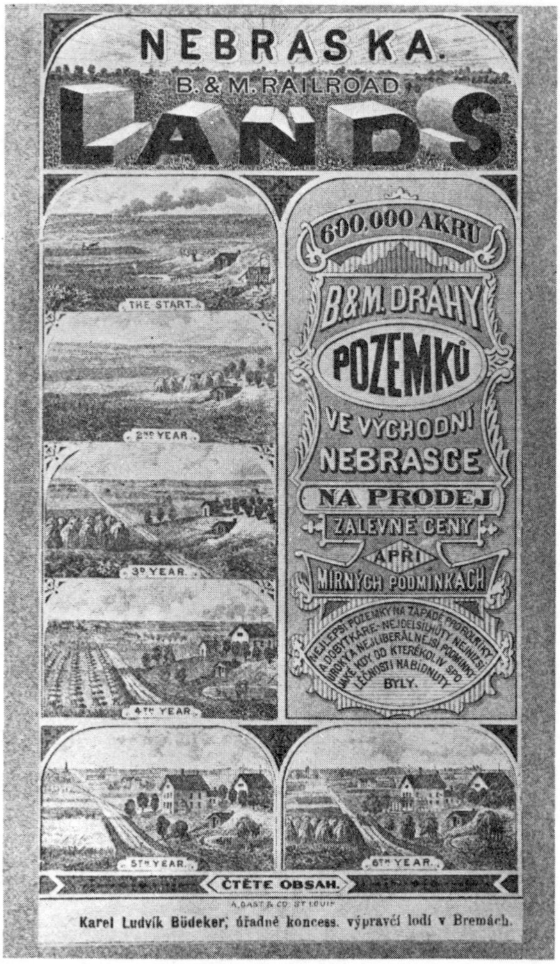

B&M advertisement used in Bohemia in 1870. Nebraska State Historical Society

Thomas Wolfe loved to include in his novels when describing the call of faraway cities. Three short roads in Illinois, the Northern Cross, the Central Military Tract, and the Peoria & Oquawaka were absorbed by the company. They built the Hannibal & St. Joseph, the Burlington & Missouri in Iowa, the Burlington & Missouri in Nebraska, and all were merged into the Burlington System. The Burlington constructed lines to the Twin Cities, to St. Louis and to Denver, acquired the Colorado & Southern and the Fort Worth & Denver to make connections to the Gulf. The final merger included the Great Northern, the Northern Pacific, the Spokane, Portland & Seattle, and the Burlington Northern subsidiaries, the Colorado & Southern and the Fort Worth & Denver.

Many short lines of bankrupt roads never completed were also picked up in Nebraska and Iowa and completed by the Burlington.

After the turn of the century, the tradition of Burlington "firsts" continued. Perhaps the most outstanding was the spectacular *Zephyr,* the first diesel-electric, streamlined, all-steel train which ran a trial run from Denver to Chicago, May 26, 1934, in 13 hours and 5 minutes. The Burlington's streamlined train was the greatest revolutionary development in railroading history.

The company continued to expand. In 1970, the Burlington merged with the Northern Pacific, the Great Northern, and the line those two built together, the Spokane, Portland & Seattle. The new name was the Burlington Northern; it is the longest railroad in the United States, nearly 24,000 miles.

As for the *Fast Mail,* the Burlington Northern announced its *Overland Mail* in 1972. The crack Western mail train of the 1880s and 1890s is back. The all-mail train runs from Chicago to San Francisco, 50 hours each way.

Without a set plan in the beginning, the Burlington had linked Chicago, St. Louis, Kansas City, Omaha, the Twin Cities, and Denver on its own line. Absorbing feeder lines and touching other railroads, it reached the cities of Dallas, Fort Worth, Galveston, and Houston, and now through its merger with the Northern Pacific, the Great Northern, and the Spokane, Portland & Seattle, the line now reaches the Pacific.

The Burlington trademark, "Everywhere West," was an optimistic slogan when it was set in 1870. However, the Burlington made that dream a reality.

4

Building the Impossible

TODHUNTER BALLARD

The 23 miles of rails constituting the first railroad track west of the Mississippi River was never impressive in itself. The Sacramento Valley Railroad, intended to connect the state capital on the river with the gold camps of the Sierra foothills 75 miles and more to the east, was built as far as Folsom and never any farther. Some of the miners did ride its yellow coaches, some supplies were hauled up the wide valley by the puffing bell-stacked engine, but the line was not an economic success nor did it greatly ease the difficulties of those it served. Its importance in history lies in the fact that Theodore D. Judah of Troy, New York, was brought west to engineer its building.

When the boy's father died, Theodore gave up his childhood dream of a Navy life and entered a technical school in his home town, and from that classroom literally leaped into the construction of a railroad between Troy and Schenectady. Thereafter until his death he was devoted to the rail lines.

At twenty-two he built the famous track in the Niagara Gorge. His reputation spread, he built bridges and surveyed rail lines all over New England, until C. L. Wilson, president of the newborn Sacramento Valley Railroad project, sought him out and offered him the job of chief engineer.

Theodore Judah hesitated. A brother in San Francisco had written of the difficulties in which the new state wallowed, but Wilson was persuasive, keeping after him until Judah and his wife took the steamer for California.

Theodore D. Judah

The work of grading the line was begun in February 1855, a month when his native state lay under snow and frozen ground. In June Judah and three company officials lifted a flatcar onto the fresh-laid rails and the platform was pushed up the hundred yards of finished track, making them the first passengers ever to ride west of the Mississippi.

The Sacramento was extended to Folsom in record time but one of the recurring convulsive financial depressions had gripped the state and the promoters were forced to put away their grand schemes of steel lines stretching all along the coast. The Sacramento Valley road, as the wags said, started in a river marsh and ended in a dust field.

Judah was out of work. The rational thing for a man of his ability and experience would have been to return East, but he had been bitten by the California bug. He had tramped and ridden through the Sierra Nevadas, and an obsession was growing within him. Edging toward it he talked to many people about projected railroads, none of which got past the planning stage, possibly because his full heart was not in his arguments for them.

What finally became a clear mandate to him was his vision of bridging the great mountain spine with a railroad to connect the Pacific Coast with the Eastern seaboard.

Central Pacific's first passenger station, division headquarters, supply base and office was this structure on the riverbank in Sacramento. Southern Pacific Collection

Toward that end he bent every effort, and his imagination, his conviction, and his dedication fathered the feat, unequalled in the history of western rail construction, of building the Central Pacific. But Judah himself was cheated of any part in the building. The task fell not to the trained engineer but on the burly shoulders of a silk merchant, a man too innocent of experience in such a project to know that it could not be done and too pigheaded to admit its impossibility when again and again he stood on the brink of defeat. But that came later, after Judah had bulled all the necessary preliminaries through many unbelieving, apathetic audiences.

To begin, Judah took on the job of surveying a route for a wagon road from Sacramento to the new silver camps of Nevada. He had no interest in such a road and made that clear to his wife, friends and the Sacramento newspapers, but it gave him the opportunity of searching for a path by which rails could climb the barricading mountains. He found such a path, tortuous, rugged, breathtaking, but, he insisted, possible.

Next he sought out men who could be convinced to attempt the formidable project. The idea of a coast-to-coast line was not new. As far back as the days when Jefferson Davis had been Secretary of War during President Franklin Pierce's administration he had ordered the Army engineers to survey for possible routes, and they had reported five available. Had not the country been approaching civil war the first road would probably have pushed west from New Orleans then, but the northern representatives had balked at voting funds for a southern road. Now, with the war even nearer, Judah would try for his northern route.

He was up against two obstacles as high as the mountains: ridicule in the press at the notion that such a road could possibly be built, and reluctance in a Congress that barely conceded the existence of California to make appropriations in so delicate a time when all available money might soon be needed to fight a war.

Judah did not falter, and never gave up his dream. His obsession drove him to buttonhole anyone who would listen, even skeptically, until he was nicknamed Crazy Judah. Still he worked, and in September of 1859 he scraped together a convention of railroad fans who assembled in Sacramento and sent him as a delegate to Congress.

In Washington he talked himself hoarse, but the Buchanan administration was too preoccupied with the coming conflict to look closely at the value of such a linkage in the north. Disheartened, he headed back to the Pacific Coast, but by the time he had made the long, roundabout trip via Panama, his enthusiasm had rebounded. He must produce actual maps with figures on grades to prove that his vision was practical.

With a friend he returned to the mountains and in the little mining com-

Charles Crocker

Leland Stanford

munity of Dutch Flat continued his preachment that he knew of a potential route, and at last found a hearing. The druggist, a Dr. Strong, took fire at the possibilities and over the counter they drew up the Articles of Association of the Central Pacific Railroad of California. At the bottom of the sheet both men signed up for more stock than they could afford. But money was needed immediately.

California law demanded that $1,000 worth of stock must be subscribed for every mile they planned to build before they could incorporate. With 115 miles between Sacramento and the Nevada line they must sell $115,000 worth to begin with. It was a tall order but Judah was confident, and within a week the local people subscribed over $45,000.

Jubilantly Judah went to San Francisco to raise more. San Francisco still resisted him. So did Sacramento when he went there to meet with moneyed men. But Judah did not know when he was beaten. A second meeting in the capital city was arranged, this one over a hardware store, sparsely at-

Mark Hopkins

Collis P. Huntington

These four men, among the original stockholders of the Central Pacific Railroad, eventually came to dominate its operations, gaining the title "The Big Four." Southern Pacific Collection

tended by a few friends from Dutch Flat, Dr. Strong, a handful of Sacramento men, and four who made the difference. With barely a dozen men in the room, none of them likely material to launch so vast an undertaking, the four key men were Leland Stanford, a grocer, Charles Crocker, a drygoods merchant and two partners in the hardware store, Mark Hopkins and Collis P. Huntington.

Charts, pamphlets, and figures were distributed. This time Judah changed his sales pitch on an inspiration of the moment. Abandoning the adjectives with which he had painted for Congress the glories of linking the two coasts, and saying nothing about his hope that his road would reunite the country, he went for their jugular, their self-interest. He asked only for the financing of a survey which he could present to Congress and press for the passage of the Pacific Railroad bill.

"The government will finance the building of the road then, but you gentlemen will own it."

He saw the exchange of glances, saw Mark Hopkins begin to shake his head, and aimed his finger in Hopkins' face, crying,

"What have you got to lose? You are merchants. Wouldn't you like to control the traffic to the Nevada mines? How rich do you think that would make you?"

Collis Huntington lifted a skeptical shoulder. "If . . . If a road could be built over that hill, which I doubt . . ."

The years of frustration, the heartbreak of failure after failure to realize the dream closed down on Judah, made him shout at the hardware dealer.

"What do you care whether a train runs on it? If we lay a grade for a railroad and can't get cars over the hill you'll have a wagon road anyway . . . and you will control that . . . a road over which you can charge any toll you choose."

Watching their reaction, watching the greed light up the faces, Judah knew that at last he had won. Virginia City, the new silver camp in Nevada, was beginning to boom, and those who controlled the flow of supplies in and of ore out . . . who needed a railroad?

There was both triumph and his final, unforeseen undoing in his victory. Taking in the four merchants of Sacramento, Judah took a camel into his tent. Together they would drive the engineer out of the company before work on the railroad was barely begun.

The Federal law creating the Central Pacific Railroad was passed, but it specified that no subsidy should be paid the company until the first 40 miles had been built. Effectively it forced the promoters to pay that cost themselves, either out of their own pockets or finding the money somewhere.

Huntington took off for Washington to lobby for help there. Stanford, already strengthening his political connections in a bid that led to his election as governor, squeezed concessions from the counties and cities through which the rails would pass, and from the California State Legislature in Sacramento.

The ways of the engineer and the promoters parted quickly. The four partners wanted the first 40 miles laid as cheaply as possible. Judah wanted to build well, for permanence. That was not the only disagreement. Judah wanted a correct, conventional financial structure aimed at benefitting the road; the merchants were accustomed to quick profits and devious methods of achieving them.

The four came up with a wonderful compromise, independently incorporating a contracting company which, as directors of the railroad company, they hired to construct the Central. Some organization had to build it, would profit from the job, and it might as well be they themselves.

They had another idea to bring an early return. Under the railroad act the subsidy voted for each mile through the mountains would be almost twice that for the level of the huge valley. As one Sacramento paper gleefully pointed out the budding railroad kings attempted a sleight-of-hand unheard of before. They asked that the designation of the foothills be moved 50 miles west, to be eligible for the higher rate.

Judah, horrified at such chicanery, protested loudly, and the open break yawned. It was agreed that the four merchants would buy out the engineer's interest for $100,000, or he in turn could buy out each of them for a like amount. Eternally optimistic, Judah started for New York certain now that the Vanderbilt interests would back his Pacific railroad, but it will never be known if he was right in that. He contracted yellow fever en route in Panama and was dead shortly after landing in New York.

Now the Sacramento four were in full control, and each considered himself the pivot of the partnership. Actually, a better balanced gang of pirates has seldom come together in one ring. Collis Huntington, hardwareman, was the acknowledged business leader. It was he who fought new legislation through Congress, who browbeat manufacturers of rails, locomotives, equipment, whatever was needed, into selling at prices below their regular levels, who traded with shipowners to carry the massive loads 13,000 miles around the Horn.

Mark Hopkins was watchdog of the treasury, scrutinizing every item to wring from it their full share.

Leland Stanford, grocer and politician, used all his connections and know-how to milk more and more subsidies from the state legislature and all of the communities who hoped to profit when the road came through them.

But it was huge Charles Crocker, dealer in drygoods, who physically drove the steel rails over the "Hill" that 90 percent of the people in California insisted could not be conquered. Anyone who has ridden that right-of-way can understand their point of view. The grades are awesome, the curves impossibly tight, the miles of sheds a great twisting, hollow wooden serpent writhing under 50-foot snowbanks in winter and seen as clinging perilously against near sheer mountainsides in summer. Disregarding public opinion, Charley Crocker never doubted. His greatest concern was time, time to get over the top, down the Nevada slope and out across the deserts and prairies toward which his competition, the Union Pacific, was building from the Missouri to claim the lands and moneys that would reward the first line to reach those lands.

In the autobiography he later dictated Crocker confessed himself a born leader, saying, "If you will step forward and take command it is amazing how many people will follow you without question."

Charley Crocker had stepped forward most of his life, first back in Troy where he saved up a couple of hundred dollars before he was twelve and bought a newspaper agency there. At seventeen he started out to establish an iron foundry and blacksmith shop. In 1849 he joined a group of gold seekers and successfully hauled their supplies up the Missouri River when no other boats could get through. And he had done well as a drygoods merchant and politician, where he came to know both Stanford and Hopkins.

But he had not found his true place until he began to boss the construction of the Central Pacific. There he bloomed. He gloried in all of it, the hard physical labor that suited his 250-pound frame, the confusion, the ever-looming challenge.

He made mistakes before he overcame the handicap of having no training for such a task. He drove his men, saw hundreds of them die in accidents along the stretching line, in avalanches that thundered down the mountains sweeping off whole camps, in premature blasts as they used black powder to drive the tunnels and blow the rock cuts. He had luck, and Crocker was the first to admit that luck.

It took a man of sublime self-confidence to step in as head of construction with Judah gone. The survey was complete, the stakes were driven all up the brutal slopes of the "Hill." What remained was to bring the dream of a railroad to reality, and in the Golden State all bets were against it. His partners' doubts waxed and waned, but Crocker never wavered.

Actual work had been begun in January 1863, and through that summer Crocker and his crews apprenticed on the easy 18 miles to what is now Roseville. He learned as he went but the education was so expensive that the Crocker Construction Company went broke long before they reached Roseville. That was not a real problem. His partners were the controlling directors of the Central Pacific company and met his payroll and expenses from the company treasury, since they also shared in the ownership of the construction company.

By the time Roseville was reached Judah was dead, and his title as engineer taken over by his assistant, S. S. Montague, an able helper. Crocker's superintendent, J. H. Strobridge, third man of the team, was a slave-driving bully with ham-like fists that made his orders law. After the early false starts these men built the Central Pacific with swarming thousands of Chinese laborers.

In the beginning the operations were plagued with labor troubles. The men of the Pacific Coast were an independent lot, most of them gold miners who had had their own claims. When the placers were worked out, the

Coast had sunk into depression and the men had taken whatever jobs they could find, but with the discovery of the Nevada mines anyone who could cross the mountains could make four dollars a day. Many who signed up to work on the railroad did so only to make money enough to take them on to Virginia City and Crocker's crews were always shorthanded with the flow of departures. He hired anyone and everyone, the lame, the halt, even children, and still they needed more.

It was Stanford who suggested using Orientals. Strobridge was strongly opposed but Crocker overruled him. He valued his own Chinese servant and he remembered how the little yellow men had fruitfully worked the placers after the American miners had given them up in disgust. They hired five hundred as a trial and were astonished at the diligence and speed of the new recruits. A second contingent was taken on and when they too proved an unhoped-for success the call went out to hire every Oriental to be found in any

Central Pacific construction boss James H. Strobridge (in dark suit) stands on flatcar after his crew laid a record 10 miles of track in one day. Southern Pacific Collection

of the Chinese settlements. Still there were not enough to meet Crocker's rush to beat the Union Pacific, and his older brother organized a company to import men directly from China.

This act fed the disrepute of the Central Pacific, alienating the local labor. Although the Americans refused to work on the road for long they did not want the Chinese in the jobs, pre-empting the potential labor market. There was other carping by such big business as Wells Fargo who did all they could to block the road. Still others who knew the Sacramento merchants by reputation shouted charges that the whole conception was an elaborate fraud to steal $1,500,000 from the state legislature, to force the cities to pay through the nose for a chimera. San Francisco screamed when a $400,000 "gift" to the Central Pacific was wrung from her. Persistently the critics predicted that the road would be built only until the going got tough, then the company would close down and leave a line of tracks to nowhere as the earlier Sacramento Valley had done.

Thousands of Chinese laborers did the backbreaking tasks of building the Central Pacific right-of-way over the Sierras. Golden West Collection

But the work went doggedly on, now heading for Newcastle, 12 miles into the foothills, and Crocker had learned much. This time he contracted for only the first two miles, the other ten being divided between a dozen independent contractors, but these fared no better than Crocker had done coming into Roseville. They lost money, lost labor, finally quit, and Crocker, again backed by the railroad treasury, stepped in to fulfill the contracts.

As a result 1864 saw very little track laid. Newcastle was reached, the 20-ton locomotives that had been freighted around the Horn disassembled were put together in Sacramento and set to work hauling supplies up to the rail-head.

Then the flow of money dropped to a dribble. For two full weeks there was not a nickel in the treasury and the railroad directors' personal credit slumped to the point that they could not restock.

Bleak as the prospect was Huntington would not give in. In Washington he ganged up with General Grenville Dodge and the backers of the Union Pacific and bulled through a far-reaching revision of the Railroad Act of 1862. The new bill, which Lincoln signed as a war measure to help hold the West Coast in the Union, doubled the land grants to both roads and made the government bonds a second mortgage, which permitted the companies to issue their own first mortgage bonds.

Moreover, he finally pulled off the four partners' original bit of magic, getting through Congress a decision that the Sierra Nevadas started upward

The locomotive Humboldt *No. 10 with a construction train of rails and ties, crosses the Newcastle trestle.* Golden West Collection

at Arcade Creek. With the new act decreeing a subsidy of $16,000 per mile on level ground, increasing to $48,000 in the mountains, this was a tremendous victory for the future railroad kings.

The California papers raised the roof with a hue and cry of fraud, but they were not the equals of men who could move the base of a mountain range 25 miles to the west with a stroke of a pen. For the moment the Central Pacific was saved.

Crocker's home now was a railroad car that took him back and forth along the tracks. Colfax had been passed and three trains ran each way every day. The labor troubles that had stymied him were being solved by the blue-clad Chinese swarming like ants over the freshly graded right-of-way. From his original two thousand the ranks had swelled to six thousand and imports from China continued to pour in with every ship from the Orient. There was enough money again and Crocker's obesssion with speed rode him mercilessly. He was everywhere at once, on the train, on his big black horse beyond the railhead riding back and forth among the half-running Chinese.

The Orientals were terrified of the huge figure. He was the big boss, Cholly Clocker to all of them, probably the only two English words they really understood, and they understood them well when on payday he pulled gold and silver from bulging saddlebags and distributed it with his own hands.

But for all his and Strobridge's driving of the crews it was still a long 50 miles to the summit and problems multiplied with every foot of altitude gained. Changes were made in Judah's route, yet they could not cut costs nor improve the grade to hurry the work.

The Chinese learned quickly and well. At first they were used only as graders, wheeling their barrows of broken rock off to dump in the canyon bottoms. Then they learned to lay track, in teams of a dozen at a time running up with a rail suspended in slings between them. As the upper reaches were neared they were taught to drill, to set the black powder charges and blast out the stubborn rock.

The higher they went the more stubborn the rock became, until they tackled an outcropping dubbed Cape Horn, which almost defeated even Charley Crocker. It was solid granite and its lower sides fell away in 1,000-foot cliffs with no toeholds anywhere. Swathed in a great fur coat and hat like some mammoth bear Crocker conferred with his two assistants. Montague was for trying to locate another route even if it meant abandoning miles of track already down, but Crocker roared his veto. Didn't they know the Union was rushing west across the easy sand hills while they stalled here, freezing under the crest of the "Hill"?

"Get your Chinks," he told Strobridge. "Swing them down that face on ropes to cut us a ledge with chisels."

CENTRAL PACIFIC RAILROAD.

No. 1, TIME CARD No. 1.

To take effect Monday June 6th, 1864, at 5 A. M.

TRAINS EASTWARD.						TRAINS WESTWARD.		
Frt and Pass No 3	Frt and Pass No 2	Pass & Mail No 1.		STATIONS.		Frt and Pass No 1	Pass & Mail No 2.	Frt and Pass No 3.
5 P M leave	1 P M leave	6.15 A M, L	......	Sacramento.	......	8.45 A M arr	12 M arr.	6.40 P M ar.
5.50 5.55 } mt frt	2.15	6.55	18	Junction.	18	3	11.20	5.55 5.50 } mt. Ft
6.09	2.38	7.05	22	Rocklin.	4	7.40	11.07	5.37
6.22	2.55	7.15 meet F	25	Pino.	3	7.15 mt pass	10.56	5.25
6.40	3.30 P M arr	7.30 A M arr	31	Newcastle.	6	6.45 A M, L	10.30 A M, L	5 P M, L

Trains No. 2 and 3 east, and 1 and 3 west, daily, except Sunday.
Trains No. 1 east and 2 west, daily.

LELAND STANFORD, President.

The first Central Pacific timetable. In early-day railroading the schedules were posted on station bulletin boards. Southern Pacific Collection

It was done. Hundreds of Chinese, dangling in midair like flies against the cliff, cut a shelf that men could work on, then that was widened, blasted out, hacked at until the tracks found room to circle the rock.

In July the first trains entered Dutch Flat where five years before Theodore Judah and his friends had organized the company. In November they reached Cisco, 6,000 feet high, 14 miles short of the summit and 1,100 feet below it.

Here the granite was incredibly hard, yet the road had to pass through it either by tunnel or rock cut. The drills could not be kept sharp and power blasts backfired, leaving the rock faces they were supposed to break almost untouched.

Then Crocker's brother learned of a discovery made in Sweden of a substance called nitroglycerin. Without it the tunnel at the summit, a bore over a quarter of a mile long, could never have been pushed through. The trouble was, the new blasting agent was wholly unpredictable, it could and frequently did go off unexpectedly. No one knows how many Chinese were blown apart in the explosions. Even Strobridge lost an eye. But even with the new explosive the work went forward at less than a foot a day.

To add to Crocker's frustration, reports of the Union Pacific's steady advance continued to bring it closer, and every mile the Union built was one mile less on which the Central could collect a subsidy.

Stanford and Ed Crocker tried to help hurry progress by sending a steam drilling rig up the hill, but Charley Crocker and Strobridge would have none of the newfangled contraption and continued their hand drilling.

To fight the stubborn rock for the quarter-mile-long Summit Tunnel bore, Crocker attacked from the western slope, sent crews around by sled to work from the east side, and others to drill down through the center section and hack horizontally from there, but the heaviest winter in history slowed them further.

Balked at the crest, Crocker leapfrogged and began grading down the Truckee canyon toward the Nevada desert. The weather there was less extreme but the problems no easier to solve: pine trees eight and nine feet in diameter had to be felled, cut to lengths that could be moved out of the right-of-way, and the stumps blasted.

Behind those crews the men fighting upward from Cisco battled ice and snowbanks 35 feet high. Of ten thousand Chinese nearly half had to be diverted from the important work to keep the work zones open. That too became impossible and they resorted to tunneling through the snowdrifts, which proved disastrous. Snow tunnels collapsed on the work crews, avalanches roared down, wiping out entire gangs, sweeping them into the canyons where they lay buried for five months, until the spring thaws uncovered the bodies.

Crocker foresaw that even with the tunnel punched through no trains could use that stretch of road except in summer, which would render the Central useless for half the year. By midwinter all work stopped on the upper reaches and the concentration was on getting down to the Nevada desert and easier going.

Meanwhile the Union Pacific was snaking forward, laying many more miles than it could have had Crocker been able to get through at the top, and tension among the four partners grew to the breaking point. During the winter of 1866–67 Crocker had three locomotives disassembled and hauled on sleds across the gap he could not close, track was laid down the eastern slope and the race to beat the Union on the level went on.

Another winter as bad as the previous one closed the work on top again before Crocker devised the nearly 40 miles of snowsheds through which his trains could move when nothing could outside. But they could not be begun until spring, and the second winter stoppage added fuel to the opposition in California who insisted that the Central at best would never be anything except a seasonal line.

With the first warm breath of spring in 1868 Crocker again laid siege to the granite gap, but it took six thousand Chinese many weeks of picking at the ice before they could attack the tunnel. Sawmills were set up along the right-of-way, the great logs cut, the sheds hung against the canyonside, and at last the breakthrough made, tracks laid through the tunnel and connected with the eastern section.

A completed section of snowshed at Donner Summit in 1869 used to protect trains from slides and drifting snow. Golden West Collection

With that Herculean task behind, the question remained, could the Central Pacific beat the Union Pacific into Salt Lake City for control of traffic into the Mormon capital? Crocker drove his Chinese without mercy, out across the desert, laying track faster than it had ever been laid before: 362 miles in one year! Still it was a furious race, for Jack Casement of the Union, egged on by General Dodge, was using a familiar brand of psychology in boasting that any Irish Paddy in his labor gangs could outwork any three Chinese, and the Irish were breaking their backs to meet the challenge.

Stanford had moved to Salt Lake City to cultivate the Mormons. The surveyors of both lines had passed each other and were miles away from their meeting point, paralleling the already completed rails with advancing stakes, and now the grading crews had passed each other.

The spot at which the two companies would join their tracks into a transcontinental railroad was still being argued out in Washington and Congress decreed that Promontory Point, just west of Ogden, should be the place. Once this was established the hurry was over.

On May 10, 1869, the Golden Spike at last united the rival roads in the middle of Utah with many dignitaries attending the ceremony. But Charley Crocker who had physically beaten the "Hill," built the Central over mountains that everyone had said could not be crossed by trains, was not present. He remained aloof in Sacramento. The fun was over and Crocker knew he would never face an equal challenge again.

That the Big Four were financial pirates is a well-known fact. Most of the men who built the West would fail the test of modern-day business morality, but they did open the country, they did give us railroads, and highways, and mines. Their methods may be questioned but it cannot be denied that the Charley Crockers accomplished what they set out to do.

Sixty years later the Southern Pacific Railroad employees erected a memorial statue to Theodore Judah, the only tribute accorded to the man who had the dream that materialized at Promontory Point. If he had lived to see the completion would he have been proud of the accomplishment, or would he still have pointed the accusing finger at those who amassed enormous fortunes as the fruit of his imagination?

5

The Wedding of the Rails

NELLIE SNYDER YOST

What was it the engines said,
Pilots touching—head to head,
Facing on the single track,
Half a world behind each back?

Bret Harte, inspired by the sight of the two wood-burning locomotives, nose to nose on the slender rails that spanned a mighty continent, dashed off these lines as the final preparations were made to drive the Golden Spike, a milestone as momentous in 1869 as the landing of a man on the moon was to be a century later. The wedding of the rails, however, had been achieved at a far greater cost in toil, suffering, and human lives.

On May 1, 1869, the heads of the Union Pacific and Central Pacific railroads had set May 8 as the official date for the joining of the rails at Promontory Point, Utah. On the evening of May 7 California's Governor Leland Stanford, president of the Central Pacific, and his party of invited guests, which included Chief Justice Sanderson, Governor Safford of the Arizona Territory, Dr. J. D. B. Stillman of Sacramento and others, arrived at Promontory in a two-car special train.

There they were informed that the Union Pacific special, bearing officials from the east, would be delayed due to storm damage to the tracks in Echo

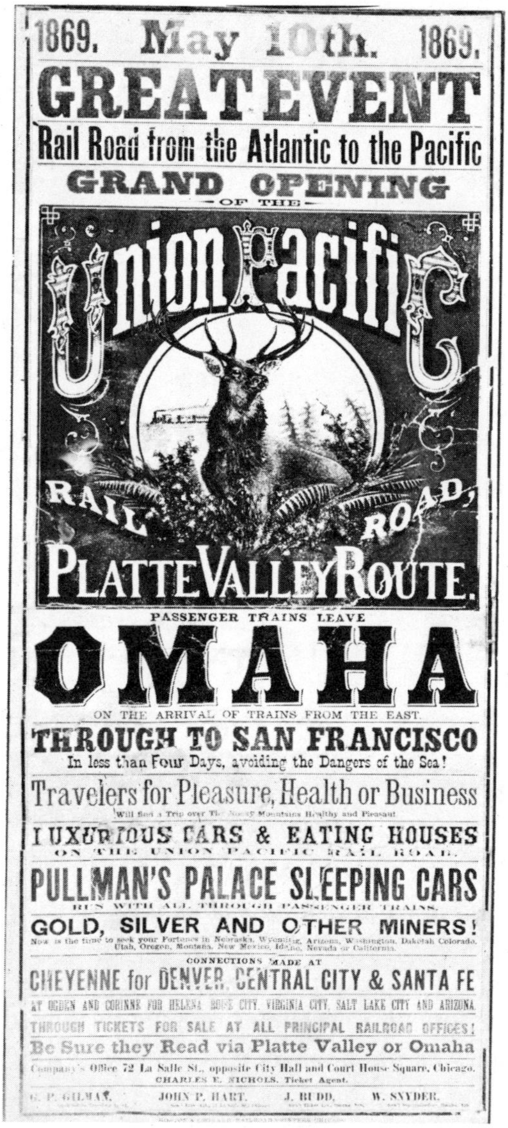

Newspapers and station bulletin boards carried this advertisement poster announcing the completion of the Union Pacific. Union Pacific Railroad Photo

Canyon, east of Ogden. The date for uniting the rails was then set up to May 10 and the Central's party took advantage of a Union Pacific invitation to spend the two extra days inspecting their line as far as Weber Canyon, just west of Echo where the tracks were out.

The storm damage, though real enough, was not the only reason for the Union Pacific's delay. At Piedmont, Wyoming, 83 miles west of Green River, Vice-president Thomas C. Durant's special had been held up by a mob of unpaid tie cutters who demanded their wages before they would allow the train to pass. Virtual prisoners of the lumberjacks, Durant wired Oakes Ames, president of the Union Pacific, that he must have the money to pay the men before he could go on to Promontory. And Ames, hard pressed by the road's financial difficulties though he was, someway raised the money and wired it to Durant, who paid the men and headed on for Promontory where, in spite of all its difficulties, the UP special steamed up to the gap in the rails at ten o'clock on the morning of May 10.

The final preparations for the ceremony that would officially unite the rails had begun at dawn that day with the arrival of two construction trains, one from the east, one from the west. The engines stopped where the rails ended at the edges of the 56 foot gap in the single track line. Railroad workers, Chinese from the west, Irish from the east, all dressed in their Sunday best, piled off the flatcars, and the trains were backed onto newly laid sidetracks.

Soon after the work trains had delivered the laborers, the Central Pacific special bringing Governor Stanford and his guests back to Promontory pulled in. The meeting place was located near the east side of a level circular valley, some three miles in diameter and surrounded by mountains. Stanford's train moved up to within a few yards of the end of the western rails, where it waited until the Union Pacific special hove in sight and came to a stop on the east side of the gap.

Governor Stanford and his guests then alighted from their cars and proceeded over to the other special, where Durant invited them aboard his private car, one of the most elegant of its day. There the western delegation shook hands with Sidney Dillon, chairman of the Union Pacific Board of Directors, Chief Engineer Major General Grenville M. Dodge, Director John Duff, the Casement brothers, Jack and Dan, the contractors who had built most of the Union Pacific road, Bishop John Sharp of the Church of Jesus Christ of Latter-Day Saints, and others.

By then the waiting crowd had swelled to more than one thousand people. Four companies of the 21st Infantry were on hand and two bands, the headquarters band from Camp Douglas at Salt Lake City and one brought along by a large representation of Utahans from the capital city's Tenth Ward. The latter, turned out in gay new uniforms, was equipped with $1,200 worth of brand-new instruments from London.

The guests included bankers and railroad builders from both coasts, workers from all parts of the railroad, civic leaders, newspaper reporters, a colorful variety of camp followers and settlers who had walked or driven across the nearby countryside for their first sight of a locomotive and passenger train.

The two engines which had brought up the official trains now stood near the ends of the rails, facing each other across the gap. There the unnamed

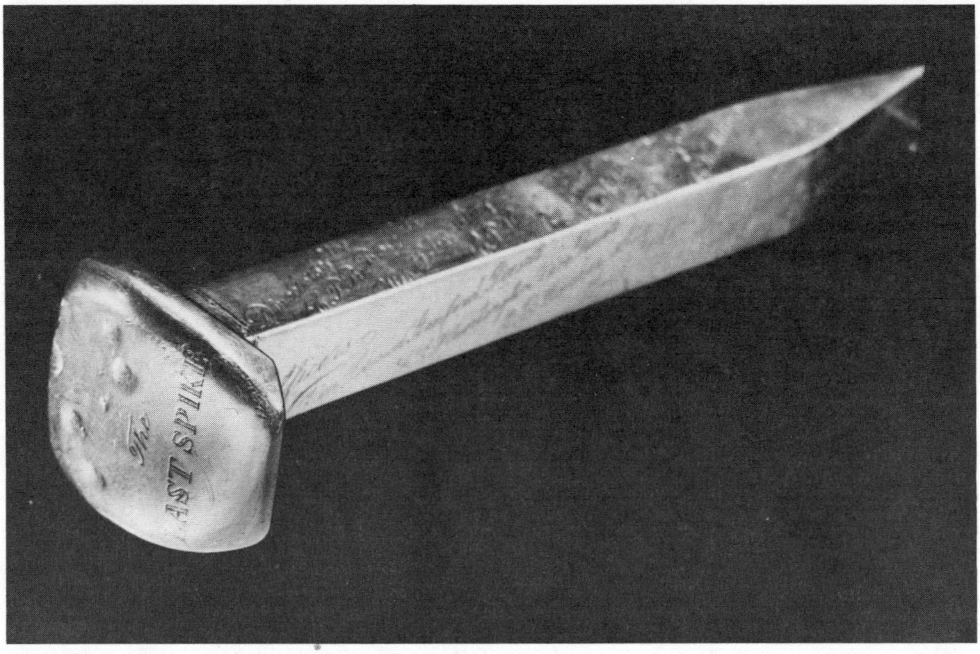

The Golden Spike. Southern Pacific Collection

Union Pacific engine, identified only by the number 119, and the Central Pacific's *Jupiter,* both polished to mirror brightness, waited under full heads of steam.

The Golden Spike, carried to the scene in Governor Stanford's private car, had been crafted from about $400 worth of gold by a firm of San Francisco jewelers. The bill, which included the engraving of 381 letters at four cents a letter, was $25.24. On the spike's head was inscribed *The Last Spike.* On one of its four sides were the words: *The Pacific Railroad; Ground Broken January 8, 1863; completed May 10, 1869.* On another: *May God continue the unity of our Country as this Railroad unites the two great Oceans of the world.* On the third: *Presented by David Hewes, San Francisco.* And on the fourth the names of the company officers were listed.

The engraver had originally used the date of May 8 as the completion date, but when the delay occurred, the date was changed at the last moment to read May 10.

Enshrined in state beside the Golden Spike was the last tie. Made of highly polished California laurel, it was eight feet long by eight inches wide and six inches thick, bound with silver and inscribed with the date of the completion of the railroad and the names of the Central Pacific directors. The beautiful tie had been presented to Stanford by West Evans, contractor for the Central Pacific.

Painting by Thomas Hill showing the outstanding citizens and railroad builders present at the driving of the Golden Spike. Painting now hanging in corridor California State Capitol, Sacramento. Union Pacific Railroad Photo

According to Union Pacific accounts of the historic occasion, as soon as Stanford's special rolled to a stop, Chinese laborers from the Central's construction gangs rushed in to level the ground in the gap, readying it for the last ties and the joining of the iron. On orders from W. B. Hubbard, Western Union superintendent, wires from the nearest telegraph pole, on top of which a nine-year-old boy was perched for a bird's eye view of the proceedings, were run down to a special operator's kit on a small four-legged table beside the gap. Seated at the table, W. N. Shilling of the company's Ogden office waited to tap out a blow by blow description of the final act to the waiting nation. A silver-headed spike maul, wired so that its blows would activate the telegraph key, lay waiting.

While the crowd cheered, the last tie was carried into place by Superintendents J. H. Strobridge of the Central and S. B. Reed of the Union Pacific. Now all was in readiness for the laying of the last rail and the driving of the Golden Spike. As the Chinese laborers carried that last rail toward the gap, photographers waited under the black hoods of their big box cameras.

And at that instant someone in the crowd shouted, "Now's the time. Take a shot."

Although the Chinese knew very little English, they were well acquainted with the word "Shoot" in all its tenses. At the same instant they noted the cameras pointed at them. Dropping the rail as if it had suddenly turned red hot, they scrambled for cover. After some urgent coaxing, they came back on the job and laid the last rail upon the ties.

Some historians do not agree that the Chinese were there, or that the event described took place. Best, however, relates that Superintendent Strobridge later in the day brought in the Chinese boss of all his track-laying gangs, numbering 10,000 at the end of construction, and introduced him to the official party, "who gave him a standing ovation in honor of the outstanding performance of his countrymen." In view of this it does not seem unlikely that some of the Chinese trackmen were chosen to lay the last rail.

It was almost noon when General Dodge lifted his hand for silence and introduced the Reverend Dr. John Todd of Pittsfield, Massachusetts, who then led the prayer which formally opened the ceremony. Just before the introduction of the minister the telegrapher had tapped out to impatient inquirers from all over the nation: KEEP QUIET. WHEN THE LAST SPIKE IS DRIVEN AT PROMONTORY WE WILL SAY DONE. A few minutes later he added: ALMOST READY. HATS OFF, PRAYER IS BEING OFFERED.

All Western Union wires had been cleared for the Promontory news and finally, as an eager nation waited, the messages began clicking out into space. At 2:40, Eastern Time, the telegrapher tapped: WE HAVE GOT DONE PRAYING. THE SPIKE IS ABOUT TO BE PRESENTED. This proved to be a long ceremony, for there were many spikes. One of silver, one of silver and gold, another ribbed with iron, clad in silver and crowned with gold, and the last, the Golden Spike. Various states, Arizona, Idaho, Montana, and California, as well as the Comstock mine, had donated spikes and all had to be presented with appropriate speeches. There were speeches, too, by Governor Stanford, General Dodge, and others. The crowd cheered them all, then cheered for the Star-Spangled Banner, which floated free from the top of a telegraph pole, the railroad, the officers, the men who raised the money, the engineers who found the routes and the laborers who built the tracks.

Governor Stanford was to strike the first blow that drove the Golden Spike and the signal that it was about to be driven—three dots by the telegrapher—was given. The governor then stepped forward, took the silver-headed maul and, while the crowd and the nation waited in a breathless hush, swung—and missed. The telegrapher, however, had already tapped out IT IS DONE.

Best describes the historic scene a little differently. There was much wrangling between the officials of both railroads, he writes, before Stanford and Durant settled the matter of who would drive the Golden Spike by agreeing to take the two golden spikes available and each drive one. When the scene was set, with the officials in place and a company of United States Army Infantry troops standing at attention, Durant of the Union Pacific placed a gold spike in the already drilled hole in the laurel tie on the outside edge of one rail. Governor Stanford then dropped the engraved golden spike from David Hewes into the last empty hole in the tie. The governor next hit an iron spike, already partly driven into the next tie, with the silver-plated maul which formed one side of the telegraph circuit, the spike forming the ground connection. And that was it.

The official announcement, flashed to the Associated Press and to President Ulysses S. Grant, read:

> Promontory, Utah, May 10.
>
> The last rail is laid! The last spike is driven! The Pacific railroad is completed! The point of junction is 1,086 miles west of the Missouri River and 690 east of Sacramento City.
>
> LELAND STANFORD
> CENTRAL PACIFIC RAILROAD
>
> T. C. DURANT
> SIDNEY DILLON
> JOHN DUFF
> UNION PACIFIC RAILROAD

The two engines, *Jupiter* and 119, covered with cheering celebrants, then advanced until their pilots touched and bottles of champagne were broken on them, the bubbling wine flowing down over the Golden Spike and the laurel tie.

As soon as the ceremony was over and the tracks cleared, crews from both the Union Pacific and the Central Pacific rushed in, removed the precious spikes and the handsome tie and replaced them with an ordinary tie and iron spikes, while the officials of both roads retired to Governor Stanford's car for lunch. There they talked over the stirring experiences of the past three years, during which a continent had been spanned with two thin lines of steel. It was at this time that the Chinese boss and his men were honored by the jubilent moguls of the railroad. And one wonders if some of them spared a thought for the many men who had died that the mighty project might be completed, and whose bones now rested in a thousand unmarked graves along the way from the Missouri to the Pacific. As a final gesture of farewell, each train steamed across the junction of the rails, standing for a triumphant moment on the other side before departing for the East and the West.

Today the Golden Spike rests in a vault in the Wells Fargo Bank and Union

The locomotives are christened. Shaking hands in the center are the chief engineer of the Central Pacific, Montague (left), and Grenville M. Dodge, chief engineer of the Union Pacific. Russell photo. Union Pacific Railroad Photo

Trust Company in San Francisco. The laurel tie was also returned to San Francisco but was destroyed in the fire and earthquake that devastated that city in 1906. But neither of the sturdy engines that faced each other across the gap more than a century ago were preserved for posterity. The old *Jupiter* was cut up for scrap at Globe, Arizona, in 1901 and, no doubt, No. 119 went the same way, her end unheralded and unrecorded as she suffered the fate usually accorded outmoded equipment by unsentimental corporations.

6

Cinderella of the Prairie: The Kansas Pacific

MEL MARSHALL

Wild Bill Hickok swaggering along the board sidewalks of Hays. Bat Masterson leaning on his gold-headed cane in front of the tent that served Sheridan Station as a marshal's office. Bill Cody sitting with his crony, General Phil Sheridan, at a bottle-laden table in Drum's Saloon and somewhere west of railhead a frustrated George Armstrong Custer chasing glory and never quite catching up with it. Over them all, the shadow of John C. Frémont, the Pathfinder of the West.

Longhorns jostling and bawling in temporary corrals while the cowhands who'd driven them up from Texas to railhead caroused away the night. Ricks of buffalo hides dried flint-hard and stacked higher than the head of a tall man on horseback spread over ten acres on either side of new-laid rails. A thousand gandy dancers pounding spikes, listening between hammer strokes for the war cries of Indians on painted ponies. Over them all, the shadows of frock-coated stock manipulators in paneled Wall Street offices.

These names and these scenes jigsaw into the railroad legends of the West. Seldom are they fitted together to make a completed picture that shows all the forces responsible for the creation of so much that has come to mean the West of the prairie frontier. One of these great moving forces was the Kansas Pacific Railroad, seldom mentioned when the legends of Hickok, Masterson, Cody, and Custer are told. Perhaps this is because it did nothing as an entity to create these personal legends. The KP goes unsung because the mere fact of its existence in that place and at that time was enough to trigger events that drew the men around whom the legends grew. The part played by the Kansas Pacific was not that of an actor, but of a catalyst.

Conceived in dissension and born in bloodshed, never far from the spectre of the bankruptcy that did finally end its career, the Kansas Pacific played a key role in altering the economy and later the ecology of one-fourth of the United States. The railroad was not a likely candidate for such distinction. As railroads go, it was always a stepchild, a sort of poor relation that got a card instead of a gift on its birthday. There were good reasons why men who knew it best swore that "KP" really stood for "Keep Poor."

Western railroad legends generally center around the Union Pacific, the Central Pacific, and the Santa Fe. The fact remains that the Kansas Pacific gave first access to Eastern tanneries from the buffalo prairie and spurred the great hide-hunting boom that was to end with the virtual extinction of the once-mighty herds. It was the KP that first gave railheads to Texas cattle ranchers and triggered the short-lived but greatly storied days of trail drives north. Had the KP's cattle cars been bigger, Texas ranchers might not have switched so readily from longhorns to the short-horned Herefords; only ten or eleven longhorns could be squeezed into a cattle car, but Herefords could be shipped fifteen or sixteen to the carload.

Born in 1856 as the Leavenworth, Pawnee & Western, the railroad surveyed a route from Leavenworth, Kansas, then an important center of Missouri River steamboat traffic, to Fort Riley, in east-central Kansas. Construction was actually begun in 1862 along a portion of the route, but the drain of the Civil War on national resources forced work to stop before more than a few miles of track had been laid. Then, even in the midst of wartime frenzy, came passage of the Federal Railroad Act of 1862, with its subsidy provisions that in effect opened the U. S. Treasury to railroad promoters. The promoters responded avidly, and among those responding were Samuel Hallet and General John C. Frémont, who secured control of the LP&W in 1863.

Frémont must have eyed the road much earlier; he was a man who was always conscious of the big chance. He was also a man with a fatal character flaw that led him to spoil every opportunity on which he tried to capitalize. Insubordination had led to his removal as Governor of California by President James K. Polk in 1848; and his removal by Lincoln as commander of the Western Armies in 1862; arrogance had defeated his ambition to seek the presidency in 1864.

Certainly Frémont was aware of the chance for fame and wealth that the newly possible transcontinental railroad would offer its creators. As the son-in-law of one of the Senate's most influential members and a former Senator

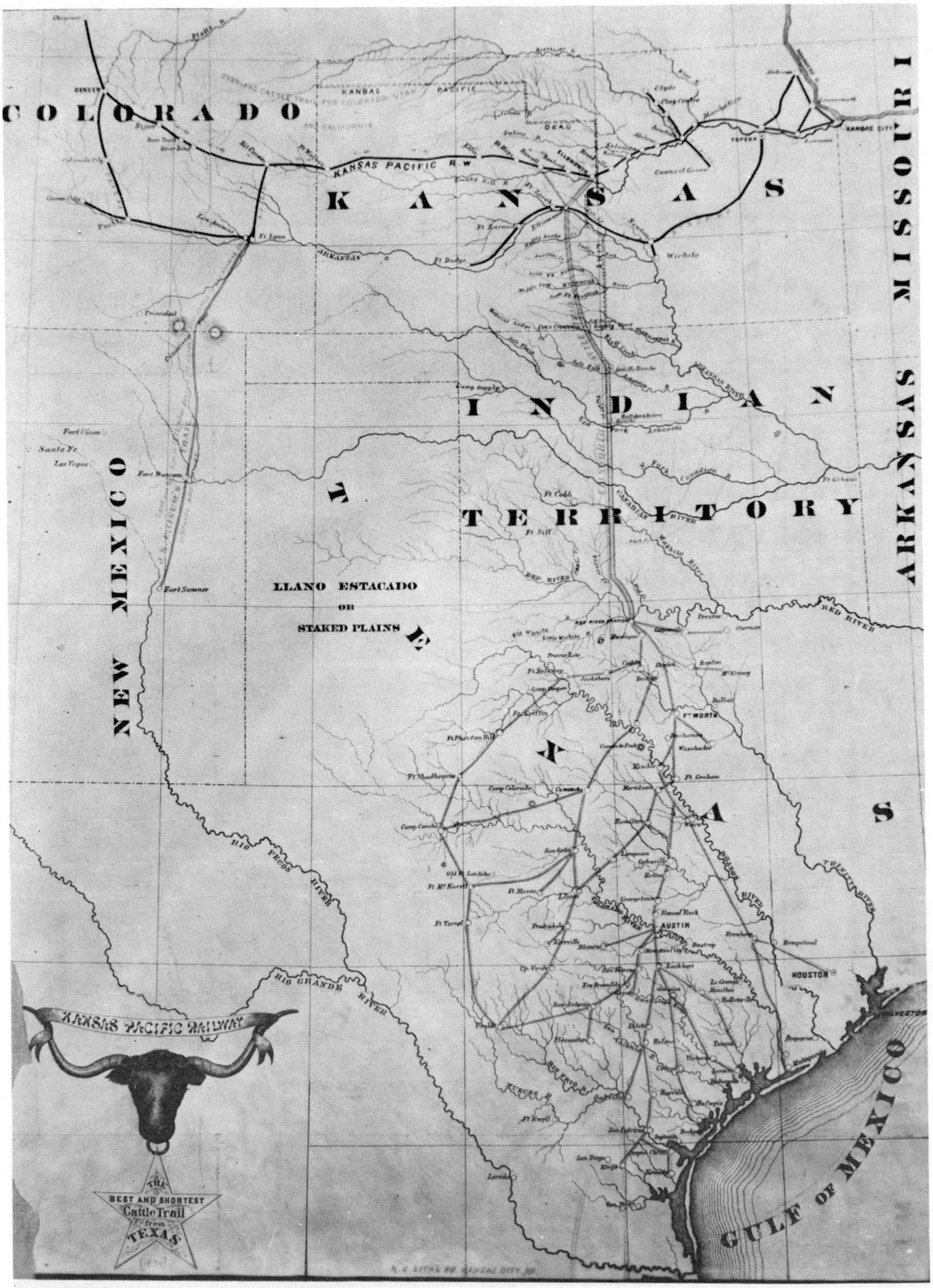

The Chisholm and Ellsworth cattle trails led north from Texas to Abilene, Ellsworth, and other cow towns along the line of the Kansas Pacific. Kansas State Historical Society himself, Frémont had the pull in Washington to get the LP&W included in the 1862 Railroad Act. He had the self-confidence to be positive that he, the Pathfinder, could win the race the Act's provision established, a race to build rails to the 100th meridian. The first road to push its tracks to that meridian would win the privilege—and the subsidies—of continuing to build west and connect with the Central Pacific, being built from California eastward, to create a transcontinental railway line.

When the Leavenworth, Pawnee & Western was officially recognized by the Act of 1862 as a contender in the race, its name was changed and it became the Union Pacific Railroad, Eastern Division. Despite this name, it had no connection with the Union Pacific, Western Division, being built farther north, along the Platte River. The northern road was promoted by the Ames brothers, Oakes and Oliver, and by T. C. Durant and George Francis Train. Not until 1869 did the UPRR, ED, become the Kansas Pacific, but to avoid confusion it will be called the Kansas Pacific here, during its construction period as well as in its later years.

Characteristically, Frémont's vision was faulty. He underestimated the magnet that the subsidies in the Railroad Act contained, and failed to foresee the methods that venally astute financiers would originate for milking the Federal Treasury. To his credit, Frémont saw only the vision of shining rails

During the construction era the Kansas Pacific line crossed the Kaw (Kansas) River near Topeka on this makeshift bridge. Library of Congress

opening new country, connecting the coasts; if he also saw personal glory, he cannot be blamed too greatly. His was not the vision of the Ames-Durant-Train combine, who saw the dollar signs of Crédit Mobilier; nor was it the vision of Crocker, Hopkins, and Huntington who saw the Central Pacific through the golden haze of their Construction & Finance Company.

Others in Frémont's group of associates did see the dollar signs and the golden haze. Dissension arose over the financing of the Kansas Pacific, and the upshot was the first bloodshed for which the KP could logically be said to have catalyzed. Frémont's chief associate, Samuel Hallet, was killed in a gunfight with O. A. Talcott, whose loyalties lay with the group trying to oust Frémont and Hallet from control of the road.

Out of the gunplay came a new board of directors which did not include Frémont. The new board, controlled by John Perry, R. E. Shoemaker, and William J. Palmer, set up the KP's own version of Crédit Mobilier or Construction & Finance Co. Under the name of Shoemaker, Miller & Co., the KP's new money siphon went into operation, playing the same game originated by the bigger nabobs of the UP and CP. Quite simply, the game was for the Kansas Pacific's new promoters to contract with their own construction firm to build the road. Shovels for which Shoemaker, Miller & Co. paid $2 were charged to the KP at $4, and so on along the list: rails, ties, wagons, wheelbarrows, mules, wages—all were padded in price, with the padding going to the promoters.

How big the operation was can be judged by figures revealed in later years. The first 394 miles of Kansas Pacific track, built over level prairie, cost $24,629,456. The final 236 miles, built after the subsidies were lost and threading through the Rocky Mountains into Denver, cost only $6,117,583. But the Kansas Pacific's promoters exercised less discretion than did those of the UP and CP, who were prudent enough to shut off the siphon before it drained away money needed to maintain their building schedules. Construction funds for the KP always seemed to be a day latc and a dollar short.

During the early days of track-laying it was either feast or famine. Wyandotte, today's Kansas City, had replaced Leavenworth as the key Missouri River steamboat terminal, and Wyandotte became the KP's terminus as well. By 1865, trackage was completed to Abilene, where work stopped for lack of cash. But penetration of the fringes of the buffalo range had been made, and anchoring of the railhead at Abilene was not necessarily bad for business. The buffalo hunters at last had a firm destination for their big Murphy hide wagons, and the cattlemen a firm target for their trail drives in a town where both hide-hunters and cowhands could enjoy the amenities of civilization.

Buffalo hides took second place to cattle during the first years of the KP's freight operation, though. Word had spread into Texas very quickly that there was now a feasible way to ship cattle east, and about the only asset Texas had in 1865 was plenty of beef on the hoof. Through the years of the Civil War, when almost all the state's able-bodied men had been riding with Confederate General John Hood or patrolling the Comanche frontier with the Texas Rangers, the big ranches in the southern section of the state had gone largely untended. As long as the war went on, there'd been no point in working the spreads, for hostilities had closed the markets where Texas cattle had formerly been sold.

Prewar, the ranchers had sent trail herds along the old Spanish military roads, east into Louisiana and Mississippi, southwest into Mexico, and over the Mission Trail west to California and the gold mines of the Mother Lode country. There had been drives north over the Sedalia Trail that cut through northern Louisiana and Arkansas to Sedalia on the Missouri, where the steers were loaded on barges and taken to the slaughterhouses at St. Louis. But with the war, the pine woods east of the Sabine River were patrolled by bluecoats whose mission was twofold: to keep Texas beef from reaching the meat-starved southeastern states and to keep Texas poor by denying it the beef markets of the north. Nor could the cattle be shipped by barge, as

The difficult job of loading Texas longhorn cattle. Kansas State Historical Society

the ranchers had done in prewar days, out of ports on Galveston Bay and Matagorda Bay, for Federal gunboat patrols controlled the Gulf of Mexico.

On the ranches, the cattle ran wild, which is a pale word to apply to Texas cattle of that era. These were not the chunky, docile steers that would appear in later years. The cattle of the 1860s were longhorns, lean and rangy, with horns that spanned eight or ten feet from tip to tip, cat-quick on their feet, meaner than panthers and as uncontrollable as so many runaway locomotives. Even during the times when they were worked regularly in herds, longhorns were never what could be called completely domesticated. They were, after all, descended from the Spanish fighting bulls of Saltilla and Miura that had been brought to Mexico three centuries earlier. Though the seed had not stayed pure through decades of casual breeding, the longhorns evidenced their ancestry in their agility and uncompromising ferocity.

Left without attention for five years, a herd of modern-day steers would fade to nothing, with perhaps a few of the more rugged animals surviving. Left to themselves during the Civil War, the Texas longhorn herds increased. When there was no grass, they ate prickly pear and mesquite brush. When there was no water, they plodded to the Gulf or the saline bayous and waded out to absorb moisture through their skins. In the hurricane season they sought shelter in the piney woods to the east, and the arroyos of the Edwards Plateau to the west. When wolves or bears or panthers threatened their calves, they fought off the intruders, and won more battles than they lost. Their ruggedness made it possible for them to survive the 600-mile trail drive to railhead.

Who actually pioneered the Texas trail drives will be argued wherever old-time cattlemen get together. Opinions are divided. Some give credit to Jesse Chisholm, with his trail from the Cross Timbers in East Texas to supply the reservations in Indian Territory with government beef. Others award the accolade to Goodnight and Loving, who drove from the Forks of the Brazos into New Mexico with steers for the military garrisons there. The question will never be settled, for Chisholm's first drive and that of the Goodnight-Loving partnership started only weeks, perhaps only days apart, and the precise dates were never accurately recorded. But even before these pioneers there had been trail drives from Texas, a fact often overlooked or forgotten by those who date cattle trailing from the mid-1860s.

This was, of course, the time when the modern cattle drive from ranch to railhead began. When word spread among the Texas ranchers that their longhorns could be trail-herded to Abilene and from there shipped in stock cars over Kansas Pacific tracks to the slaughterhouses in St. Louis and Chicago, the railroad's business rocketed. In 1867, only 35,000 longhorns made the trip. The following year, ten times that number, over 300,000 bawling, plunging,

Kansas Pacific's Kansas Express *at Abilene after its arrival from end-of-track at Ellsworth.* Union Pacific Railroad Photo

half-wild longhorns arrived at the KP's Abilene railhead. On occasions there were from 30,000 to 40,000 head at once jammed into hastily erected shipping pens waiting for the cattle cars to roll.

By 1871, the KP was handling 600,000 steers a year from Abilene and Hays. After that, the Santa Fe, a hundred miles closer to Texas, began to cut into the Kansas Pacific's lucrative traffic. When the first north-south feeder line, the Texas Pacific, began operating out of Fort Worth in 1876, both the Santa Fe and the KP lost steam. While the KP boom lasted, it had been big. The best estimates agree that between 1866 and 1876, 10,000,000 steers worth $200,000,000 at railhead, traveled to the stockyards to become beef.

Cowpunching was not a job for weaklings. Many an ex-cavalryman, fresh from military duty with Hood or Longstreet or Thomas, found he'd had an easier time riding herd on the Federal cavalry than on these raw longhorns. Just rounding up the steers for trailing was a task rough enough to shake out the faint-hearted and lily-fingered. Taking the herd north, 600 to 800 miles depending on its starting point, with the final lap through unpredictable Indian Territory along the Chisholm Trail, was a job that called for men as ornery and tough as the steers they handled. If the cowboys weren't meaner than the longhorns when they started out from Texas to railhead, they'd gotten meaner by the time they reached Abilene.

Contemporary accounts, probably only slightly exaggerated, tell of periods as long as a month when a thousand cowhands—most of them from Texas—

were waiting at Abilene for cattle cars on which to ship their herds. For a brief span in history, Abilene became the biggest, brawlingest, lustiest cow town of them all, the prototype of the Western frontier settlement on a scale of wildness never quite equalled elsewhere. At its zenith, Abilene's attractions included such favorites as the Alamo Saloon, where each of the three shifts that worked seven days a week was manned by twenty-five bartenders. The Alamo was one of forty saloons, twenty dance halls, fourteen gambling houses or poker rooms that kept the cowboys entertained around the clock. There was also an unrecorded number of brothels, scattered all over town until the city fathers enriched the language with a new phrase by ordering them to move to "the other side of the tracks."

When the action slackened in Abilene and shifted to Dodge City, on the rapidly building Santa Fe line, not all the riffraff attracted by the boom moved to Dodge. Into Abilene, hired by the city selectmen from his job as marshal at Hays, came Wild Bill Hickok. Like a number of early gunfighters, Hickok seems to have run afoul of the law before becoming one of the West's most notable law-enforcers, but his early troubles in Nebraska had been cleared up long before he arrived in Kansas.

Along Texas Street in Abilene, Hickok's embroidered shirts and fancy vests became sights as familiar as the pair of long-barreled .36 caliber Navy Colts he favored. Hickok brought to Abilene the unorthodox style of gun-packing that was often imitated, though never quite successfully, by later gunmen. He wore his holsters high under his long frock coat, the guns butt-forward, and since Wild Bill lived to be shot in the back while playing cards in a Deadwood saloon many years later, it's logical to deduce that he could sweep out both weapons in a double cross-body draw faster than the hip-draws used by the antagonists he faced. Just as insurance, he also kept a double-barreled .41 caliber Williamson derringer in each fob pocket of his vest.

Hickok must have been a proficient gunfighter. Legends credit him with having killed eleven or seventeen or twenty-seven men, the number varying with the distance separating those recounting the legends from the places Hickok lived. He cleaned up Abilene with only one fatal gunfight; the Hickok reputation was so big that few cared to draw against him.

As the decade of the 1860s rolled to a close, trail herds wore out their welcome in Abilene. By request of the town officials, cattlemen began shipping from other railpoints, most of the business going to Hays, 110 miles west on the KP. By 1867–68, Hays was not only getting a major share of the cattle-shipping business, but by virtue of being deep into the buffalo prairie it also became the center of the hide trade. The hide boom really began when the Kansas Pacific lost the race to the 100th meridian, and as a result lost the sub-

James B. "Wild Bill" Hickok.
Kansas State Historical Society

sidies it would have been paid for extending its rails to connect with the Central Pacific. While the road's promoters debated whether to build on to Denver or sell out, the end of track was at Sheridan Station, a few miles beyond Hays.

There had been 1,200 or more men working on construction of the KP, and they were fired without notice and without provision being made for them to return east. Some moved down to work on the Santa Fe, which was then pushing its tracks toward the Arkansas River. Others went north to help lay UP iron, snaking along the Platte toward the joining at Promontory Point with the CP tracks. About half the jobless gandy dancers tied up with the outfits of professional hide-hunters who'd moved just ahead of the KP rails as they stabbed deeper and deeper into the heart of the prairie range occupied by the big central buffalo herd.

Up along the Platte, the Union Pacific had tapped the hide market first when it reached the vicinity of the northern buffalo herd. Professional hide-hunters had been working this herd long before the rails arrived. Since 1840 they had been sending about a half-million hides a year to the tanneries in New England, the hides hauled by wagon to Missouri River steamboat landings, then barged downriver and transshipped to the East Coast. Still farther north, the Canadian herd was untouched by any except the Indians, and to the south the Texas herd had felt no impact from hunters other than the Comanche and Kiowa and by a few ciboleros from New Mexico, who took only a few hundred hides a year. Until the KP thrust its rails into the middle of Kansas, the big central buffalo herd had grazed undisturbed except for the 20,000 to 30,000 animals a year taken from its millions by the Prairie Indian tribes.

Hunting as practiced by the hide-men bore no resemblance to sport. They left the showy business of running buffalo from horseback to the Indians, who had to get close enough to kill with lance or bow and arrow. Even Buffalo Bill Cody, who ran the animals and shot from horseback to entertain foreign and eastern dignitaries in later years, followed the sensible methods of the professional hunter at this point in his career. Cody had a contract with the KP to provide twelve buffalo carcasses a day for its track crews, and hired others to do the hauling and butchering. It was usually a

A buffalo hunter's home. Nebraska State Historical Society

short day's work for Cody to ride out from railhead and scout around for a small bunch of buffalo, dismount and knock over a dozen animals, and ride back to camp, leaving his hired hands to do the rest of the job.

Cody hadn't conceived his Wild West show then, of course. He had toyed with the idea of land promotion, and had plotted a townsite he intended to develop along the KP right-of-way past the point where construction stopped at Sheridan Station, west of Hays. It was really the sudden stopping of track-laying that provided the manpower that large-scale hide hunting required. Men laid off from the KP crews who didn't go to the Santa Fe or UP quickly found jobs with the hide-hunters. Skilled marksmanship wasn't a requirement. Skinners and teamsters were in as great demand as shooters, and these were jobs any able-bodied man could handle. Even the shooters needed very little training. The technique was to rest their big Sharps .50s or Henry .44s on bipod stands, or to shoot from a prone position, or sitting with the gun resting on the knees, from a range of 150 to 200 yards. Buffalo invariably graze with their heads into the wind. All the shooter had to remember was to approach quietly from behind the herd, and to pick off the rearmost animals first, so that the herd's leaders wouldn't be alarmed.

With this method, it was possible for even a mediocre marksman to drop twenty or thirty buffalo at one stand, and when the herd finally spooked, to follow it the quarter-mile or so that the buffalo usually moved, leaving the fallen carcasses for the skinners to work on. When the wet hides were stripped and folded, teamsters hauled them to the base camp, where they

Buffalo hides piled high at Dodge City. Kansas State Historical Society

A herd of buffalo stopping the train

were pegged hair-down on the flat prairie, to dry hard and stiff in the sunshine. These flint hides were what the KP and other buffalo country railroads hauled east to the tanneries. At Hays and Abilene the flat-piled ricks of flint hides awaiting shipment often stood ten feet high and covered the prairie for a half-mile on both sides of the tracks. The smell was terrible, especially on a warm day.

Buffalo on the right-of-way presented real problems to the Kansas Pacific, trying to maintain a schedule between its eastern stations and the railhead where it connected with the Overland Stage for Denver and the Barlow-Sanderson stage for Santa Fe. Typical are a couple of train reports of the years 1867–68. One train, 20 miles east of Hays, waited eight hours while an immense herd streamed across the tracks, the procession of buffalo never stopping or growing thin enough to allow the engineer to proceed. Another train ran late between Ellsworth and Sheridan Station, a distance of 120 miles, because for that entire stretch it was traveling through a single herd of buffalo that repeatedly blocked the right-of-way.

More than one trainman of the day remarked on a characteristic peculiar to buffalo when in the vicinity of a moving train. If the animals were on the north side of the tracks, the animals were not bothered by the locomotive's huffing and whistling. However, if they were on the south side at the train's approach, they bolted madly across the tracks to get north of the locomotive. After a few derailments, some crumpled boilers on the tinpot locomotives of the period, and a number of instances when light wooden cars were butted off the rails, the trainmen learned to let the buffalo cross while the train waited.

Like all railroads traversing the buffalo range, the Kansas Pacific tried fencing its right-of-way between strands of barbwire. This buffalo wire was made to special order, double-gauge stout with extra-long barbs, and each road had its own distinctive wire twist or barb pattern that identified the wire as railroad property. This was not a matter of pride or prestige, but to discourage settlers from "borrowing" right-of-way fence wire to enclose their own fields or homesteads. But the use of buffalo wire was a short-time experiment. The buffalo paid no attention to fences, whether made of barbwire or railroad ties. The wild buffalo of the 1860s were virtually unfenceable, whether the fence was designed to keep them out or hold them penned. A lot of people tried to build buffalo-proof fences, but none succeeded.

To publicize its route, to attract buyers for its stocks and bonds and settlers for the subsidy lands it had for sale, and to pick up a bit of petty cash, the KP ran several "buffalo excursions." For ten dollars, according to advertisements in the papers in Chicago, St. Louis, Kansas City, and other metropolitan centers, the would-be buffalo hunter could buy a round-trip ticket from Lawrence, Kansas—between Kansas City and Topeka—all the way to railhead, 410 miles west at Sheridan Station. The trains left on Tuesday and returned on Friday, making stops along the way where buffalo were encountered to give the hunters riding the coaches plenty of opportunities to blaze away. The carcasses, like those of the animals brought down by hide-hunters, were left to rot where they lay. But this kind of shooting was a minor factor in the buffalo's almost total extermination.

Early figures are inexact and their accuracy unverifiable. Guesses about the number of animals in the four major buffalo herds range from a high of 100,000,000 to a low of 60,000,000, with the higher figure probably nearest to being correct. The central herd, ranging between the Republican and Arkansas rivers in the country opened by the Kansas Pacific, quite possibly contained as many as 20,000,000 to 25,000,000 buffalo. This is the concensus of the best-qualified contemporary observers, men who traveled the prairies before the hide-hunters went to work.

It took just twelve years after the big killing began in 1867–68 to wipe out all four herds. The northern herd had come under pressure from the time the UP tracks opened its range, and the KP followed closely in time when it penetrated the territory of the central herd. Both northern and central herds were almost gone by 1875, and the hunters had begun fanning out north to the Canadian herd and south to the Texas herd. After 1880, hide-hunting became a mop-up operation, and by 1885 only 700 to 800 buffalo were left alive, about 200 in Central Texas, the remainder in the Yellowstone country of Montana, a scattered few in Wyoming.

Buffalo hunting by train was considered a prime sport in frontier times. The shipment of buffalo hides and bones became big business to the western railroads. Library of Congress

A year-by-year tally of the buffalo kill is impossible. Railroad practice in early days was to rent freight cars to shippers, and what went into the cars was not recorded by the roads. By 1872–74, when public concern was beginning to be expressed over the possibility that the buffalo would be exterminated, some figures on hide shipments were put together. The Kansas

Pacific, Union Pacific, and Santa Fe combined shipped almost 1,500,000 hides in those two years, and estimated that an equal number moved east in that same period in cars whose contents were not recorded.

General Nelson A. Miles, commanding the Army's Southern Department, south of the KP tracks in Comanche country along the Arkansas River, figured that about 4,375,000 buffalo were killed in his department between 1871–74. An informed guess would be a total kill of 6,000,000 to 7,000,000 animals a year in the entire Great Plains basin between 1867–77. Then the hide shipments began dwindling, ending completely in 1882–83. By then, the Kansas Pacific was shipping 10,000,000 pounds of sun-bleached buffalo bones a year to eastern plants, to be ground up for fertilizer. The buffalo era was over.

Even before the buffalo vanished, the Indians had gone. When the Kansas Pacific started building track in 1862, the Sioux, Cheyenne, and Comanche, then the dominant Plains tribes, were and had been openly at war with the pale-eyes. By 1865 the minor tribes had professed peace, but only the Cheyenne had an organization able to enforce discipline on an entire people, and the Cheyenne intensified their fighting after the 1864 Sand Creek massacre. Some tribes—Blackfoot, Osage, Pawnees—had in truth made peace with the whites; these provided most of the Army's scouts, and many an inept cavalry commander had his bacon—and usually his scalp as well—saved by the experienced Indian scouts. Ineptness is the only word that fits the average cavalry commander coming new to the guerrilla fighting tactics of the Cheyenne, Comanche, and Sioux. The mass-formation, hell-for-leather charges they'd learned to rely on during the war with the South were useless against the Indians on the prairies.

Central Kansas, KP territory, was the province of the fierce Cheyenne, who now had besides Sand Creek the new bitterness created by the invasion of the fire-horses on their steel tracks, the settlers and hide-hunters who followed the rails. It was a toss-up which group the Cheyenne hated most: railroaders, hide-hunters, or settlers. Since settlers were few and hide-hunters scattered, the brunt of the Cheyenne wrath fell on the track-workers and survey crews, whose mobility was limited by the roadbed.

How many gandy dancers and transit men lost their lives along the Kansas Pacific right-of-way was not recorded then and is undiscoverable now. Payroll records in the modern sense did not exist; workers were paid in cash, and if a man failed to show up after a day or so his name was simply scratched off the paymaster's book, no questions asked, no reason sought. Estimates of the number of KP men killed by Indians range from a score or so up to the hundreds, with the truth probably being a hundred or so. In one of the few raids documented, Kansas Governor S. J. Crawford telegraphed to General Sherman in September 1867: INDIANS ALONG THE SMOKY HILL . . . LAST WEEK FIRED INTO CONSTRUCTION TRAIN ON THE RAILROAD, ATTACKED AND CAPTURED PARTS OF THREE GOVERNMENT TRAINS, ATTACKED MOST OF THE WORKING PARTIES . . . KILLED ONE CONTRACTOR AND EIGHT EMPLOYEES AND WOUNDED MANY MORE.

Even the presence of two thousand troops along the right-of-way and the issuing of 1,500 rifles and 50,000 rounds of ammunition to railroad workers from the Federal arsenal at Fort Leavenworth did not completely insure the safety of the track gangs. The greenhorn gandy dancers from the peaceful East could never quite believe in the reality of the Indian threat, and too often the troopers were as innocent of Indian ways and tactics as the men they were there to protect.

This innocence extended up to the top echelons of command. Colonel George Armstrong Custer—General Custer, to give him his brevet rank—was, as the expression went, "a greenhorn from go." Both Custer and his immediate superior, General Winfield Scott Hancock, had made their reputations during the Civil War with conventional cavalry tactics. It was a case of the blind leading the blind when Hancock, with Custer second in command, led a thousand troopers in a punitive expedition against the Cheyenne and Arapaho who'd been harassing the KP's track crews and survey gangs. Their supplies were hauled in slow-moving mule-drawn wagons, their equipment included pontoon boats to be used to ferry rivers that existed only on maps.

Five minutes' conversation with any experienced buffalo hunter would have revealed to Hancock and Custer that the cavalry, slowed to the speed of its supply train, could never hope to catch up with the fast-riding Cheyenne. As for the pontoon boats, another factor that held down their mobility, the hunters could have told them that in August only one or two of the prairie rivers couldn't have been forded by wading horses fetlock-deep. The expedition marched out, spent a month in the field, burned a deserted Cheyenne village, but saw no Indian warriors.

Superior firepower and superior manpower took their toll of the Indians over the years, of course. So did the slaughter of the buffalo. General Phil Sheridan had been right when he told the Texas legislature, which was debating a bill to protect the buffalo, "If you want the prairies to be free of Indians, let the buffalo be killed. Every dead buffalo means ten starving redskins." Deprived of the animal that provided them with food, clothing, shelter and trade goods, the Plains Indians waned, and by the beginning of the 1880s were confined to reservations. With the Indians and the buffalo gone from the Great Plains, the ranchers with their cattle, the settlers with their plows, moved in by the thousands, not only along the Kansas Pacific, but beside the rails of its competitors to the north and south.

For a short while there was business enough for all. The Kansas Pacific had solved its money problems temporarily by floating a massive issue of bonds on the European market. This gave the road funds to push its tracks on to Denver. Having lost the race to the 100th meridian to the UP, the KP had to go it alone from Sheridan Station to Denver, building with crumbs instead of subsidy cash. The crumbs were pretty substantial, coming from the sale of KP bonds and stock, haulage traffic, and the sale to settlers of subsidy lands along its route. But compared to the money that had flowed through its coffers during subsidy days, the funds available to build west from Sheridan Station were crumbs indeed.

The Kansas Pacific roundhouse at Armstrong, seething with live steaming locomotives in this 1869 scene. Donald Duke Collection

Now, history began to turn full-circle. The original promoters of the Leavenworth, Pawnee & Western had been forced out by the maneuvers of Frémont and Hallet. In turn, Frémont and Hallet were pushed aside by the financiers headed by Perry, Shoemaker, and Train; this trio was soon joined by William J. Palmer, who had been trained in the tough railroad operating school of the Pennsylvania, competing with Vanderbilt, Drew, Fisk, and Gould. It was Palmer, as operating head of the KP, who was responsible for the road's growth after 1865. He finally pushed KP iron to Denver, the first through train schedule between Kansas City and Denver beginning in September of 1870.

Palmer also negotiated the deal that brought about both the construction of the KP's subsidiary, the Denver Pacific, that ran north from Denver to Cheyenne and also a connection with the transcontinental line of the Union

Pacific-Central Pacific, finally giving the KP a link with the West Coast. Another Palmer brainchild was the Arkansas Valley Railway, a projected Kansas Pacific subsidiary to push trackage southwest of the KP mainline via the Arkansas River valley into New Mexico, Arizona, and potentially, California; this would have put the KP into direct competition with the Santa Fe. Like the northern KP branch line, the Junction City & Fort Kearny Railroad, which operated briefly between those two points, the Arkansas Valley line died a quick death.

History's circle closed fast on the Kansas Pacific after it completed its trackage to Denver and began branching out with feeder lines. The gold panic of 1873 affected the prairie and mountain states as greatly as it did those along the eastern seaboard. There were no more buffalo hides for the KP to haul to the tanneries, the Colorado gold mines it had counted on for big freight tonnage were curtailing operations or closing down completely, and the Santa Fe, a hundred miles closer to Texas ranches, was cutting deeply into the cattle shipments that had been a Kansas Pacific mainstay. The KP hung on, more than ever earning its "Keep Poor" nickname, until in 1876 a grasshopper plague wiped out the crops of settlers throughout the Central Plains.

Bankruptcy, close for several years, could not be staved off. In the East, Jay Gould was moving into railroads with the profits he had made through gold manipulations, which had brought on the 1873 panic. Already in virtual control of the Union Pacific, Gould saw the profit potential in the KP. The potential was built in, no matter how he played his hand. With control of both the UP and KP, he could either blackmail his UP associates and stockholders with the threat of KP competition and sell one road to the other at an inflated price, or he could operate both roads independently, but with a collusive and exorbitant rate structure. There was no way Gould could lose.

Acting in concert with the Kansas Pacific's European bondholders, Gould manipulated the appointment of Henry Villard as referee in bankruptcy for the KP. Villard had already been serving the European consortium as trustee for a bankrupt railway in Oregon. Now, he moved into the Kansas Pacific, forced out Perry, Shoemaker, Train, and Palmer, and delivered the road to Gould. Without delay, Gould informed the Union Pacific stockholders that they had a choice of merger or war. The UP chose peace.

After the merger, in 1879, the whistles of the Cinderella of the Prairie wailed no more. True to its destiny as the stepchild of Western railroads, the Kansas Pacific ended as it had begun, as the Union Pacific Railroad, Eastern Division.

7

Across the Top: Building the Northern Roads

WILLIAM O. TURNER

The march of rails across the northwestern states might be chronicled in terms of stock issues, mergers, financial coups. It might be sketched in dates and distances, elevations and gradients, trestle heights and tunnel lengths. But the story is basically one of men. It can best be told in terms of some of those who, with all their human frailties and contradictions, did the work of giants.

Magicians of finance in private Pullman cars and shovel bums in blizzard-buffeted rag camps, they were driven by gaping appetites for money and power or just by a need for day wages. But they had a steel core in common—a commitment, a determination to be where the action was. It was not in their natures to sit back and watch history made, to read about it in the newspapers. They had to live the making, to feel its sweat and aching failures and final triumph. When they had got the steel down, two thousand shining miles of it, they had opened a new empire. It included the richest mines, coniferous forest, wheatland, and the finest deep water harbors on earth. They, the builders, were part of it and it was forever part of them.

First of all, back in 1853, there was Isaac I. Stevens. A West Point graduate, number one in the class of 1839, he was handsome, tireless, monstrously ambitious, and gut tough. He had been wounded in the Mexican War. More recently, as brevet major of engineers, he had done some im-

Isaac I. Stevens. Washington State Historical Society

portant map-making for the War Department. Now he was on his way overland to the newly formed Washington Territory as its first governor. He had also been commissioned to find a route for a northern railroad that would reach from the Great Lakes to Puget Sound.

He left St. Paul with a party of more than a hundred dragoons, guides, engineers, scientists, and two hundred unbroken mules that the St. Louis quartermaster pawned off on him. Stevens had a double hernia and had been cautioned by doctors to stay out of the saddle, but he made the whole five-month trip on the back of an Army mule. Meeting subsidiary parties on the way, he made a thorough study of the country. He was a good engineer; the material he accumulated was pertinent, accurate, and voluminous. He made one mistake. He assigned Captain George B. McClellan to find a pass over the formidable Cascade Range. McClellan showed the dilatory timidity that was later to characterize him as commander of the Union Army. He failed to find a crossing that he would recommend for a railroad or even a military wagon road. Stevens was furious with him and stated in his report that he believed Snoqualmie Pass would be suitable. The problem of the Cascade crossing was the weak spot in the report, however, and it continued to plague location engineers for years. It was not solved until the late 1880s, after the first trains were following a roundabout route to Puget Sound by way of the Columbia gorge.

On the whole, it was Stevens's persistence that did more than anything else to smooth the way for a northern railroad. He turned out to be a dictatorial and rather unpopular governor, trying to run Washington Territory as he would a military command. His term was notable for hurriedly conceived treaties which led to the Indian War of 1855–56. He seemed almost to welcome the war. He shaped a raggedy-rump militia into a fighting force that defeated the hostile tribes in a campaign that made the outmaneuvered regulars look like a bunch of cub scouts. He then resigned as governor and got himself elected territorial representative to Congress. Principal among his reasons was his determination to get congressional sanction for a railroad across the northwestern states.

Secretary of War Jefferson Davis was against a northern route as were the southern Congressmen. They argued that the Northwest could be served adequately by a branch line from a central route. Stevens scoffed at this compromise and fought them vigorously. He prepared an 800-page report, complete with illustrations, and had thirty thousand copies printed and circulated. About 1860, he introduced a bill calling for a charter for a northern road. It was tabled, but in 1864, two years after the central route had been approved, the Northern Pacific was chartered. Stevens didn't live to enjoy this victory. A brigadier general of more than ordinary competence, he had got his brains blown out leading a charge at Chantilly, flag in hand.

For five years while the central route was under construction, the northern route remained a sleeping project. In 1869, Jay Cooke, who had done more than anyone else to finance the Civil War by marketing loans for the Federal Government, got interested. He sent surveyors out from St. Paul. They reported that the engineering problems in crossing the Rockies were no worse than those already solved by the Central Pacific in the Sierras. Moreover, the northwest country between Minnesota and the coast was not the desolate, snowbound wilderness that most Americans—probably including Jay Cooke—had thought it was. It was unimaginably rich in farmland, cattle country, minerals, and timber.

Cooke agreed to finance the Northern Pacific by selling $100,000,000 in stock and another $100,000,000 in bonds. His commission was to be 2 percent, payable in stock. He undertook an elaborate promotional campaign aimed at investors in the United States and Europe. Construction began in 1870 in Minnesota and at Kalama, Washington Territory, moving north toward Tacoma.

No satisfactory pass through the Cascades had been found; so the plan called for track to go down the Columbia to Portland, then north to Puget Sound. It would have to follow the south bank; the north bank was considered too rugged and the danger of slides too great. The main obstacle to the plan was the Oregon Steam Navigation Company. It ran steamboats down the Columbia with rail portages along the route and it controlled most of the right-of-way along the south bank. The NP had little choice but to buy it, paying $5,000,000 for boats, portage roads, and rights-of-way.

The NP, however, was quickly in financial trouble. The Crédit Mobilier scandal during the construction of the Union Pacific had made the public suspicious of anything and everything regarding railroads. Jay Cooke found few buyers for NP stock. He began to shovel his own money into the company. In September 1873, Jay Cooke and Company went broke and took the NP with it. The thud shook financial exchanges around the world. The panic of '73 was on.

Desperate for cash, the NP sold its Columbia River holdings back to the original owners for twenty cents on the dollar. In the east, construction stopped at Bismarck, North Dakota. In the west it jolted to a halt at Tacoma. There was not enough money to pay workers, who promptly tore up some of the track.

The company reorganized with Frederick Billings as president, a solid, energetic man. But the 1870s were lean years; there was no money for more than a little token building here and there. The port towns of Puget Sound were up in arms. They had never liked the idea of trains reaching them by way of Portland; now that work stopped altogether, they visualized themselves doomed to dependence on branch lines from the central route. To appease them, the NP began laying track eastward from Tacoma, raising hope that a Cascade crossing was at last on the way. But after moving twenty-five miles up the Puyallup Valley, construction stopped.

Henry Villard. Burlington Northern photo

It wasn't until the end of the decade that Billings raised $40,000,000 and got the NP moving again. Track moved westward out of Bismarck across Montana. Work also began at the junction of the Columbia and Snake rivers northeastward toward Pend Oreille.

Now another giant comes into the story, a man called Henry Villard. Born in Bavaria, he had come to the United States at the age of eighteen. Before he was thirty he had become one of America's most distinguished journalists, celebrated especially for his front-line reports during the Civil War. After the war he married the daughter of the famous abolitionist, William Lloyd Garrison. Through Garrison, Villard got a job with the American Social Science Association. His work included a study of corporation finance that proved to be invaluable preparation for his future.

In 1874, German stockholders in Ben Holladay's Oregon railroad ventures believed they were being treated badly and appointed Villard to look after their interests. Villard met with Holladay and the two seemed to dislike each other at once. Holladay was big, gruff, blustering. Villard was a dapper little man of cultivated tastes. Holladay agreed to Villard's demands and then reneged, a typical Holladay way of doing business. But he had underestimated the little German. After a brief and decisive legal fight, Villard stripped the living legend not only of his two railroads but of his Oregon Steamship Company as well. Stockholders and creditors installed Villard as head of all three companies.

Meanwhile, Villard had been sitting in on another high stakes game with Jay Gould and Sidney Dillon of the Union Pacific. Again representing German stockholders in a complex legal battle, he got the best of Gould and Dillon, too, and emerged with a large personal fortune. This he used to buy out the stockholders of Holladay's crumbled empire so that he, Villard, was solely in control.

Next, he took an option on the Oregon Steam Navigation Company, which controlled the Columbia River right-of-way. He then bought 25 miles of track that ran to some coal mines east of Seattle. He combined these holdings into the Oregon Railway & Navigation Company—known thereafter as the OR&N. He also bought Dr. Dorsey Baker's famous wooden track railroad between Wallula and Walla Walla. The wood-and-strap-iron rails had been replaced with steel by this time and Villard paid more than $300,000 for 32 miles of track and one small train. In 1880, he began construction to fill the gaps in the track on the south bank of the Columbia, linking Portland and Walla Walla.

During this period, Villard did more than anyone else to bring settlers into eastern Oregon and Washington. He set up immigration offices at ports of entry on the East Coast and in several European cities. As a result of

Track was laid on a crib along the edge of this stream as the Great Northern bulled and twisted through northern mountains. Burlington Northern Photo

his propaganda (and that of Holladay before him), the Willamette Valley and the valleys to the south and east were filling up with farmers. The country around Walla Walla was also booming. The first attempts at irrigation began. They were small scale but results made it clear that the desert east of the Cascades could be converted to soil that would grow wheat, oats, barley, hops, and even fruit trees.

Villard visualized branch lines that would tap this potentially rich country and feed his railroads. He even talked of branches into the mining country of Montana, Utah, and Wyoming. The great threat to his plans for expansion was the revitalized NP, now building again at a merry rate. The only thing to do, Villard decided, was to get control of it.

He began by leasing it the OR&N tracks, giving it a route down the Columbia. He then quietly bought up NP stock. He ran out of money and organized his famous "blind pool." This was done by writing letters to eighty financiers, asking them for capital, not telling them for what. Amazingly, he raised $20,000,000, enough to buy the shares he needed and give him control of the NP. He threw Billings out and had himself elected president.

In 1883, on the north bank of the Deer Lodge River 60 miles west of Helena, Montana Territory, Henry Villard had the satisfaction of seeing the east-west linking of NP tracks. Ex-president Grant and other celebrities arrived on special trains. Actually, the crews had finished the work a day ahead of schedule, so they obligingly ripped up half a mile of track and laid it again for the celebration.

Congress had given the NP the largest land grant in history. For every mile of track laid in the state of Minnesota, the company got twenty odd-numbered sections of free land. In the territories it got forty sections—25,600 acres for every mile of track it put down! As it built, it did its best to promote settlement along the route, selling the land for $1.50 an acre and up. In spite of this, it was in constant financial trouble. In January 1884, three months after the triumphant joining of the rails, it was broke again.

Villard, for the time being, was ruined. He went to Germany to recuperate. In 1887, he was back in the United States and again became a powerful figure in the Northwest. In 1889, the NP elected him to its board of directors but he never again had control.

The bust of '84 shook the OR&N loose from the NP again. The OR&N president was Elijah Smith. The NP was headed by Robert Harris. The two got into a series of quarrels over freight rates, schedules, and policy in general. The flames were fed by a bitter feud between Portland and the Puget Sound towns.

The Columbia River approach made Portland the principal Northwest port. It was growing fast and its booster groups were doing all they could to have the NP declare this its permanent route to the sea. Villard had agreed with them; but now that he was out, the Sound ports renewed their demands that a pass be found and track laid over the Cascades. The conflict grew

Nelson Bennett. Washington State Historical Society

sharp and enormously complicated. For one thing, the Columbia route was proving to be not quite so good as its backers had claimed. It was plagued by slides and heavy snows. On one occasion a train was trapped by a blizzard and its passengers were prisoners in it for four days.

Reorganized again, the NP decided to build up the Yakima Valley and through Stampede Pass directly into Tacoma. The plan called for a tunnel two miles long at the summit, one of the most ambitious bits of engineering yet undertaken by an American railroad. Asking for bids, the company made it clear that it meant business by laying down a deadline. The work must be finished in exactly twenty-eight months. The contractor must agree to forfeit $100,000 plus 10 percent of the gross price if he was even one day late.

Nelson Bennett, who had laid track for the NP in Montana and for a hundred miles between the Columbia River and the town of Yakima, got the bid. Thus began a construction story that is still told in the Northwest and in railroad circles everywhere.

Great Northern workmen are shown shoveling snow preparatory to laying track somewhere along the spine of the Cascades. Burlington Northern Photo

Photograph taken inside Stampede tunnel shows Nelson Bennett's method of digging the heading in advance. Washington State Historical Society

Canadian-born Bennett had come up the hard way. Before he got into railroad building he'd been a teamster, freighter, Pennsylvania oil well digger, miner, and a brakeman on the Chicago & North Western. Thick-built and barrel-chested, he was all bone, gristle, and determination. His brother, Captain Sidney Bennett, was just as tough. The captain was the on-the-job boss. On February 1, 1886, the Bennett brothers began moving men and supplies into the Cascades.

The end of track was at Yakima.* This meant that thousands of tons of heavy machinery had to be transported by wagon over 82 miles of the most rugged mountain terrain imaginable. Road had to be built every foot of the way. There were plunging streams to bridge or ford, canyons to skirt, jungle-thick forest to cut through. Mud was so deep that the road had to be paved with heavy plank. Sawmills were set up to provide it. Some 16 miles of the route were so steep that twenty-horse teams couldn't make the grade and block and tackle had to be rigged. Men shoveled through canyons packed with eight feet of snow. Over the last few miles, snow was so solidly packed that sleds had to be built. Men at the summit got around on snowshoes. A blizzard dumped three feet of new snow in one night. There was day after day of driving rain.

Among the equipment hauled over this teamsters' hell were five donkey engines, two arc light plants, machine shop and sawmill machinery, two complete ventilating systems with giant exhaust fans, tons of pipe, miles of rail, fifty dump cars, and two small locomotives. In March the Yakima *Signal* reported the arrival of a 7-ton boiler at the end of track. It was too heavy to be risked on the wagon bridge that spanned the river and had to be dragged across by eighteen horses. After that the newspaper reported its progress almost daily for the four weeks required to reach the east portal. At times it climbed only a mile a day.

Jittery about the 28-month deadline, the Bennett brothers began work almost as soon as the first party reached the tunnel site. To their dismay, they found a 175-foot waterfall at the exact spot the surveyors had marked for the east portal. This was on a stream that flowed from a lake on top of the mountain they had to tunnel through. Some of the engineers wanted to change the location of the portal. Since that would require the approval and would also mean delay, Nelson Bennett wouldn't hear of it. He dammed the stream and moved the waterfall. Behind the fall, he found 10 feet of solid ice that had to be chopped away to get to the face of the mountain.

* Actually, the NP bypassed Yakima when greedy real estate men tried to charge a huge price for a depot site. Tracks were laid four miles north and a new town of the same name was laid out. The NP paid the expenses of the hotel owner for moving his building to the new site. The whole town followed, putting buildings on rollers and pulling them by forty-mule teams.

Approaches were graded and boring began at the east portal. A few days later another bore was started on the opposite side of the mountain. Hand drills were used at first and progress was agonizingly slow. When boilers and compressors arrived, Ingersoll compressed air drills were put into use on the east side. Hand drilling continued in the west bore until an air pipe line 3½ miles long was laid over the top of mountain. Both bores were lighted by electric arc lamps, an innovation marveled at in local Washington newspapers.

On March 17, the Yakima *Farmer* reported that "the latest new town of the West" had sprung up near the east portal—also electrically lighted. The buildings included Bennett's bunkhouses, mess hall, and stables along with two saloons and "several commodious business houses" erected by enterprising citizens. One of these was "a large structure one story and a half high, presumably for a sporting hall."

From the beginning, the Bennett brothers had serious problems excavating the tunnel. When the bore was 60 feet into the mountain, the Yakima *Signal* stated that the rock was in "a decomposed state." There had been cave-ins and the newspaper expressed "serious apprehensions" that the work could not be completed within the deadline period. The Yakima *Republican* referred to the unstable formation as "soapstone." The *Farmer* called it a "seam of coal" and reported a 30-foot cave-in.

The tunnel was 16½ feet wide and 22 feet high. The digging technique was to bore an 8-foot heading or "arch." This was kept 30 feet ahead of the crews who followed to clear out the bench. After a slow start, Nelson Bennett found that he would have to average about 14 feet of completed tunnel per day if he was going to beat the deadline and avoid the $100,000 forfeit.

East of the mountains, rails pushed westward through sage and rattlesnakes from Yakima to Ellensburg. On the west slope, they climbed upward along the Green River. Slash camps reached the west portal of the tunnel with graders not far behind.

The effect of the rails across central Washington was already abundantly apparent. The Palouse *Gazette* reported "strangers arriving on every train, looking for homes and farms." Other news items enthusiastically hailed the new prosperity. A Klickitat County rancher loaded three hundred and forty horses into seventeen freight cars, bound for Geneva, New York. The first cattle were shipped east from Ellensburg. A month later, a reporter wrote, "Cattle trains going east are getting too numerous to keep a correct account of." In a few weeks' time the NP sold more than a hundred lots in Ellensburg. A "brick block" was being built in that town along with the large number of frame residences.

NP President Harris and his board of directors had always understood the

Zigzagging switchback in the Cascades similar to the one used over Stampede Mountain until the tunnel through it was completed. Washington State Historical Society importance of the Puget Sound ports; now they began to grasp the tremendous potential of the "inland Empire." In their enthusiasm they decided that it would pay to connect up this area with Tacoma and Seattle as quickly as possible. They announced they would build a switchback over the top of Stampede Mountain to be used until the tunnel was completed. The work was promptly completed by several contractors, one of them Nelson Bennett.

The grade was 300 feet to the mile and the crossing must have been one of the trickiest in railroad history. Eight miles of track were required to get a train over the 3½ mile summit. The crossing took an hour and a quarter. It required two special mountain engines equipped with hydraulic brakes, one engine on each end of a train. Special crews took the trains over and there were special rules, strictly observed. Equipment was minutely inspected before each crossing. There were three switches on each side of the mountain and a man was stationed at each. Each switchman was given a written receipt for the train when it had passed his switch.

The first train direct from St. Paul to Puget Sound zigzagged over Stampede Mountain and arrived in Tacoma in the summer of 1886. The newspapers mention a rip-staver of a celebration. Tacoma, with a population of less than 8,000, had thirty saloons.

Dormitory cars for Great Northern construction crews are shown in Montana in 1887. When they reached the mountains, these cars had to be sawed down to clear the tunnels. Burlington Northern Photo

Trouble continued to plague the Bennett brothers with the tunnel, however. There were cave-ins, cracking of the arch, failure of the ventilating system. On several occasions, men were killed by premature explosions of dynamite. Dozens of injuries kept the doctor busy and the camp hospital full. Finally, there was labor trouble.

Wages started at $1.75 per ten-hour day for a shovel stiff and went up to $2.50 for a skilled worker on an eight-hour shift inside the tunnel. Supervisors got $5 per day. All hands were charged seventy-five cents a day for board. The chief cause of discontent was the length of the shift the laborers put in. They wanted their work divided into eight-hour shifts like that of the drillers. There were other complaints, including one that Captain Sidney Bennett was too quick to fire workers who didn't drive themselves hard enough to suit him.

There was a strike that lasted two days. The sheriff came up from Ellensburg and settled it by gunning down one of the leaders and arresting some others. When the crews had gone back to work, Nelson Bennett tried to smooth things over by putting in a bonus system. Every man on the crew was paid an extra twenty-five cents for every foot of progress beyond the necessary daily average. Skilled workers got fifty cents per extra foot.

The new system brought immediate improvement in the tunnel's progress. Good-natured rivalry between the east and west crews developed and each tried to outdig the other. There were still many setbacks, however. In May 1887, progress had to be recorded as a negative 146 feet, the result of a flood

James J. Hill. Burlington Northern photo

and a cave-in. There was more trouble with premature blasts. A total of thirteen men lost their lives before the tunnel was finished.

But the Bennetts kept pushing. They completed the work just seven days ahead of the deadline. Mrs. Nelson Bennett, who had vowed that "the first man through the tunnel would be a woman," was on hand for the last blast, which was set in the east bore. It broke through, but the hole into the west bore was very small. She plunged into it and got stuck. Men caught her hands and hauled her through but pulled her out of most of her dress in the process.

To the amazement of laymen, including several newspapermen, who had expressed bewilderment as to how you could start a tunnel on either side of a mountain two miles thick and have the bores meet accurately, Nelson Bennett announced that his line was off just one-quarter of an inch.

The Northwest at last had its railroad. But by this time there was still another line on its way, the Great Northern. Its story is the story of the greatest railroad man of them all.

James J. Hill was high-handed, tight-fisted, cantankerous. At times, however, he was also generous, even downright kind. He was thorough to a fault. He knew all there was to know about planning, financing, building, and operating a railroad. Most important of all, he was imaginative. He saw the potential of the Northwest more clearly than anybody else on record. He saw that it could support another road, even without a land grant.

He was born on a Canadian backwoods farm in Ontario, September 16, 1838. His father was an Irish Protestant, his mother of Scottish descent. Early in life, James developed the habit of reading everything he could get his hands on. In spite of the fact that he lost an eye in a boyhood accident, this appetite never left him. When he was fourteen, his father died; but James stayed in school, working in a grocery store for $4 a month. By the time he was seventeen, he was well educated in English, Latin, Greek, and mathematics.

In 1856, he left home, knocked around the States for a few months, and turned up at St. Paul, a booming little city of about 5,000. Hill got a clerk's job for a riverboat company and quickly was put in charge of the St. Paul office. He tried to enlist in the Civil War but was rejected because of his blind eye. By the time the conflict was over, he had set himself up as an independent agent representing various steamboat, railroad, and freighting interests. He also operated a warehouse, bought and sold furs, and dealt in hay.

He had a great curiosity about the country west and north of St. Paul, especially the Red River Valley, which offered a route to new land developments in Canada. He spent a good deal of time exploring, often on snowshoes. He built a steamboat and put it into service, breaking a transportation

Track laying machine used on the Great Northern. Burlington Northern photo

monopoly long held by the Hudson's Bay Company. Then he developed a new route to the river from St. Paul, using the tracks of a jinky-whistle railroad grandiosely named the St. Paul & Pacific.

The road owned less than 20 miles of track. It was overcapitalized, shabbily built, badly managed, and was losing money by the barrel. It did have a land grant, however, good only in the state of Minnesota, that entitled it to ten acres for every mile of track it laid. The NP owned most of the St. Paul & Pacific's stock. When Jay Cooke's panic of '73 left both lines broke, James J. Hill saw his chance. Patiently, over a period of five years, he planned, negotiated, raised capital. In 1878, he got control of the St. Paul & Pacific.

The line was out of cash, but Hill somehow got enough credit to start laying track along the Red River toward Winnipeg. There were many financial and legal difficulties. For one thing, the NP planned to build over the same ground. Hill managed to talk its board of directors into changing their plans. Physical obstacles to construction were considerable, especially since the work had to be done in a hurry, before the Minnesota land grant expired. One section of the road had to be completed by August 1878. Another had to be done by the end of the year.

Hill bossed the job in person, insisting that track be laid at a minimum rate of a mile a day. A crew struck and quit. He brought in a new one. Mosquitoes attacked in clouds, causing horses to bolt and oxen to bellow with pain. Dust and bad water caused an epidemic of the bloody flux. Men fell from heat prostration. Many cursed Hill and quit. Others liked the shaggy-headed, one-eyed old slave-driver. He called them by their first names. In a pinch, he grabbed a shovel and worked for hours at a time. They stayed with him and got the track down in time for the land grant to be certified.

Hill's line now connected up with the Canadian Pacific, which was building westward across Canada. His trains had a through run from St. Paul to Winnipeg and his road was now an immensely valuable property. He never again had trouble getting credit.

He now became involved with the Canadian Pacific for a short time. He advised on routing and construction and was elected to the board of directors. A few years later he resigned because he felt that his U.S. railroads created a conflict of interest.

A lot of people, including some of Hill's stockholders, thought he was crazy when he announced that he was going to push his railroad (now called the St. Paul, Minneapolis & Manitoba) across the roof of the United States to Puget Sound. The NP had already covered that ground. Moreover, Congress would not authorize another land grant. If the NP, with its huge grant, was constantly in financial trouble, how could Hill's project end in anything but disaster?

Hill was not at all upset by such criticism. He knew more about the NP than its own board of directors. He knew it was overcapitalized and much of it badly built. Its steep grades made operation expensive. Some of the country it spanned was not productive. Its management was inefficient. He would build a transcontinental as it should be built.

He familiarized himself with the country along the route—every foot of it. Most of it, he explored personally. The rest he learned about by study of detailed reports submitted by his hand-picked representatives. He studied the land with an eye to construction problems and also for its capacity to feed his freight cars. He learned all he could about the ore deposits, the farm and grazing land, the timber. He built slowly, east to west, inspecting the work himself and insisting that every foot of track be laid "to last a hundred years." He drove short spur lines north and south from the main road to protect his rear from the NP. He took steps to bring people into the country along his route, many of them immigrants from Europe.

Without a grant, he had no land to sell off, but there were homesteads to be had for the taking. The Great Northern, as Hill's road was now called, set up a land department to help settlers with legal details. It would carry them from anywhere in the United States to points along its route for $10 apiece. In some cases, homesteaders with large families and furniture were rented boxcars for practically nothing.

Building with a view to future operating costs, Hill insisted on finding gentle grades over the mountains. When it came to crossing the Continental

Divide, he determined to rediscover a lost trail that was said to be easier than any other. Lewis and Clark had seen it and named it Marias Pass, although they did not cross by it. Later explorers failed to find it until Isaac Stevens made his 1853 survey and one of his subsidiary parties came upon it. Then it was lost again—not even Indians could find it. Hill detailed his top location engineer, thirty-five-year-old John Stevens (no relation to Isaac), to search it out.

After months of exploring the area that is now Glacier National Park, Stevens was overtaken by winter. Traveling on snowshoes, he and an Indian guide were caught by falling temperatures that reached 40 below zero. The guide quit and went back, but Stevens pressed on and sort of blundered into the pass. Forced to spend the night at its summit, he found himself in snow so deep that he was unable to build a fire. He kept himself alive by pacing back and forth until daylight, wearing a trench in the snow. Some years later, he was honored by the erection of a statue in Summit, Montana, at the exact site of his cold camp. It was Stevens, too, who located the Great Northern's route over the Cascades by discovering another pass, which today bears his name.

The Great Northern was completed in 1893. Trains rolled into Everett, Washington, in January and into Seattle in July. It was a year of depression

Snow sometimes slowed but seldom stopped construction. Photo shows bridge on a switchback near the summit of the Cascades. Burlington Northern photo

Edward H. Harriman. Union Pacific Railroad Photo

for most of the country and for most railroads. The NP surprised nobody by going broke once again. But the Great Northern showed a profit from the first, thanks to Hill's efficiency in construction and operation.

The NP was in receivership. With some backers, including J. P. Morgan, Hill bought up enough stock to give him control. Boss of both northern transcontinentals now, he reorganized the NP and quickly had it on its feet.

But James J. Hill wasn't satisfied. Having reached the great timber stands of the Cascades and the pine of northern Montana, he began working on a plan for a rail network that would give him access to the lumber-hungry Midwest. Beyond that, he envisioned his lines hauling cotton from the South and steel from the East to Puget Sound to be shipped to the Orient. What he needed and set out to get was the Chicago, Burlington & Quincy.

E. H. Harriman, head of the Union Pacific, guessed Hill's plan and tried to beat him to the punch. Hill outmaneuvered him and got the Burlington. This was the beginning of a power struggle between the two men that lasted as long as Harriman lived.

Harriman was a shy, frail, mild-mannered man who wore thick spectacles and looked like a schoolmaster. As a young man he made a fortune on the New York Stock Exchange. He moved into railroading with instant success and eventually organized a syndicate that gave him control of the Union Pacific. He was also a heavy stockholder in the Central Pacific and the Southern Pacific and a principal voice in their management. Defeated by Hill in their initial encounter, he developed a plan to steal the NP from under Hill's nose.

Before Hill realized it, Harriman had bought up almost enough stock to pull off his coup. Hill, backed by J. P. Morgan, began buying furiously. A battle that made stock market history was on. Before it was over, NP stock had hit $1,000 a share. There was a brief panic on the stock exchange and a good deal of public criticism of the operation of "robber barons." To avoid disaster, Hill compromised. He allowed Harriman a seat on the NP board of directors. Hill, however, remained solidly in control of the railroad. In the next battle, he took the offensive, invading territory where Harriman had reigned unchallenged.

Hill wanted a line directly into Portland. The present route over the Cascades to Puget Sound and then south was too long. The old OR&N tracks down the south bank of the Columbia now were controlled by Harriman's UP. The north bank had always been considered unsuitable for a railroad, but Hill disagreed and began to build there.

Huge logs from Washington's densely timbered mountains made their way to lumber mills over the fledgling Great Northern in 1892. Burlington Northern photo

Harriman immediately moved to block him, organizing paper railroads and making surveys that conflicted with Hill's and led to legal tie-ups. Harriman had no intention of building; he was merely trying to stop Hill. At one point, where Hill had begun a tunnel, Harriman made a show of beginning at the other end by putting a few men to work with, it is said, two picks, a shovel, and a wheelbarrow. Hill won the contest in court but at the cost of time and money. In another instance, Harriman had legal control of a stretch of right-of-way but Hill beat him by tunneling underneath it. On occasion Hill and Harriman crews met in hand-to-hand battle, swinging pick handles. With all the delays, it took Hill three years to complete his road, but complete it he did. Harriman was beaten again.

Fresh from the Civil War, General William J. Palmer built the Kansas Pacific across the prairies, then pushed his narrow-gauge Denver & Rio Grande south from Denver with destination Mexico City. Golden West Collection

By this time Hill was seventy years old and had announced that he was retiring. Actually, he was just getting warmed up. He fixed his good eye on central Oregon now. For one thing, one of the world's best stands of ponderosa pine was there. He envisioned Hill trains hauling it to market. Besides, central Oregon was the way to San Francisco.

A man calling himself Sampson turned up in the Deschutes River country and began taking options on some rather strange barren tracts of land. He was an outdoorsman, he explained, a sort of early-day conservationist. He wanted to latch onto some hunting and fishing land before it was spoiled. A little later this same Mr. Sampson showed up in Portland, where he bought the stock and charter of the Oregon Trunk, a paper railroad that owned not one foot of track or anything else. Mr. Sampson then disclosed that his real name was John F. Stevens. He was none other than the location engineer who had found Hill the lost pass over the Continental Divide. His task was to lay out a railroad from Hill's Columbia River tracks to a little settlement called Bend in the heart of the ponderosa country.

Harriman realized that the real plan was to build on through to San Francisco. This time he countered with more than token building and legal tie-ups. He chartered a new line called the Deschutes Railroad and set out to get track laid over the route before Hill could. Thus began the famous Deschutes War with Hill's crews building up the east bank of the river and Harriman's up the west.

They were huge crews. The Deschutes is a narrow river. There were frequent battles with clubs, axes, rocks. Guards were hired and armed with rifles. Men were killed. When construction reached Deschutes canyon, where the river writhes between pressing walls of rock, dynamite was used as a weapon. Blasts were set to bring murderous showers of rock down on the enemy. Great boulders demolished work trains. More men were killed, dozens injured.

The confrontation came to a head at a piece of land that both roads had to cross. The legal complications were enormous, but a court finally held that Harriman's title to the property was valid. Hill made peace. He agreed not to build the Oregon Trunk beyond Bend and to permit Deschutes Railroad trains to run on Hill track from this point into Bend. That hamlet, formerly called Farewell Bend, became a lumber center and soon had a population of more than 5,000.

Hill had by no means given up, of course. He established a boat train between Portland and Astoria, Washington; then he put two steamships into service between Astoria and San Francisco. The service was efficient enough to cut heavily into freight and passenger business of Harriman's trains. Finally, Hill laid plans to connect his Great Northern with the Western

Pacific so his trains would at last have a way into San Francisco. The project was completed, but not until after Hill's death in 1916.

Stewart Holbrook, perhaps the Northwest's most popular historian, sums up James J. Hill as well as anyone has. In his *Story of American Railroads,* Holbrook says, "I can think of no other single American who had quite so much influence on quite so large a region." It is a tribute that shaggy old Jim Hill, the Empire Builder, would have appreciated.

8

The Baby Road

STEVE FRAZEE

"A railroad is an ordinary railroad until it reaches the Rocky Mountains," said Jesse Fleming, chairman of the Moffat Tunnel Commission. "When it reaches the Rocky Mountains it isn't an ordinary railroad in any sense of the word."

When Fleming made that succinct summation in 1918, the Denver & Rio Grande Railway had been proving his point for almost half a century. Fondly by its partisans, contemptuously by the great transcontinentals, the D&RG was called the Baby Road. It was narrow gauge, the rails only 3 feet apart, instead of the customary width of 4 feet 8½ inches.

Then, too, the D&RG was indeed an infant when it entered the field of competition dominated by some of the most ruthless pirates the United States has ever seen.

The Rio Grande soon developed into a very tough baby.

"Steal everything in sight" was the motto of railroad magnates in 1870 when the Rio Grande was incorporated. General William Jackson Palmer, founder of the Baby Road, was cast in a different mold from most of the financial buccaneers of his day, men like bearded, tubercular little Jay Gould, Cyrus K. Holliday, Tom Scott, Edward H. Harriman, and others.

Palmer had emerged from the Civil War as a brevet brigadier of cavalry. Slender, dapper, impeccable in manner, utterly proper in attire, precise of

Denver's first Union Station, built in 1871, served the infant Denver & Rio Grande Railway and the Kansas Pacific. Denver Public Library—Western Collection

speech, Palmer conveyed the air of an aristocrat. Appearances to the contrary, he was a tough-minded operator.

And he was possibly the most optimistic man who ever challenged the Rocky Mountains.

Before the war he had been private secretary to the president of the Pennsylvania Railroad. After the war, as construction manager of the Kansas Pacific, he brought that line across the Kansas plains into Denver.

Palmer became hooked on the Rocky Mountains. Some of his writings about the massive wedges of granite verged on the poetic. He was also hooked on railroads. He envisioned a narrow gauge for Colorado Territory that would serve the area in an ideal way. The road would be free from dissensions, rate wars, internecine throat cutting, employee troubles—all the ills that plagued ordinary railroads.

General Palmer was Utopian in his statements about plans for towns, schools, employee facilities, and over-all operation of the Baby Road. But even before he dived into the business and got his nose bloodied, he also indicated a hard sort of realism when he wrote that the hot competition of American business created a great temptation to be a little unscrupulous.

In 1870 Denver had less than 5,000 inhabitants, but it did have two transcontinental rail connections. Built largely by local subscription, the Denver Pacific came down the 107 miles from the Union Pacific's main line at Cheyenne, Wyoming. It reached Denver on June 22, 1870.

After a long stall in Kansas, during which time the Kansas Pacific had demanded $2,000,000 of Denver citizens to build into their town, the KP had been caught short by the building of the branch line that connected Denver to Cheyenne. Two months after Denver got its branch line completed to the Union Pacific, the Kansas Pacific arrived in Denver—and said no more of the two million bucks.

Now, westward from Denver lay some incomplete roadbeds and a few miles of trackage, but no railroad that actually penetrated the tremendous

A tiny D&RG narrow-gauge engine takes on water at Florence, midway between Pueblo and Canon City on the Royal Gorge Line. Denver Public Library—Western Collection

barrier of the Rocky Mountains. South of Denver was nothing but oxen roads.

General Palmer had a splendid, optimistic grasp of the great void where no rails disturbed the ecology. The Baby Road was incorporated October 27, 1870, as the Denver & Rio Grande Railway. It was projected to run from Denver southward on the plains beside the Rampart Range to the Arkansas River near Pueblo. From there it would veer west to the Labran coal fields near Florence and then on to the struggling town of Canon City.

From Canon City the road would plunge into the mountains by way of the awesome Grand Canyon of the Arkansas, later to be called the Royal Gorge. Once out of the Gorge, the road would follow the Arkansas to low (9,010-foot) Poncha Pass near the present town of Salida. Thence the rails, 30 pounds to the yard, would head south beside the geologically recent, sharp-spined Sangre de Cristo Mountains down the vast inland plateau of the San Luis Valley to the Rio Grande River, justifying the second part of its name. Following the course of the Rio Grande River, the Baby Road would go on to Santa Fe and then to El Paso—and, in time, to Mexico City.

This was the course outlined in the charter granted by Congress. There was nothing small in General Palmer's thinking.

There were also seven branch lines in the planning. One would go over the Rockies to Salt Lake City, Utah. In the meantime, if anyone in the mountains of Colorado had a few cheeses to haul or a pile of ore stacked up in some remote canyon, the Rio Grande would build additional branch lines to haul such freight.

In the fall of 1871 the Baby Road reached Colorado Springs, 76 miles from Denver. Capitalists in the Eastern United States were putting up construction money, along with British, Scotch, and Dutch investors. Money would always be tight with the Rio Grande. The history of the railroad was to be solvency one day, even prosperity on paper, and receivership the next day.

Besides stocks and bonds, there were many ways to help finance railroad construction. One of General Palmer's associates, A. C. Hunt, former Territorial Governor of Colorado, knew a thing or two about real estate, as did Palmer himself. Using dummy companies and affiliates, the Baby Road bought choice land along the intended route before anyone else knew where the line would run. On public lands the United States Government supplied the 200-foot right-of-way, with 20-acre sites for depots every 10 miles.

Wherever possible the company established its own towns and sold the lots. This of course was nothing unusual. All railroads in the West followed the principle of exacting tribute from any source that could pay.

Colorado Springs was a colony town of the Baby Road. Old Colorado City was close by. Land comprising the new townsite cost Palmer's company eighty cents an acre. Advertising in England extolled the wonders of the new town so effectively that Britons began coming to Colorado Springs in surprising numbers. The place was soon known as Little London.

With 76 miles of light iron on ties so recently wrested from the forest that birds were still crying plaintively about them, the Rio Grande was well on its way. Southward it wended, now toward Pueblo, where Jim Beckwourth, Mountain Man and Crow war chief, had founded a trading post in 1840.

If you had a town in the 1870s it was almost immoral not to have a railroad. One way to help get one was to issue bonds and contribute to construction costs. Pueblo, with perhaps 400 inhabitants, was quite anxious to have a railroad. The citizens were worried by the fact that Canon City had voted $50,000 in bonds to have the Baby Road come their way quickly.

Always deliberately vague about their surveys, Rio Grande officials made noises about missing Pueblo by 25 miles. By then Pueblo had already voted $100,000 in bonds to help bring the line to town.

Baby Road officials let it be known that if another $50,000 was raised, the survey crew could be persuaded to continue south. Pueblo citizens approved the additional bond issue. The Rio Grande went into town June 19, 1872. On July 3 the first excursion train arrived from Denver, loaded with nabobs who had refreshed themselves with champagne during the 118-mile run over spongy roadbed.

The jubilation was thunderous. The oratory was soaring. All was good will and love between the Baby Road and the hamlet of Pueblo. The honeymoon was short lived. Almost before the hangovers had cleared up, the Rio Grande moved its station to a new town across the Arkansas, to company owned South Pueblo.

Double cross, screamed Pueblo citizens. They at once reneged on the bond issue. The Baby Road sued to collect—and lost the case.

No matter. Business was good. Pueblo began to boom. General Palmer claimed that by the end of 1872 the town had grown from a population of 500 to 3,500. Rio Grande revenue and freight haulage on the wobbly track between Pueblo and Denver went up and up.

Construction costs, however, had been higher than anticipated. The Baby Road was not in the chips by any means. The little engines, weighing 12½ tons, costing about $8,500, were burning expensive, inferior coal from the fields of northern Colorado. One writer facetiously claimed that passengers on an early run from Denver to Pueblo had been obliged to disembark to gather buffalo chips to feed the firebox. Such apocryphal yarns would be told about the little narrow gauge wherever it went.

Palmer was going to get the coal problem settled, at least. Long before the first dirt had been moved in Denver he had checked the potential of the Labran coal fields near Florence. Close by, also, was an oil field which would become the oldest continuously producing field in the United States.

Grading toward the Labran coal deposits had continued while the Rio Grande had been dallying outside of Pueblo, waiting for that town to get with it financially.

The Baby Road reached Labran in 1872. The construction outfit that had done the work was the Union Contract Company. For two years the Rio Grande had no title to the branch line because it was unable to pay the construction company. The railroad made good use of the line, however, on a rental basis.

Canon City was a mere 9 miles away and the roadbed was complete to the town, but no rails were down. The people of Canon City, understandably, howled considerably and gnashed their teeth like beavers at the delay in getting service. The explanation was simple enough, though General Palmer was not about to give it: the Baby Road did not have money enough to lay track.

Back to basics. If you want the railroad, ante up another $50,000 in addition to the $50,000 already pledged, General Palmer said to Canon City. Fremont County seethed over what seemed like outright blackmail, but the county did vote on the proposition. It carried by two votes. That was just "too damn close" to be the true expression of the people, declared the county commissioners, and held the election null and void. No extra fifty grand for the greedy Baby Road.

Then the town of Canon City held its own election and approved the additional bond issue—in land. The Union Contract Company actually footed the tab to finish the line into Canon City. To the general public it appeared that the construction company and the railroad were separate and individual entities, especially when one considered that the contracting outfit had retained control of the Labran branch after the Baby Road could not pay for the construction costs.

As a matter of fact, the Union Contract Company and the Rio Grande were one and the same, with interlocking directorates, interlocking funds—when any were available—and common interests. Such inter-organization took a heap of bookkeeping, to be sure, but it was legal, albeit a mite confusing to the casual viewer.

Now, in 1874, the Baby Road was in Canon City. It would be several years before the rails went on west on the originally planned route through the Royal Gorge. General Palmer's eyes were directed south. New Mexico had a lot of people, a lot of undeveloped land, and plenty of potential traffic for the Baby Road. Get there first and you had it all.

The ascent of Veta Pass (now La Veta Pass) in 1877 was one of the greatest engineering achievements of the time, and was the highest railroad pass in the United States before the turn of the century. Denver Public Library—Western Collection

Both the Kansas Pacific (UP owned) and the powerful Atchison, Topeka, & Santa Fe were courting Pueblo now. The two lines organized dummy companies and promised to build into Pueblo. So enchanted were Puebloans at the idea of having their town a rail center that they went to the polls again to the tune of $400,000 to bring about the dream. Such sanguine action was typical of the West.

Publicly, General Palmer professed to be happy over the plans of two rivals to serve Pueblo. After all, a lot of their freight would have to be hauled over the Baby Road, he said. The Santa Fe, the Kansas Pacific, and the Rio Grande would be a big cheerful family group, sharing profits in a gentlemanly manner.

Palmer knew better. His public utterances always had to be run through the coding machine.

The Panic of 1873 stopped the Santa Fe temporarily and left the Kansas Pacific far away on the wind-blasted plains. Historically, recessions in financial centers of the East send their ripples only slowly toward the West.

The year of 1873 was not a prosperous one for the Baby Road, but it survived.

Southward was the dream of General Palmer. On to Santa Fe. He kept looking over his shoulder to see where the Kansas Pacific and Santa Fe were. For lack of money the Baby Road was not building anywhere. In 1875 Palmer went to France and tried to raise capital, without any luck.

In 1876 the Santa Fe reached Pueblo. General Palmer hurried off to Boston, the control center of both the Santa Fe and UP. There he negotiated an agreement to split profits from all eastbound traffic with the other two railroads. The Kansas Pacific promised not to build into Pueblo, while the Santa Fe left the impression that it would not build beyond Pueblo. This was more of a truce than a contract. It was good for only two years, and all parties knew that they would breach it whenever it was to their advantage.

At any rate, the presence of the Santa Fe in Pueblo stirred the Baby Road into action. With or without funds, General Palmer would always find some way to lay track.

South of Pueblo were the coal fields of Trinidad, and, of course, distant Santa Fe. The Baby Road built south, letting the Union Contract Company pay for construction. Trinidad was delighted at the approach of the railroad, even after the Rio Grande began a branch veering west from Cuchara toward La Veta Pass.

Experienced at infuriating every established town it neared, the Baby Road did it again. Instead of going into Trinidad, the Rio Grande set up a new town, El Moro. It was on a large tract of company-owned land just 5 miles northeast of Trinidad.

Frustrated towns with railroad fever could really bellow. Trinidad citizens never forgave the betrayal. Later, they got their chance for revenge.

Again the Baby Road was operating on a line it did not own. While the Rio Grande used the road, the Union Contract Company took the income from the operation. This of course was only a switching of money from one pocket to another.

As might be expected, there were bitter public outcries about the Baby Road, not only because of rates, but because of its far reaching self-interest in land ownership and townsites. Prolific writers to newspapers complained about schedules, insulting conductors, lack of safety, and most of all about gouging on passenger and freight charges. Ten cents a mile was considered by some an outrageous cost for passengers. Others complained that one could get freight from New York to Denver for less than it cost to haul the same cargo from Denver to Pueblo. Then, too, the Rio Grande had discriminatory rates for transporting coal.

The Pueblo newspaper had no use at all for the Baby Road, while the

Denver *Rocky Mountain News* and the Colorado Springs *Gazette* were its staunch supporters. Both these papers printed criticism of the road by writers, and then always tried to refute the attacks.

One irate farmer said that ox teams would put the Rio Grande out of business. They went about as fast and did not run off the track nearly as frequently as the Baby Road engines.

Livery rigs beat the railroad all hollow, another critic said. They were cheaper and safer.

All such complaints went past General Palmer's ears like a gentle zephyr. You could not build a railroad to Santa Fe and other places yet unknown if you took time to listen to petty gripes.

Listening to bondholders was another thing. In the years 1875 and 1876 the Rio Grande was in a monstrous financial jam. Reserves for paying interest had been used for construction. Palmer talked bondholders into putting their unredeemed coupons into trust against ten-year certificates at 7 percent. He worked some more legerdemain by issuing capital stock to the Union Contract Company and promising first mortgage bonds also.

When you get in so deep, all you can do is keep plunging. In Palmer's case it meant keep spiking them rails.

A trustee for Dutch investors thought it was high time to untwist the tangled financial affairs of the Union Contract Company and the Rio Grande. He filed for a hearing in receivership. The court denied the petition. General Palmer stroked his elegant mustache, took a deep breath, and sent his gandy dancers on westward.

La Veta Pass was the first mountain crossing of thc Baby Road. The Rio Grande would go places later that would make La Veta Pass look like a gentle swale in a cow pasture, but still there was a spectacular muleshoe curve on La Veta that made flatlanders gasp. Passengers praised the breathless beauty of the summit, from which they could see mountains and more mountains, valleys, and more pure distance than one could shake a stick at.

The Baby Road wised up in a hurry. From then on the Rio Grande sold scenery.

La Veta Pass often proved to be a hellion in winter, but it was a rare beauty in summer.

Tipping down from the pass, the Baby Road went on to old Fort Garland, where only a short time before Kit Carson had been the commanding colonel. Now the line was fairly in the lower reaches of the San Luis Valley, where it had planned to go all the time, though by the Poncha Pass route at the upper end of the valley.

By June 1878 the railroad had an honest name. It had reached the Rio Grande River at Alamosa. Santa Fe was only 160 miles away. It would be a

Royal Gorge three miles east of the narrow part of the canyon; the Arkansas River is to the right. It was in this defile that the Rio Grande & Santa Fe fought a long-drawn noisy but bloodless war for the right-of-way. Denver Public Library—Western Collection

long time before the Baby Road could build its Chili Line on south. Big trouble was brewing on the eastern side of La Veta Pass.

The new manager of the Santa Fe Railroad was William B. Strong, a young, vigorous, competent man. He and General Palmer felt each other out and talked about such things as pooling profits, consolidation, and even a sale of controlling interest in the Baby Road to the AT&SF. All they did was talk. As long as Palmer had anything to say about Rio Grande policy, the Baby Road would stay as independent as possible. Broke, maybe, but independent.

Strong got orders from the president of the Santa Fe to build over Raton Pass, a 7,800 foot saddle just across the Colorado line south of Trinidad. And not far from the end of the Baby Road's track at El Moro.

General Palmer got wind of the project in a hurry, since the Rio Grande controlled the telegraph lines in Colorado. The Santa Fe was going to grab Raton Pass and with it all the rich traffic of New Mexico. Palmer ordered John A. McMurtrie, his chief engineer, to start grading on Raton at once.

Near the top of the pass old Mountain Man Dick Wooten ran a roadhouse. He favored the Santa Fe, perhaps because its engineers had been attentive to him, and had also bought his whiskey. Wooten provided A. A. Robinson, the Santa Fe's chief engineer, with some men and plenty of salty advice. Robinson's force was augmented by a considerable number of men from Trinidad who remembered well their grudge against the Rio Grande.

McMurtrie had rustled up his grading crew, just about as large as the forces of his rival. The two competing outfits reached the pass about the same time on a misty morning before daylight.

McMurtrie's gang chose to rest until they could see what they were doing. The Santa Fe men leaned not upon their spears. With pick and shovel and hoe and an ample supply of Dick Wooten's whiskey they worked by night, scratching out what they called a railroad grade.

When the Rio Grande men arrived at the scene of activity, they were less than an hour too late. The two groups exchanged threats and insults but refrained from a rumble. Though the Baby Road crew did make a half-hearted show of grading on an alternate route up the pass, appropriately called Chicken Creek, the game was over. The AT&SF had won Raton Pass. Their right to it by virtue of prior grading was upheld in court.

After that, no matter how the Rio Grande branched out like a malformed octopus, the main thrust of the railroad always would be west. Having lost Raton Pass, General Palmer now became anxious to push up the Arkansas River to the fabulous silver mines of Leadville. The first step was to beat the treacherous Santa Fe to the Royal Gorge.

Meanwhile, the Santa Fe had also decided to beat the treacherous Rio Grande to the big canyon. Already the AT&SF had a dummy railroad for the purpose, the Canon City and San Juan. The Rio Grande claimed priority on the Gorge by virtue of surveys run in 1871.

Both lines had work parties in the Royal Gorge when war began April 19, 1878. Shortly before General Palmer had found out that the intentions of the Santa Fe to run west into the mountains had solidified. W. R. Morley, assistant chief engineer of the Santa Fe, received orders to grab the Gorge and use the same tactics that had proved successful on the Pass of the Rat.

Wasting no time, Morley went into Pueblo on a Santa Fe special and

A great deal of threatening language and a show of force characterized the war between the Denver & Rio Grande and the Santa Fe Railway for the rights to Royal Gorge. State Historical Society of Colorado

tried to charter a Rio Grande engine to take him to Canon City. But there was no engine for Brother Morley. He got on the train for Canon City, and there he sat, and the train did not move—until after he got off.

Morley made the 40-mile ride on horseback and the horse died as a result of the sprint. Remembering how they had been sandbagged by the Rio Grande, Canon City citizens rallied to Morley's assistance. In a very short time he had a grading crew throwing dirt around at the mouth of the Gorge with such enthusiasm that it appeared that they were going all the way that day.

A large work crew of the Rio Grande showed up soon afterward. Everything was curses, noise, excitement, threats, but no shooting.

Both railroads went to court. Meanwhile, work crews outflanked each other in the canyon. The Baby Road lost the first court decision, but that was only a start. Rio Grande men built barricades across the Santa Fe grade, constructed stone forts overlooking the survey line, and hired plug-uglies by the dozen. Day and night the forts and barricades bristled with rifles. Wages were $2 a day, $3 for the night shift.

Santa Fe crews continued to work. The pooled resources of all the railroads in the United States would not have been enough to pay the costs of carving a ledge in the sheer walls of the Royal Gorge. The builders simply appropriated part of the riverbed in many places, rock walls and backfill.

Where the squeeze was too tight for both river and railroad, the Santa Fe hung a bridge parallel with the pounding water, suspending it by means of inverted V trusses that reached from wall to wall. The Hanging Bridge is still there today.

In the hallowed halls of justice the case dragged on. There were decisions,

Train time at Salida as a westbound narrow-gauge passenger train prepares to tackle Marshall Pass en route to Gunnison. Donald Duke Collection

appeals, reversals, more appeals and new suits. After one court ruled that both railroads could use the Gorge, the armed forces were withdrawn, but they charged back into the canyon a little later when new lawsuits erupted. Lawyers waxed fat and court reporters got writing cramps.

General Palmer was a fighter, but the Santa Fe was a super heavyweight. Palmer was forced to yield to the pressure of his bondholders. In December 1878 the Baby Road was leased for thirty years to the Santa Fe. Rather than ending the Royal Gorge War, the leasing merely intensified hostilities.

In control of the 337 miles of the little narrow gauge, the Santa Fe began a deliberate policy to ruin the Baby Road. Freight rates skyrocketed. Carloadings went down like a lead balloon. Passenger revenue fell off. Profits went to hell.

Palmer charged that the Santa Fe's action constituted lease violation. He sued and got a court decision to that effect. The Santa Fe appealed to a U. S. District Court. Then on April 21, 1879, the Supreme Court of the United States ruled that the Rio Grande did have priority in the Royal Gorge, but that the Santa Fe also could use the route. This meant two tracks where possible and joint trackage where the crowding walls pinched tight.

It appeared to be a victory for the Rio Grande, but there was still that matter of the lease to the Santa Fe. Palmer decided not to wait for a decision in a court he distrusted. He regained his railroad by force.

A special packed with armed men started from El Moro, the Baby Road's synthetic town at the southern end of track. Station by station the raiders gobbled up all Santa Fe employees who refused to take a quick oath of allegiance to the Rio Grande. Only two holdouts were killed.

In Colorado Springs the sheriff and a dozen deputies descended on the railroad station. Company B of the 1st Colorado Cavalry went along. The muzzles of a lot of Winchesters peeped through the windows at the sheriff and his force. Then, without firing a shot, the Santa Fe men capitulated. After all, Colorado Springs was a Rio Grande town.

Pueblo was another matter. Behind barricades in the roundhouse there was a formidable force of good old country boys from Kansas and a passel of imported gunmen from Dodge City. They were led by Bat Masterson, Sheriff of Ford County, Kansas.

The *Ford County Globe,* June 10, 1879, stated: "In response to a telegram from headquarters of the AT&SF railroad, Sheriff Masterson opened a volunteer recruiting office in this city, and half an hour from the receipt of said telegram he was whirling westward with an engine and one coach containing sixty men, at the rate of 40 miles an hour."

The Santa Fe mercenaries did not come off well in the encounter at the Pueblo roundhouse. There was a mighty potential for carnage. It simply did not happen. When the Rio Grande men charged an outlying building, one Santa Fe man was killed. The roundhouse fell without serious resistance. Just what did happen will never be clear, but the strong odor of bribery clings to the event and it is very likely that the Santa Fe men succumbed to it.

Masterson and company had left Dodge City on June 9. They were back on familiar sawdust by June 12. The Dodge City *Times* reported: "Sheriff Masterson and party of fifty men returned from Pueblo on Thursday morning. He had been placed in charge of the railroad property there, but surrendered his authority upon writs being served by U.S. officers. The Denver & Rio Grande has possession. And 'our boys' didn't smell any powder. Their voice is for peace."

General Palmer had regained his railroad, but he was still vastly uneasy about what might happen when the U. S. District Court ruled on the lease violation. He pulled a card from the bottom of the deck and sent the Rio Grande into receivership. Everyone rushed back to court.

Now the Santa Fe delivered the oldest threat in the railroad business: parallel construction. The company threatened to run from Pueblo to Denver beside the tracks of the Rio Grande, and from Canon City to Leadville, and also into the San Juan country—in fact, just about anywhere the Baby Road planned to build in the mountains.

Though the AT&SF was having financial troubles of its own, it is likely that the threat was more than a bluff.

The whole scene changed quickly. Jay Gould, railroad predator without peer, had been watching the Santa Fe–Rio Grande feud with wolfish interest. He had quietly merged the Kansas Pacific and the Union Pacific and now he bought into the Rio Grande and promised to lend the Baby Road money.

The temperature in the boardroom of the Santa Fe dropped about twenty degrees.

It grew even chillier when Gould casually mentioned doing a little paralleling from Pueblo into AT&SF territory in Kansas and on east to St. Louis. Very busy at stacking the center of the line against the Rio Grande, the Santa Fe had left one end unguarded. After due consideration, the Santa Fe decided not to tangle with Gould, to give up the Royal Gorge route, to forget the San Juan country, and to go west by way of New Mexico.

The Royal Gorge War was officially ended by the spring of 1880. It had cost both sides plenty but at least bloodshed had been minimal. The Rio Grande agreed to defer building to Santa Fe for ten years and to forget the threat of a parallel road eastward through Kansas.

The Baby Road paid for all the work the Santa Fe had done in the Gorge and beyond, and now the narrow gauge was free to run wild in the Colorado mountains.

A narrow-gauge passenger train ascends the steep four percent grade of Marshall Pass between Mears Junction (in the valley below) and the Summit. State Historical Society of Colorado

Breaking out of the long canyon of the Arkansas, the Rio Grande tracks reached Cleora, a town founded by the Santa Fe. Naturally, the Baby Road went right on through and founded another town two miles to the west, Salida.

Former Governor Hunt, ever the Rio Grande advance man in land matters, had heavy real estate investments in Salida. The Board of Trade of the new town quickly offered free lots to Cleora merchants. Saloonmen were summarily exempted from the giveaway, and thereby the Board of Trade hit a high note of piety never again achieved in Salida.

Building remarkably fast up the Arkansas, the Rio Grande reached Leadville in 1880 and began to haul ore. After smelters were built in the Carbonate Camp, silver ingots weighing up to 500 pounds made the freight platforms groan.

In 1881 the Baby Road went over Marshall Pass (11,000 feet) into the booming Gunnison country, and then kept right on going to the anthracite coal mines of Crested Butte.

That same year a branch from the Gunnison line went over Poncha Pass and down the San Luis Valley to the Orient iron mine. The Orient was owned by the Colorado Coal & Iron Company (now the thriving Colorado Fuel and Iron Steel Company) and its mainspring was—General Palmer.

Not long after the founding of the Colorado Coal & Iron Company, Palmer was proud to announce that the mills were making steel rails for the Baby Road. The Rio Grande was then no longer dependent on importation of iron rails from England.

Palmer's adeptness at mixing his own corporate affairs with those of the Rio Grande sometimes made the railroad bondholders unhappy. In one instance he made private use of Baby Road equipment to serve his personal timber interests near Colorado Springs.

Building was always the order of the day when Palmer was in control.

Dipping in and out of New Mexico by way of Chama, the Rio Grande reached Durango, Colorado, in 1881. Durango was a company town just a short distance down the Animas River from Animas City, which now had to move. The Baby Road loved brand-new real estate.

Still running as a tourist attraction is the narrow gauge from Durango to Silverton. The road was completed in 1882. Today it is probably the most profitable narrow gauge in the world. At Silverton the Baby Road was 500 miles from Denver, as the tracks meandered. Altogether, in 1882 the Rio Grande had 1,100 miles of track, 123 of which were three-rail between Denver and Pueblo. With three rails, both standard and narrow gauge could use the same line.

Though it seemed that the Baby Road ran spurs or branches in any direction where a prospect hole beckoned, General Palmer had a strong drive westward. The Rio Grande reached the Colorado River at Grand Junction in 1882, having gone from Gunnison down the river of the same name and through the Black Canyon, a defile so narrow, precipitous and deep that one standing in the bottom can see stars in the daytime.

It is reported that the last mile of Black Canyon roadbed cost more than the entire Royal Gorge construction. Colorado terrain being what it is, the Baby Road could scarcely go anywhere without scraping through a grim canyon beside tumbling white water, or looping back and forth on a plunging mountain like a drunken reptile. Passengers were warned to keep their heads from protruding from the windows, no matter how great the scenery. It was facetiously said that one coat of paint was all the wooden coaches could take because of limited clearance on rocky curves.

In 1883 Palmer resigned from the presidency of the Baby Road and then from the board. He was building too fast to too many places, his bondholders said. He then gave his attention to the Denver & Rio Grande Western, a line he controlled in Utah. It ran from Ogden to Green River and there met the tracks of the D&RG.

Colorado now had a continuous interior railroad from Denver to Salt Lake and on up to Ogden, the Rio Grande Western being leased for 30 years to the Baby Road. It was 735 miles from Denver to Salt Lake on the mountainous meandering of the Rio Grande system.

Rate wars with the Union Pacific and the Central Pacific broke out as soon as the Rio Grande began to operate in Utah. And then arguments over the lease of the Rio Grande Western to the Rio Grande flared up in childish quarreling. At one point the Rio Grande's new president had a mile of Baby Road line east of the Colorado border torn up, creating a fatal gap in the 735 miles of rails. A lacuna like that was too much, so the quarrel was patched up and the rails connected again.

There was also a Rio Grande Southern, built by Otto Mears, an incredible man who ran toll roads and rails over terrain considered impassable.

By 1888, with 1,673 miles of narrow gauge, the Baby Road had reached about every mining camp of any consequence in the Colorado Rockies. Though the mining industry was beginning to fade by then, two of the greatest camps in all the West were still to arrive, Cripple Creek and Creede, in the first two years of the 1890s.

Suddenly conservative, the Rio Grande did not build into either of them. Other lines went into Cripple Creek and reaped rich haulage. The Rio Grande was already at Wagon Wheel Gap on the Rio Grande River, just 9 miles from Creede when that hell-roaring camp exploded on the mining scene.

The Baby Road stayed at Wagon Wheel Gap in spite of the pleas for service from men like David H. Moffat, who had heavy mining investments in Creede. Moffat at last built the 9 miles of road with his own money, and then sold it for a fancy sum to the little reluctant dragon.

Mountain railroading was never simple and safe. Rio Grande trains were sometimes buried to the windows by snow on high passes. Washouts thundered down narrow canyons and left miles of track and cross ties suspended like a crazy rollercoaster. Rounding curves, engineers were frequently confronted with 15-ton rocks that had fallen from the canyon walls.

The life insurance of train crews was invalidated by waiver in their policies as soon as they left the main line of the Rio Grande in Brown's Canyon, between Salida and Nathrop, and went up through Box Canyon on the Calumet branch. The grade was steep, the curvatures tight. On the trip down with iron ore from the Calumet mine the trains were hard to hold. Flanges jetted fire from the light rails on curves and the busy brakemen kept one eye peeled for a soft place to jump.

Whatever the hazards, the Baby Road met them head-on and kept the doughty little Baldwins steaming where eagles screamed.

Most of the Rio Grande branch lines remained narrow gauge until abandonments as late as the 1950s. On the more important trackage standard gauging had been going on since 1882, but in 1920 the Baby Road still had 800 miles of slim track. Twice that distance was standard gauge.

From Denver to Salt Lake in the 1920s was still a long, circuitous way by any railroad. The main line of the Rio Grande was Denver to Pueblo, through the Royal Gorge, up the Arkansas to Salida, on to Malta (near Leadville), over Tennessee Pass, down the Eagle River to the Colorado, and then on west by way of Green River, Utah, and Soldier's Summit.

As early as 1867 far-seeing men had advocated a tunnel through James Peak, west of Denver. Later, David Moffat had fought to get the project started. He owned the Denver & Salt Lake, a railroad that went west from Denver over 12,000-foot Rollins Pass and on toward Salt Lake—as far as Craig, Colorado. That road still deadends in Craig, but for many years other railroads were kept uneasy by the threat of the Denver & Salt Lake being extended westward until it earned an honest name.

In 1922 tunnel plans jelled at last by means of political log rolling and the issuing of public bonds. The 6.2 mile Moffat Tunnel was started through James Peak. The man for whom the bore was named had then been dead for eleven years. East Portal is 50 miles west of Denver. The tunnel was completed in 1928, a single track bore.

By using the tunnel and the tracks of the Denver & Salt Lake as far as Bond, Colorado, and by then building a 38-mile connecting link down the Colorado River to its main line, the Rio Grande could reduce the distance from Denver to Salt Lake by 175 miles.

It was six years before the Rio Grande did build the connecting link, the Dotsero Cutoff. In 1934, at long last, Colorado had an almost direct line railroad from Denver to Salt Lake.

Today only freights use the Royal Gorge route.

So little is left of the narrow gauge branches from the days of steam that the name Baby Road no longer fits. After all, the infant is 105 years old.

The Durango-Silverton line still runs in summer. Colorado and New Mexico joined to buy the narrow gauge from Antonito, Colorado, over Cumbres Pass, to Chama, New Mexico. This is part of the old Chili Line that eventually did get to Santa Fe, but so late that it played no significant part in Rio Grande history.

Railroad buffs can still ride the preserved part of the old Chili Line, though it has no schedule.

9

Highballing on Wooden Rails

GLENN R. VERNAM

Whenever old-timers of the Pacific Northwest gang up for a session of yarn-spinning, especially if the company should include any of yesterday's railroaders, it is ten to one that the evening will not pass without some mention of Washington's first pioneer railroad.

Then it is that the listener will hear strange and wonderful tales of the West's most amazing transportation system. Nostalgic voices will speak of pint-sized, wood-burning locomotives operating over a 32-mile line of crude wooden rails to serve a territory half a continent away from the nearest other steam traffic. Other yarns will recall the dog which took the place of a cow-catcher, the thousand plug hats used to forward the wheels of progress, and the myriad similar ruses employed by the individual who conceived, financed, built, and operated this fabulous venture.

Only the spirit of the frontier could have given birth to the various accounts of how rawhide strips were sun-shrunken over the rapidly fraying wooden rails to form a protective armor against metal wheel flanges. This will be solemnly described as serving very well except in wet weather, when its stretching propensities allowed it to pile up in wavelike billows between the spinning wheels, while the train stood still. Or its wholesale disappearance, that legendary winter, when deepening snows and bitter cold held the Inland Empire in its frozen grasp for month after month. It was then, the raconteurs will maintain, that the ravening wolf packs swept down to fill their gaunt bellies with the rawhide designed to forward the march of civilization.

Further accounts depict the strap iron that was used to replace the rail covering devoured by the wolves. Nailed flat on top of the rails, this material had the bad habit of working loose to curl upward behind the advancing wheels. Reflective memories delight in portraying the car bottoms repeatedly pierced by upthrust trackirons, thus galvanizing into dramatic action various innocent passengers so rudely harpooned from below.

Fantastic derailments are brought to light, along with stories of schedule disruptions through the train crew's weakness for a little impromptu hunting along the way; special freight rates that were higher because of the goods being carried on the foremost car, and thus arrived ahead of the general cargo; a track crew that worked from horseback; Walla Walla's canvas-covered depot; a special car for General Sherman, which turned out to be a shipment of wheat with the topmost sack reserved for the general's seat.

The remarkable part is that most of these stories are essentially true. Though perhaps hard to conceive by minds atuned to jet propulsion, atomic power, and continental streamliners, such a railroad did exist. And most of its eccentricities need little embellishment by the yarn-spinner's fertile mind to set them apart as unique in railroading history.

Baker's Rawhide or Strap-iron Railroad, as it was commonly called, ran along the Washington-Oregon boundary from Wallula, at the bend of the Columbia River, to Walla Walla, Washington. It was designed chiefly to carry freight between the inland settlements and the Columbia River boats, which connected with the seaport of Portland, Oregon. Its creator, Dorsey Syng Baker, was one of those legendary visionaries to whom America owes most of her spectacular advancement.

This Dr. Dorsey Baker was a man of parts. He must have been an outstanding character, even for those days of rugged individualism and unconventional deportment. Tales of his idiosyncrasies and business ventures are as varied as those of his railroad.

Born in Iowa in 1823, his medical studies enabled him to come to Oregon as a doctor with the migration of 1848. The medical profession, however, soon succumbed to the magic lure of Dame Fortune. The following spring, we find him joining the throng bound for gold mad California. There, he apparently found what he was looking for. At any rate, the early '50s saw him back at Portland, well set up in the hardware business. During this period, he built a flour mill at Oakland, Oregon, for which he is reputed to have imported the state's first regular millstones.

On the heels of the rush to central Idaho's new gold fields, his vision soared

Dr. Dorsey Syng Baker. Oregon Historical Society

over the Cascades to encompass an empire in the making. That was in 1861. He immediately enlisted William Stevens and John Boyer as working partners in establishing an extensive outfitting enterprise at Walla Walla. Here, his business acumen was again demonstrated. Prospectors, hangers-on, and starry-eyed venturers were flooding into the country. They all needed supplies. Dr. Baker was there to furnish the necessary needs.

By the following year, he was able to lengthen the wings of his vision. This consisted of joining with Senator Crockett and Captain Ankeny in building the steamboat *Spray* to inaugurate boat traffic on the Snake River between Lewiston, Idaho, and Celilo Falls on the Columbia. Other boats were al-

Walla Walla in 1866. Penrose Memorial Library, Whitman College, Walla Walla ready plying the length of the lower Columbia. The falls and miles of unnavigable cascades at Celilo had, however, blocked any further ascent of the stream, as well as discouraging serious thought of upriver traffic.

But Dr. Baker was not one to let obstacles interfere with a dream. With his Snake River boat in operation, he promptly built a mile-long wooden tramway along the Washington side of the Cascades. This connecting link would enable him to portage his cargoes between the upper and lower river boats. In due time, he was making scheduled deliveries all the way from Portland's deep-sea port to the head of navigation on the Snake.

This, then, was the man who consulted his oracles and decided the virgin Northwest needed a railroad. New settlers were casting their eyes on the fertile miles rolling away into the distance. Frustrated gold seekers found their thoughts turning to the more enduring wealth of productive fields. Many had already located in the Walla Walla Valley and off toward the Blue Mountains. Others were spreading out to distant points away from the river. All found their rich acres turning off phenomenal yields of wheat, wheat which was steadily demanding a more practical route to market. A rail line seemed to be the answer, a speedy transport connecting this new farming bonanza with the lower Columbia steamboats.

Dr. Dorsey Baker, ever the man of action, looked the scene over, evaluated his resources, flexed his wings and decided to grab Progress by the forelock. The fact that he had never operated anything more complicated than small boats and ox-team freight outfits, didn't bother him in the least. Neither did the knowledge that nothing faintly resembling railroad equipment existed within a thousand miles. What of that? The country needed a railroad; a railroad should be a profitable enterprise; so a railroad Dr. Baker would build. That's all there was to it.

This decision was born the spring of 1871. Without any more to-do, Baker promptly caught a boat for Portland. There, he visited Ladd's bank and placed an order through their representatives in Pennsylvania for two small, narrow-gauge, camel-back locomotives, one hundred pairs of car wheels, and a thousand plug hats. Then, while waiting for the order to go through and delivery be made via sailing ship around the Horn, he laid out the 32 miles of future roadbed and contracted for his track material.

This last was to be a native forest product. An ex-lumberjack from Wisconsin, named Tarbox, engaged himself for the job. He took a party of loggers up onto the headwaters of the Yakima River to get out the logs. His plan was to float their cut down the river to the sawmill Baker was meanwhile constructing on the east bank of the Columbia shortly above Wallula.

Unfortunately, however, 1871 proved to be an exceptionally dry season.

Due to shortage of water in the river, the log drive proved to be a failure. Dismayed but not discouraged, Baker went ahead with his sawmill and grade building, assuring all and sundry that this little difficulty would soon adjust itself.

Whether his was the kind of faith that moved mountains, the gods of fortune had taken him under their wings, or it was just plain luck, we don't know. Nevertheless, about the time the sawmill was ready for operation, early the following spring, who should show up but an old bullwhacker in search of a job. Baker sized up the man, who gave his name as D. W. Small, and quickly decided he was as efficient as the string of oxen he had yoked to his wagons. Without further parley, he gave Small a contract for delivery of the logs.

Nor was he to regret this decision. Small's ability proved itself within a matter of days. His loaded wagons raced with time to finish their task before the frozen ground gave way to softening roadways. And with the mounting supply of logs on the rollway, the sawmill screamed its way to full-scale production.

Meanwhile, the tracklayers were stringing square-sawed ties and spiking down the six-by-six timbers that were to serve as rails. With equal dispatch, the rolling stock finished its long journey around Cape Horn and up the Columbia to Celilo Falls.

Here, Dr. Baker again showed his acumen by unpacking the shipment of plug hats in the presence of the many Indians always found in the neighborhood of the falls. White man's finery was invariably big medicine to the natives. Now, coupled with the strange devil wagons, they were irresistible. With such an inducement to offer as a bonus for labor, Baker had little trouble in hiring the help needed to portage his engines and car wheels around the cascades to the upriver boat. At Wallula, the western terminus of the new railroad, twenty-span ox-teams hauled the locomotives up onto the twin, yellow strips of freshly laid track.

Admittedly, the whole procedure was highly unorthodox and against all the rules of ordinary railroading. But Baker was no ordinary man; for him, it worked. The sawmill provided lumber which local carpenters fashioned into car bodies. These, mounted on the imported wheels, were soon shuttling back and forth behind the diminutive engines. Track laying speeded up with material trains displacing the plodding ox-teams. Erstwhile skeptics scratched their heads and began hunting for loopholes in some of their earlier uncharitable predictions.

Mile after mile, the new line unrolled eastward across the dusty sagebrush plain. The snorting locomotives performed well, as did the rest of the system.

Yet, halfway to Walla Walla, it was seen that the unprotected wooden rails were not durable enough for extensive use. Even at this stage of the game, they were already becoming seriously damaged at the river end of the route.

Perhaps it was then that some experiments were made in facing the rails with dried rawhide. History and fable are ever hard to separate with definite exactness. And we do know that dried rawhide has the durability of many metals. In pioneer times, it took the place of numerous unpurchasable items. But whether or not its use as a running surface on the Baker Railroad, and subsequent destruction by the hungry wolves, assumed the proportions accredited to it by latter-day raconteurs is still food for argument among historical purists.

We do know, however, that long before the road was completed, Dr. Baker had boated in a shipment of strap iron to reinforce his track. This iron was in strips, an inch and a half wide, bored for the nails that were to spike it down on the railtops. And a very good running surface it made; that is, until continued vibration worked the spikes loose and allowed the straps to curl away from the pounding wheels.

Eventually, the pioneer builder was forced to replace his makeshift track with 26-pound, all-metal rails shipped around Cape Horn from Wales. This uncalculated conversion was naturally somewhat expensive. It evidently unravelled the seams of the good doctor's budget. At any rate, by the time the road reached Whitman, six miles west of Walla Walla, his finances were scraping the bottom of the barrel.

The Walla Walla, *first locomotive on the Baker road.* Penrose Memorial Library, Whitman College, Walla Walla

But Baker was a practical man. He might have been even slightly guileful. Anyway, at this point, he bluntly announced that lack of funds was forcing him to make the smaller settlement his eastern terminus. It was a decision that shook Walla Walla to its scab-rock foundations. The local citizenry raised its lusty voice in a howl of protest. They were in no mood to surrender the railroad to the neighboring village. Following a hasty meeting, a group of their leading businessmen put up $25,000, to bring the road on into the budding city.

This move erased the last hurdle. And, as later developments proved, confirmed the wisdom of everyone concerned. Baker's homespun railroad was soon found to be the chief impetus needed to place Walla Walla in permanent leadership as the main distributing center for that area. At the same time, the railroad fully justified its builder's faith in broad visions. The Bonanza Line, as he named it, was unique among railroads in that it always paid dividends and was never in debt.

Moreover, its many confirmed iniquities, from first to last, spawned the legends that, even a hundred years later, still highlight the bold saga of the Pacific Northwest. Here it was that lighting was eliminated by confining train schedules strictly to daylight hours. Most of the freight was hauled on the plank-floored flatcars, thus conforming to Dr. Baker's ideas of economy, convenience, and contempt for the weather. The more privileged passengers were allowed to bounce and rattle on the long benches running along both sides of an undecorated boxcar.

Various cattlemen had been moving their herds to the lush grasslands of the Inland Empire during the intervening years. With barbwire still a thing of the future, their cattle held little regard for progressive industry bisecting their range. It was quite a problem. Incidentally, we might suppose that the doctor's studies had given him some inkling of how any mediocre animal immediately became a valuable purebred upon being killed by a train. Anyway, he could easily see that his blunt-nosed locomotives were not equipped for clearing the track of trespassers, without possible damage. Characteristically, he went into a huddle with himself and came up with the answer. He forthwith had a small platform built on the front end of each locomotive. Then, with a dog trained to ride the platforms and answer a blast of the whistle, he was assured of a clear track. The whistle's warning call was all that was needed to send the dog racing ahead to disperse any heedless interlopers on the railroad's domain.

It worked, like all the Baker innovations, for a time. But even animal minds are not always fully in accord with the schemes of man. At any rate, the dog developed an incurable habit of lying down between the rails, when its task was finished, there to await the slower moving train's arrival and take him aboard. One fateful day, when his lead and the train's progress were at too much variance, he dropped off to sleep. Perhaps the engineer was also asleep. Time has erased some of the details. All we can truthfully say, at this late date, is that the mangled body of Fido persuaded Dr. Baker that a more conventional cow remover would be advisable.

The law, at that time, demanded that each car be posted with the required freight rates. Baker complied by tacking his freight rate notices, of $5 per ton to or from the river, on the car roofs. Fast, or preferred, shipments were hauled on the leading cars; the track maintenance man carried a poleax and bag of nails behind his saddle; the repair shop was under the engineer's seat.

A typical Dr. Baker story concerns the occasion when General Sherman demanded a private car for that stage of his journey, while making his tour of the West. The fiercely independent and democratic doctor had an abiding dislike for imperiousness and class distinction. His sarcastic reply to the general's request ended with a brief motion toward the topmost sack on a flatcar load of wheat. "If your holiness demands privacy," he snapped, "nobody will crowd in on you up there." Sherman, it is further stated, hastily reversed his opinion about associating with the common passengers.

But whatever his failings and peculiarities, the Bonanza Line was unquestionably both a financial success and a keystone in the Northwest's railway development. Dr. Baker subsequently sold a six-sevenths interest of his one-man creation to the Oregon Railway & Navigation Company, with himself remaining president of the road. That was in 1877. Two years later, the pioneer railroad was converted to standard gauge and made an integral part of OR&N.

Time has dimmed the physical features of that rare breed of men who carved an empire out of a wilderness, with rawhide, scrap iron and sheer bold daring. Future ages may tend to obscure their accomplishments. Yet they will always live in memory. And head-high among those craftsmen of American destiny, in that Valhalla of visionary individualists, we may hope to find Dorsey Syng Baker looking back through the ages at his 32 miles of splintery wooden rails, which opened the old Washington-Oregon Inland Empire to world-wide commerce.

10

High Iron by Christmas or The Great Christmas Race

ELLIS LUCIA

For several years now in the 1860s, railroad fever had been spreading in epidemic proportions through the Oregon Country. Completion of the first transcontinental iron trail to California would leave Oregon, the original Promised Land of the pioneers, sidetracked, with the flow of people and goods funneled into the big brawling land to the south.

It was a prospect that stuck in the craw of proud Oregonians and particularly the Yankee business interests that ruled Portland and therefore, much of the new state which had entered the Union just a few years ago. Moreover, prospects of a railroad directly linking the Pacific Northwest with the East were dim for the immediate future, since the terrain between here and there was wild and rugged, and the population strength of the Northwest simply wasn't sufficient to warrant such an investment.

What made good sense would be a West Coast railroad tying together the two main cities of Portland and San Francisco, and all those waypoints in between. The present slow stagecoaches offered little comfort, not everyone enjoyed sea travel, and both passengers and goods suffered frustrating delays from the bad roads of the long rainy season and the ravaging storms which lashed the Northwest from October into the spring. There was a fortune to be made in such a railroad, although the investment would be substantial—a fact of no little concern to Oregon interests which had no Comstock or Mother Lodes on which to rely. The prospects of a great treasure trove in Federal land grants and direct railroad profits had business tycoons along the West Coast and in the East jockeying for positions at the faro table and wooing the conservative, bullnecked, and independent Oregonians in such amazing fashion as to raise their suspicions against any newcomer who talked railroading.

Companies were formed in both Oregon and California, under such highly original names as the Oregon & California Railroad and the California & Oregon Railroad. Some survey work had been accomplished, primarily on the southern end, but then power politics alias human greed bogged down everything in a snarl of quarreling and bickering that would likely stall the Iron Horse for years to come. Building a railroad through western Oregon's cluttered terrain of deep forests, swift rivers, mountains, and adverse weather conditions would be no simple or inexpensive task. Yet the main difficulty at this moment was the Oregonians themselves who were exhibiting their characteristic independence and the ability to shout loud and long if things weren't to their liking. About the only point they could agree upon was that they wanted to finance and construct their own railroad; they wanted no interference from the Californians. Beyond this, everything fell apart in all directions, for just about everyone wanted the railroad to run through his town or farm, within spitting distance of his front door, so his kids could wave at the engineer without going off the porch and thus getting soaked by the rain.

Nobody in the state could speak with much authority about railroads. A lot of folks on the farms and in the villages had never seen a train, nor heard the lovely wail of the Iron Horse echoing through their tall timber. The only railroads in the territory were the short portage lines around the cascades of the Columbia Gorge, built to accommodate steamboat passengers and freight, shuttled along wooden rails and for a long while powered by obstreperous mules. Then the Oregon Steam Navigation Company which virtually monopolized the rivers with its steamboat fleet brought in the *Oregon Pony,* a tiny 5-ton steam engine which could muster speed of 20 miles an hour on the iron-faced rails. That was the extent of steam railroading in Oregon and Captain John C. Ainsworth who held the helm of the mighty steamboat empire was happy to keep it that way—unless, of course, the Oregon Steam Navigation Company could retain controlling interest in any railroad so that it wouldn't knock the steamboats out of business. The O.S.N. had a good thing going in its river fleet. Everyone rode the steamboats, for there were many rivers, flowing all directions, the roads were awful, and the skippers boasted that the colorful sternwheelers could run "anywhere it's damp." And the Oregon Steam Navigation Company, lacking serious competition, could set passenger and freight rates to suit the mood of Ainsworth and his partners, known as "The Triumvirate."

Still, the railroad pressure continued building. Ainsworth knew that sooner or later, the O.S.N. would have to turn to railroading. Presently, there were two major factions, commonly called the East Siders and the West Siders, indicating the route any California-bound railroad would follow. The north-flowing Willamette River bisected the great Oregon Valley of the same name for over a hundred miles in the general direction of San Francisco, as the Sacramento River did a similar valley on the southern end. Any such railroad would run through these mighty valleys, but the big debate in Oregon—much of it strongly linked to local civic pride and prospective economic riches—was whether the road should go on the east or west side of the Willamette River.

The West Siders were composed largely of powerful Portland interests which held the state's economic and political clout. No small force was the Oregon Steam Navigation Company; much of the West Side's leadership came from Captain Ainsworth and his influential friends among the money changers. The East Siders were mainly anti-Portland people who were trying to develop a competing town called East Portland on the river's opposite shore, and settlers living and doing business upriver and in the hinterlands of the great valley, the area snobbishly called "Upstate" by the Portlanders. They had little capital, but much lung power and unlimited dreams. They also had the dubious asset of one Simon G. Elliott, a bumbling California county surveyor who passed himself off as a top-grade railroad "civil engineer" and manipulator of high finance. Elliott had earlier surveyed the right-of-way between Marysville, California, and Jacksonville, Oregon, where the effort went broke, but not before it caught the eye of a young newspaper editor, Joseph Gaston, who dreamed of riches for himself and threw in with the Ainsworth crowd as the best prospect for an Oregon-owned railroad system.

Both factions added to the confusion by adopting the name Oregon Central Railroad Company, one "of Portland" and the other "of Salem," the state capital. They rushed to get their incorporation papers in order, each hoping for endorsement by the state legislature. The duplication of names created a furor which wound up in the courts, along with the issue of just which company was the legal heir to the railroad construction project and the rich Federal land grants that were the sweepstakes prize. Gaston had penciled in an early filing date before completing the West Side papers. This became the point of white-hot contention, for although the East Siders filed later, their papers were all in proper order. Yet the influential West Siders gained the endorsement of the legislature as the legal company amid howls from the East Side element which took the frontier war to the halls of the U. S. Congress,

Big Ben Holladay, transportation giant of the early West, invaded the Oregon country to build a West Coast railroad to California. Ellis Lucia Collection

where there was heavy pressure to extend the deadlines for filing and also for construction of the road.

Into the fray at this point waded Big Ben Holladay, spoiling for a fight, his pockets jingling with the coin of the realm from having peddled his great Overland Stage Company to Wells Fargo for over $2,000,000. Railroads were the coming way of life in the West, the King of Wheels realized, and he wanted "out" before his Overland was valueless. Wells Fargo couldn't see it—there would always be stagecoaches—so Holladay generously stepped aside to let them find out the hard way.

By now Old Ben was a Western legend, full-blown, rich, and roaring in the operation of stage, express, and freight companies, river steamers, ocean vessels plying waters clear to Australia, the greatest government mail contractor of them all; road builder, land developer, owner and operator with huge investments in mines, banks, swank resort hotels, meat packing plants, ranches, and distilleries. He owned a string of mansions from coast to coast, including one in Washington, D.C., where he threw fancy parties and tossed his weight around. He had great influence with the country's leaders, Presidents notwithstanding, and was internationally recognized. Holladay was a man to be reckoned with, who would go to any length to have his way and add to his power and his pocketbook. But he also got things done when they needed doing.

The West Siders shuddered when the bearded transportation king stepped ashore from the steamer *Oriflamme* in the company of Simon Elliott. What was he doing here? Holladay had operated steamers into Portland for years, but his visits had been infrequent. Now he talked as though he might locate here. Secretly, he had long desired to get into railroading. He'd tried to have a part in the Union Pacific project, building the transcontinental route near his Overland Stage line, through stock manipulations and political and business intrigue, but was outmaneuvered by his long-time enemies. For some time now, he'd been observing the West Coast endeavor from his Bush Street mansion in San Francisco with amusement, especially the machinations on the Oregon end. When Elliott came pounding on his door, seeking capital, it was the answer to any prayers Big Ben might have said to his own particular gods. Opportunity was knocking and Ben was never one to shrug it aside.

West Siders' fears were quickly realized as Holladay made an inspection of the East Side right-of-way and also sneaked a look at what had been accomplished across the river. Conditions were much as he expected. Both sides held spectacular ground-breakings a year or so earlier, with bands, orations, and free liquor, in hopes of gaining supporters. There'd been a little grading, but then the projects ran out of steam and plunged into the present turmoil which was to Ben's advantage. Yet the East Siders welcomed Holladay warmly, even though some of them realized that the Magnificent Barbarian was a dangerous dealer who played for high stakes and would trample on anyone getting in his way. Observing and listening to the personable King of Wheels, East Siders failed to find any resemblance to a coiled rattlesnake. Besides, he was their only hope. The fact of prime importance was that Holladay was a mover of mountains and at this moment, building that mainline railroad along the east bank of the Willamette was the foremost matter at hand. There was also the hard-hitting impact that Holladay's very presence made upon the West Siders. The Portland crowd feared his power, knowing that when Big Ben declared all-out war, he would go to the far limits to win.

Holladay lost no time swinging into action by gaining control of the East Side company from Elliott and his partners. This wasn't as Elliott had planned it, but Ben quickly recognized that the surveyor was a weak man who made many mistakes. The Portland *Herald* cheered the move:

Ben Holladay Esq. has purchased a controlling interest in the contract for construction of the Oregon Central Railroad (East Side) and will hereafter lend his energies to advancing work upon the line. Mr. Holladay is one of the most energetic men on the Pacific Coast and we consider that his taking interests here is the best sort of an indication.

His showmanship and personal magnetism drew supporters to his swelling ranks. Amazed Oregonians, unused to the style in which Holladay flung money about, stared in fascination. High stakes in terms of millions of dollars were beyond their comprehension. Right off, Ben sent to San Francisco for several hundred Chinese laborers to get the railroad moving again. He purchased a great tract of land opposite Portland and then declared open war against the West Side business element by roaring:

"This will be the city of the future. I'll make Portland nothing but a rat hole, with grass growing on Front Street."

Yet he bought a grand home in the enemy camp, near the center of Portland, where he entertained lavishly with excellent cuisine, rare wine, music and dancing, for Big Ben recognized long ago that there is much more to politics than politics. His main concern was over what the state legislature might do about recognizing the East Side company as the legal heir to the Federal land grants. The legislators were gathering this fall of 1868 in Salem, and Holladay couldn't chance a lengthy court fight, for time was of the essence. Still, changing the fanciful heads of the lawmakers, especially when you were an outsider, would take some doing.

Ben purchased a riverboat, turned it into a private yacht, and took it upriver to Salem. He also bought a hotel and set up offices in the capital. Lawmakers, lobbyists, state officials, and others of influence received personal invitations to come aboard Holladay's boat when they wished to cut free from their tedious duties at the statehouse. Delicious meals were served at all hours, while the clink of glasses echoed amid the great fir trees and the decks were said to be "drenched with champagne." Charming and beautiful ladies roamed the decks, willing to share a man's table and to provide additional favors in the private staterooms below. Everything was on the house; the glamour of Holladay's hospitality could be resisted by very few. Big Ben knew full well that lawmakers liked to be entertained. He'd seen plenty of it in Washington, and what it got you. This was Oregon's first paid lobby and a kind of political shenanigans never before witnessed in the state. The horrified West Siders, yelled their disapproval over Holladay's efforts to buy the legislature. They could only pray that in the end their fellow Oregonians would see the light and approach the railroad business with level heads, not with hangovers from the quantities of wine they were consuming.

It didn't work that way. The legislature made a complete about-face

Ben Holladay handled his business dealings and manipulations concerning the Oregon-California railroad from this plush mansion in Portland. He lavishly entertained here and at a villa on the Oregon coast. Ellis Lucia Collection

in favor of the East Side. Legislators argued that Holladay, by reputation and financial depth, was the best bet to do the job—and Oregon needed that railroad. The resulting holler finally reached Congress. Ben had much influence in the Capitol, but newspaper editor Gaston's persistent broadsides to discredit Holladay and his East Side company proved to be a powerful counterbalance. Finally Congress became fed up with this frontier feuding. It extended the land-grant filing time, then added a crowning touch: the grant would go to the company laying 20 miles of track and having a railroad in operation, able to pass inspection, by Christmas Day 1869. Let 'em slug it out on the frontier!

Both sides rolled up their sleeves. The weeks sped by as they surveyed, cleared land, and graded their rights-of-way for the crucial 20 miles of track, while their leaders wheeled and dealed with landowners and beat the brush for additional financing. A wet spring cut into construction and the summer season was all too short to make the progress needed for that deadline set by Congress. Holladay was, as predicted, throwing everything into the race, for he needed a victory to bolster his transportation empire. His image as America's King of Wheels was also at stake.

East Siders and West Siders both were having problems with capitalization, but Old Ben managed to strengthen his hold on the Oregon Central by gaining the support of Milton S. Latham, head of the highly influential London and San Francisco Bank. Shortly, Latham was recommending Holladay's Oregon railroad bonds to British and German investors so that Holladay got the long-term capital he needed.

Throughout that critical summer, Holladay was spending more time than he preferred away from the railroad project, grubbing for additional funds and dealing with his affairs on many fronts, including the problems of a socially ambitious wife, two uncontrollable daughters, and a pair of wild and drunken sons. Still, the Chinese were making progress amid the stumps of the muddy right-of-way. Almost every ship brought more laborers and more construction gear, from picks, shovels and axes to hundreds of wheelbarrows. Holladay was pouring every cent he could scrape together into the project which soaked up funds like the earth of Oregon did the heavy rains. He had a payroll to meet and had taken consignments on huge quantities of railroad equipment, including 2,000 tons of iron rails—enough for 25 miles of track. He had to keep the work going all along the line, not displaying any signs of weakness which would cast doubts with his investors and encourage the West Side. The Ainsworth forces were pressing him on other fronts, for Ainsworth and Company had their own forceful connections. They threatened to establish a competing line to Ben's West Coast steamship fleet, beginning with a fine vessel purchased on the East Coast. If they tried putting her in operation on the West Coast, Holladay warned that he would "blow her out of the water." A large block of steamship stock was also forced back upon his hands by the California Steam Navigation Company. Ben suspected this, too, was Ainsworth's doing, since the grizzly steamboat man who once had Mark Twain for his pilot held strong connections in San Francisco.

With all the demands on his time, Holladay reluctantly left Simon Elliott in charge of construction, although he had long suspected Elliott wasn't half the engineer, or money raiser, that he pretended to be. Ben hired a high-ranking civil engineer, Robert L. Harris, to inspect the right-of-way and give him a full report. The worried Elliott dogged Harris's footsteps. Hearing this, Holladay boarded the next steamer for Oregon. Harris told Ben flatly that things were one grand mess, that no self-respecting locomotive and cars could negotiate the road. The work was sloppy and would never pass inspection. The grading was uneven, while cuts through the hills were only wide enough to accommodate the track and their slopes so steep that heavy rains and passing trains would cause serious sliding. There were no provisions for drainage and south of Oregon City, the old territorial capital, where the line rejoined the river after a wide swing to the east, the stump-grubbing was "not

Thousands of unskilled Chinese laborers, called coolies, were brought north from California by Holladay to carve the route of the Oregon-California railroad through thick timber and muck of the heavy autumn rains. This is one such gang of Orientals pushing south toward California. Ellis Lucia Collection

properly done." The railroaders had to chisel the way around the rock bluffs near the Willamette Falls. This grading was lagging behind schedule. All along the route far more clearing of the hefty Oregon firs would be required. Harris's conclusion: much of the work had to be redone and the project was for the most far behind schedule. Meanwhile, the West Siders who drew the easier route through the broad Tualatin Valley boasted of some 20 miles graded to the village of Hillsboro. It appeared that before long they would be laying iron, while Joe Gaston continued soliciting funds and selling more bonds.

Many priceless weeks had been lost from Elliott's bumbling. The setback would cost a pretty penny in time and dollars. Cursing, Holladay took over the job of construction boss. More and more he was realizing that railroad building was a far cry from stagecoaching, and more expensive. The two-fisted one-time boss of the plains ranged up and down the right-of-way, bellowing like a locomotive, spouting steam and fire with every breath. His black stallion and his long heavy legs carried him along every foot of the route, through muck and mire and across acres of downed trees and fast-running streams, his sharp eyes catching every detail of the work being done by the laboring gangs. Certainly the East Siders had drawn the toughest way through those deep forests, bogs, streams, the swift-flowing Clackamas River, and the formidable barricade at the Willamette Falls. The weeks flew by at highball speed as night and day, the gangs swung their sledges and leaned into their shovels and wheelbarrows to move the many tons of earth on the Portland section; and as trestles and bridges began taking shape over the many creeks, defiles, ravines, and rivers that must be crossed.

Already it was mid-September and Holladay knew he needed every second to meet that Yuletide deadline. The country was drenched by the first autumn rains; the land was again turning mucky. Some mornings there was ice upon the puddles. It was a helluva time to build a railroad. And still the West Siders were out ahead of him.

One night marauding renegades of the West Side crossed the river to set fire to many great stacks of ties and piling, yanked up survey stakes, and wrecked sections of the grading. From then on, Holladay ordered twenty-four-hour patrols and guards posted at the supply depots.

Ben's big sawmills along the river spewed forth more ties, bridge pilings, settings and lumber. In his new Brooklyn yards, the first railroad cars ever built in the Pacific Northwest were being fashioned of Oregon timber. Each ship brought more men, more gear. Hundreds of kegs of railroad spikes were in one shipment alone. Then, in late October, the *Moses Taylor* arrived with some 200 tons of railroad equipment, including the first rails rolled on the Pacific Coast. It was a day of celebration, as a large crowd gathered. A brass band and booming cannon welcomed the ship. The rails were swung ashore and then came the driving of the first spike. But the ceremony was brief, although Holladay provided a quantity of free champagne. He couldn't afford the time; he still had a railroad to build in seven weeks, and his locomotives hadn't yet arrived.

Ben fired Elliott who fled the territory, replacing him with a competent railroad construction man, John F. Kidder. But Holladay was still very much in the driver's seat, checking that the work was done right and that no man was loafing on his shovel. He tongue-lashed the crews, putting his own powerful muscles to the cause wherever he saw the need, for unlike the West Side leaders, Ben had never been a desk man. He believed in being with the action.

His main concern now was that 370-foot trestle bridging the Clackamas River, 12 miles to the south. It required a tough piece of engineering skill that would consume all the remaining time. Roaring, pushing, shoving, cursing—Holladay drove the crews to keep at it. By torchlight the work went on, at the bridge and in the deep forests. Kidder had things organized, with expert section hands—many of them from the transcontinental project—

Holladay's route south was blocked by heavy timber and undergrowth which delayed construction while rivals on the west side were laying track along an open valley floor. This is how the line appeared, not long after completion. The Southern Pacific still uses the route carved by Ben Holladay between Portland and San Francisco as its main line. Ellis Lucia Collection swiftly laying track in proper fashion. Time was ticking away, yet the job had to be done right, although they skimped on the ballast and thick planking straddled the swampy places, sometimes two deep to hold the roadbed level.

Constant autumn storms lashed the region, one upon another, dumping deluges of rain on the railroads. The West Siders were pacing hard, although Holladay had the feeling that they were running out of fuel. His own work concerned him more, the men laboring in the bone-chilling cold at the swollen creeks and rivers, making bridging difficult. Axes sang in the forests; big bull oxen dragged great timbers to the Clackamas bridge where crews were struggling to link up the trestle. Just as the last section was bolted into place, a cloudburst struck the mountain area to the east. A boiling wall of white water surged downstream, smashing into the new trestle. The bridge shuddered on the initial shock, creaking and swaying with growing violence. A

The J. B. Stephens *was shipped from San Francisco as the Oregon railroad's first full-fledged locomotive. The woodburner is shown on the troublesome Clackamas River bridge which was knocked down by a cloudburst.* Ellis Lucia Collection

girder snapped like exploding cannon, then another and another. Men leaped for their lives as the trestle twisted, collapsed, and was swept away on the raging torrent into the Willamette River a few miles downstream.

The West Siders, watching the trestle remains float downstream toward the Columbia, were gleeful. It touched off a rousing celebration in the Portland saloons and the sedate parlors of the local nabobs. This put Holladay to the wall; he might never recover. The entire span must be rebuilt—this time more solidly—and little more than a month remained before Christmas.

The tired bridge builders were ordered back into action while additional manpower was hurried to the scene. A little pony locomotive, the *Betsy,* was rafted across the flooding Clackamas so that track-laying could continue on the southern end. But there was also good news, something to lift all their spirits. Holladay's prize possession arrived on the bark *Webfoot.* An elegant locomotive, the *J. B. Stephens,* named for one of the early East Side promoters, was the first steam engine of any consequence to be brought to the Oregon Country. Crowds turned out to admire this handsome product of the Hinkley Works which weighed 22 tons, was crowned with a balloon stack, and was brightly trimmed in highly polished brass.

"Handle her with care, boys," Holladay ordered. "She's a proud beauty, ain't she?"

The crew almost lost her in the drink getting her ashore, for 22 tons deadweight is rather cumbersome. Holladay roared he'd have all their hides if she landed with so much as a scratch. At last the beautiful woodburner was safely on the dock, poised for inspection on the spur track near the wharf turntable. Next day they fired up the *Stephens,* making a careful trial run to the Brooklyn yards a few miles away, while the shrill and happy whistle could be heard sounding victory across the river where Captain Ainsworth sat glumly in his office, drumming his desk. He had become disenchanted with Joe Gaston and all his talk, for Gaston was like Elliott, failing to deliver the goods. Capital was running low and Ainsworth doubted the wisdom of pouring any more wealth into a bottomless pit. It appeared that Holladay might win and perhaps it would be wise to make some kind of peace with Old Ben. However, when Ainsworth tried, Holladay shunted him aside. The only hope for the West Side in bringing the railroad to Portland, and therefore under the control of the O.S.N., lay in the heavily guarded Clackamas trestle, that it might not be completed or the work unable to pass Federal inspection. And Holladay seemingly even had those inspectors in his pocket.

Day after day, night upon night, Sundays and Thanksgiving included, the track-laying and -grading continued down to Parrott Creek, the far end-of-track and the required 20 miles. The finishing touches were being put on some of the sections and the *Stephens* tested them out with two of the new passenger cars. Still the Clackamas bridge wasn't finished and now they were into December. The key to it all was right there. Holladay posted extra guards in case anyone tried to blow up the bridge. The men swarmed over the trestle, working elbow to elbow, striving to erect a structure which would withstand anything the unpredictable Clackamas might throw at it. The span rested solidly on massive rock piers on each bank of the river. The heavy beams were strongly bolted, the trestle was braced and girdered in every direction to withstand the stresses and strains of both swift water and heavy passenger and freight trains.

Meanwhile, optimistic Old Ben ordered the telegraph strung, a depot erected at East Portland, and a turntable set at Parrott Creek. His race was now one against time which could disqualify his claims to the land grant, for the West Siders had run out of cash, and, therefore, out of steam, the Portland crowd realizing they couldn't win against this Herculean effort that Ben Holladay was making.

Six miles south of Oregon City, the last spike was driven into place at Parrott Creek at noon on December 23. Now but a single full day and two nights remained. The old barbarian leaned harder on his good men at the Clackamas as more girders, struts, and supports were fitted into place. The ties were down and the rails brought up as West Siders hung around, watching for anything slipshod in shortcuts that could disqualify Holladay in this final hour. Minutes and hours ticked away and then the first rails were going down, the heavy sledges ringing on the thick spikes. Another rail, another fitting, another hour gone by. Ben bawled to his men to hurry. Down the track the *J. B. Stephens* was poised, her boiler fired up, singing a happy tune, blowing steam, eager to make the run. The engineer stroked the throttle, anxious to throw it open.

The gap was closing. Ben glanced at his gold watch which swung on a 5 pound chain of Comstock quartz. Another rail . . . then another . . . the final one . . . another delay while it was cut to fit the remaining distance. Then the spikes went home, solid and sure in the gathering dusk of Christmas Eve.

Lusty shouts went up, men hugged each other, and the *Stephens* hooted long and loud. Big Ben threw down his tall beaver and stomped on it. Then he leaped aboard the locomotive, grabbing the whistle cord.

There's your railroad, Mr. Gaston!

"Get 'er movin'!" Old Ben ordered.

The fireman, grinning broadly, chucked in more cordwood. The engineer eased the throttle and clanged the bell. The locomotive gave a chug, then another as men scrambled aboard the baggage and twin passenger cars;

shouting and clapping each other on the backs as the *Stephens* moved slowly across the great bridge, its headlight piercing the dimness ahead.

The locomotive spread the word down the line, for the whistle and bell could be heard for miles. Folks dropped whatever they were doing, grabbed their young'ns, and rushed trackside to watch the train go by.

The sleek J. B. Stephens *and her Oregon-built passenger cars, described as "splendid," posed along the Willamette River following victory in the Christmas race of 1869. A reporter expressed amazement that the train could do 15 miles an hour.* Ellis Lucia Collection

On Christmas Day, Holladay celebrated by giving his particular friends and their families, and his close aides, a private trip over the line. Everything seemed to be in proper order and the roadbed solid enough. A few days later, he held an official inspection for the Federal committee, along with local dignitaries and newspaper reporters. The delegation was impressed by the work, especially the intricate trestle over the Clackamas which would indeed stand for many years. They were astounded by the quantities of railroad equipment Holladay had amassed at the Brooklyn yards, and also the fine home-built rolling stock which a writer for *The Oregonian* described as "splendid passenger cars."

A reporter for the Portland *Herald,* who rode in the cab, enthused:

"Such was the condition of the track that we were able to make the return to Oregon City at the rate of 15 miles per hour . . . We believe the quality equals that of the Central Pacific east of the Sierras."

The following year, 1870, now with a 3,800,000-acre land grant under his money belt, Big Ben extended the railroad south to the capital in time for Portlanders to ride to the State Fair in September. He pushed the rails to Eugene, 125 miles from Portland, and by 1872 had reached Roseburg, 198 miles from his starting point. By then he had also taken over the near-defunct West Side line and extended it, giving him 245.5 miles of operating railroad.

Yet Holladay was still some distance from Jacksonville, the rich mining town at the southern edge of the state. There were mountains between, and beyond Jacksonville he faced the mighty Siskiyou Range to connect with the California line. And the Oregon & California, as it was now called, was to date of little profit, for in reality it went nowhere except for local service and wouldn't be a moneymaker until it could meet the California line building north in the Sacramento Valley.

The southbound railroad reached Salem, Oregon, the state capital, in the late summer of 1870, in time to bring people to the State Fair. It was the start of a new era for Oregonians. West Side forces by then were defeated and Ben Holladay bought out the rival company. Ellis Lucia Collection

Ben Holladay was spread too thin, for he had miscalculated the lack of profits from this unfinished operation. His German bondholders sent Henry Villard to check on things, and especially on Ben Holladay. Villard who wanted the railroad for himself forced the crusty old barbarian to the wall in what was Big Ben's greatest defeat and the beginning of his decline. Villard was then able to build the Northern Pacific across Montana to Portland from the east, completing it in 1883 through his astounding "blind pool" of investments. He extended the Oregon & California to Ashland on the Oregon border before he, too, went broke.

It took the Southern Pacific to finish the West Coast line across the Siskiyous where the gap was for years served by stagecoaches. The first train rolled into Portland from the San Francisco Bay Area in December 1887, a few months after Ben Holladay died, over roadbed that Old Ben had blazed eighteen years before. And still today, the main north-south line of the Southern Pacific follows much of the old Holladay Christmas right-of-way along the east bank of the Willamette River where the stout piers of the original Clackamas bridge remain plainly visible.

11

The Benevolent and Belligerent Octopus: The Southern Pacific

PAUL BAILEY

By 1850 a wrangling American Congress had hammered out the compromise. An aging and exhausted Henry Clay was willing to allow California to come into the Union as a state unpledged to slavery. Daniel Webster, worried lest refusal of statehood would end in an independent republic on the western shores, with San Francisco as capital, backed down on his adamant stand, and stood for California's immediate admittance. Stephen A. Douglas, flying in the teeth of the great debate over the issue of slave lands and free lands, wanted California in on any basis and, along with it, Federal aid for transcontinental railroads from Atlantic to Pacific.

With the granting of statehood, on September 9, 1850, California became the thirty-first star to the flag. The nation now stood with sixteen anti-slave states—fifteen states jealously loyal to the "institution"—with all petitioning territories free to decide for themselves as to the explosive issue. A bitter war was soon to be fought on this matter, regardless of compromise. But what the lusty new states of the Far West wanted—far more than the right to dominate and exploit the black man—was a spanning of the nation by rails. That was their cry. That was their demand.

The unparalleled rush of population westward, following the conclusion of the war with Mexico, and the discovery of gold in California, had changed the United States from an insular confederation into a great power—at least geographically. America's spread was now from ocean to ocean. Hundreds of thousands of its citizens were moving to California by land and by sea. The demand for modern transportation to shorten the endless miles of mountains and prairies would not be downed. Railroads! Give us railroads!

Politicians, ever the opportunists, were now hammering on the theme of Federal backing for a job far beyond the capability of any single human, or group of men, to accomplish. Financially the nation was groaning under the strain of footing bills for the sudden expansion. But expand it must. Demands on the public till were just as insistently and loudly voiced then, as they would be a century later.

The seer, Theodore Dehone Judah, was now crying desperately from California. The tiny Sacramento Valley Railroad had become first crutch to his great vision—a dream that would impel him into a most amazing and epochal survey—an obsession that eventually would win the hearts of enough politicians and common allies to start a railroad eastward out of California.

What Judah had conceived would someday become the segmental miracle known to friend and foe as the Southern Pacific. Its true beginnings, however, were years before Judah's dream—before the Central Pacific had crossed the Sierras—before it had spiked itself to the rails of Union Pacific, at Promontory.

In 1852, in New Orleans, two years after the granting of statehood to California, the New Orleans, Opelousas & Great Western Railroad was born. The "Opelousas," with a charter from the Louisiana legislature authorizing a capital stock of $3,000,000, was the first segment of a jointed railroad tentacle that eventually would reach the Pacific Coast. Being years ahead of the frenetic battle for America's miles by Central Pacific and Union Pacific, the New Orleans entrepreneurs had neither the idea nor plan for transcontinental structure. With the $2,994,235 they had raised by popular subscription, they started laying track from the west bank of the Mississippi toward Texas. In those early days there was no such thing as a standard gauge. Width between rails could be the choice of any builder. The Opelousas laid 80 miles of track, on the astonishing gauge of 5 feet 6 inches, and with 11-foot ties.

In 1851, the Buffalo Bayou, Brazos & Colorado Railroad had been born in Texas. From its starting point at Harrisburg (now a part of Houston), it had, by 1855, laid rails to Brazos, 30 miles away. The BBB&C chose 4 feet 8½ inches as gauge for its rails—nothing remarkable, other than the fact that this later would become the "standard gauge" for all American railways.

These minuscule beginnings were years previous to Federal aid in financing. Later the government would turn more than 155,000,000 acres of public land over to railroad builders—the prime incentives for the Illinois Central, the Union Pacific, and the Central Pacific. But the Opelousas and the BBB&C were recipients of none of this largesse. These tiny stirrings—destined to join Judah's dream, and later to emerge as Southern Pacific—far antedated Federal help. The Civil War would completely shut off view of this southern picture until after Central Pacific had joined Union Pacific in tying the northern half of the nation together with bands of steel.

Though Theodore Judah was not on hand during those decades when Southern Pacific was pieced and hammered into the dominating giant of California and the West, he was father to the lusty child in every parental sense. A dynamic little man in ill-fitting clothes, Judah had been hauled to California as chief engineer to the ailing Sacramento Valley Railroad. He was already a man of reputation and accomplishment: he had surveyed the railroad route through the Niagara Gorge and spanned it with railroad trestle. Yet, great as were these accomplishments, they would be minor scene to the visionary dream that changed him into "Crazy Judah."

Only infective fanaticism could have induced four Sacramento merchants, Collis P. Huntington, Leland Stanford, Charles Crocker, and Mark Hopkins, into sharing the wild dream of spanning the High Sierras with a railroad, and pooling their capital to make it possible. The "Big Four" were never less big than when, after the Central Pacific was truly born out of the Sacramento Valley Railroad and was laying track, they eased "Crazy Judah" out of the picture. If Judah had not died of yellow fever contracted while crossing Panama to return to his home in the East, he might later have rejoined his hard-driving associates in resumption of the California dream. But the "Big Four" completed Central Pacific without the help of the man who had started it and who had planned it. Because Theodore Judah fathered Central Pacific, he was also the living, breathing parent to the Southern Pacific—which Central became in mature, full stature.

But through those years of turbulent and fantastic evolvement of Southern Pacific, the name of Theodore Judah was all but forgotten. No towns, no stations, no sidings were named after him. Not until six decades later did Southern Pacific get around to erecting a monument to Judah, in front of its Sacramento station, financed by donations from railroad personnel who had scarcely heard of the man. Tardily, the summit of the Sierras, pierced by SP's highest tunnel, was named Judah Ridge. For the dynamic Judah, this mountain remembrance is probably the most appropriate.

If lobbyists were to move out of Washington, D.C., the national capital would probably lose half its population. Democracy, in America, long ago surrendered itself to a government of pressure groups. Wheels that squeak the loudest are wheels that get the grease. In the subtle art of lobbying for public favor and public funds, the railroads set an early and effective pattern. Pleading help for his Central Pacific, Judah successfully faced Washington. He was quickly joined by the fast-learning and doubly persuasive Collis P. Huntington. And through the years, as Central Pacific metamorphosed into Southern Pacific, Huntington remained in the East as dogged battler and advocate for a rail empire he and Stanford, Crocker and Hopkins were carving out of the West. The success of this Sacramento hardware merchant in persuading Washington Congressmen and New York bankers to financially back the plunges and speculations of himself and his three partners has no parallel in American capitalistic jugglery. As with Judah, the railroad became Huntington's life. He served it faithfully.

First, the new Central Pacific must be extended to San Francisco Bay. Weary travelers from the East must no longer be boated down the Sacramento River to San Francisco. Freight should remain on the cars until seaport was reached. It was Charles Crocker's job to continue laying ties and rails in never-ceasing expansion throughout California. It was Stanford's and Hopkins' task to acquire rights-of-way, rolling stock, and smaller railways that might be absorbed into the ever-expanding dream. Their task too was to collar the California financiers for the local capital to augment everything Huntington could coerce from the East.

All of them were young men. At the railroad's inception Stanford was thirty-six, Crocker thirty-eight, Huntington thirty-nine, and Hopkins, the oldest, was forty-seven. Judah was only thirty-four years of age when he brought the "Big Four" together. As a group they were single-minded in purpose, ruthless, and aggressive.

Charley Crocker, with his mercilessly driven army of imported Chinese laborers, clawed Judah's Central Pacific through the Sierras and out to Utah to join rails with the westward constructed Union Pacific. When snows of up to 30-foot depth annually buried the trackage in California's high mountains, he covered 40 miles of its bitterly won right-of-way with timbered shedding. The trains, bearing immigrants and freight to California, snaked through a strange world of blackness and shadows in miles of mountain sheds and tunnels before emerging into the lush Sacramento Valley, and the river level that carried the payloads on to San Francisco Bay. Judah's dream of a transcontinental railroad became a reality, but financial success to the Big Four seemed as far away as when these young merchants had begged and borrowed the first of the endless funds necessary to push the railroad eastward.

They possessed 690 miles of rails and ties, an adequate number of high-wheeled, funnel-stacked, wood-burning locomotives—hauled around the Horn by ship to California—and an impressive assortment of freight cars

The completion of the Southern Pacific's southern route was cause for celebration in 1879. Donald Duke Collection

and passenger coaches. But they also possessed a debt that would have staggered less reckless mortals. The immense revenues they envisioned had failed to materialize. They had anticipated recouping all losses on the haulage alone from Nevada's booming Comstock. With collapse of the silver mines through water-flooding, this revenue was wiped out. The four men were so discouraged they offered to sell out at ten cents on the dollar. But no one could be persuaded to assume the colossal burden of debt that went with Central Pacific.

Forced to the necessity of holding on, and tapping new sources of revenue, it was "borrow and plunge" to expand the dream from Sacramento to Oakland and San Francisco, and north and south through California's great central valleys. This was the time of feverish railroad building throughout America. Scores of companies were incorporated, and made their grab for Federal and state lands. Local lines, tiny roads with short hauls of less than a hundred miles, a locomotive or two, some cars, and usually some discouraged entrepreneurs, had sprung up everywhere. Stanford and Hopkins, determined to stifle competition before it could raise its ugly head, bought or forced the local lines out of business, grabbed up their trackage and rights-of-way, and brought them under the tattered umbrella of their expanding but precarious empire.

After completion of Central Pacific into California, the young railroad never ceased laying rails. Charley Crocker moved his Chinese labor camps back to the Pacific Coast. By acquisition and by construction, Central Pacific reached San Francisco by way of Stockton, Miles Canyon, and the local lines that made up the pioneer Oakland and Alameda rail-ferry service. To give validity and authority to Crocker's frenzied rail-laying north and south, the Southern Pacific Railroad Company, and the Oregon & California Railroad Company were additionally organized by the four partners. California was slowly filling up with settlers. Oregon already was populous enough to serve a rail line profitably. To hesitate now in expansion would be to lose forever to some equally ambitious competitor.

By 1870 Southern Pacific had pushed its rail lines southward to Modesto, through the great San Joaquin Valley. Four years later they were at Sumner (east Bakersfield). Already a new dream—for a second transcontinental line—was on. Ultimate destination would be Texas, and by linkage and acquirance of the failing BBB&C, and the Opelousas, on to New Orleans and the sea routes. A side bar to the dream would be to push north and east from El Paso to Kansas City and Chicago.

But these goals were still many land miles away. In California, Southern Pacific was bogged down with a problem. Charley Crocker, in getting a railroad out of San Joaquin Valley, and up and through the mountains, faced a challenge in the southern Tehachapi as grave and difficult as the one he had surmounted in the northern Sierras. Crocker drew on the best engineering talent of the day. Sam Montague took over duties as chief engineer, but it was Bill Hood, Montague's assistant, who shouldered the task of clawing the railroad out of San Joaquin Valley, through the Tehachapi Mountains, and out again to the desert plain. The idea of lifting trains nearly three thousand feet, over a distance of but a few miles, was a brutal assignment—but Bill Hood managed it.

With the Chinese construction crews who had scratched through the northern end of the Sierras for CP, Hood put them to work with their picks and earth carts in this dramatic confrontation with the southern end of the same lofty and stubborn mountain range. Five tunnels and a lot of mountain carving were necessary before the roadbed had reached a point high enough to where the real construction could begin. In two huge circles, and thirteen more tunnels in and out of the ridge—the railroad actually crossing under and over itself like a convoluted snake—the Tehachapi problem was solved. The earlier trains of Hood's day would disappear into one of the black holes, to later emerge out of another higher hole to cross over its lower point of entry. When the long trains of a later day, with their huge cab-in-front locomotives, snaked through the Tehachapi loop, the front end could be seen emerging from one tunnel, while the tail of the snake was disappearing into the tunnel below.

Earthquakes and technical necessity, rather than snow, would later force modification of the Tehachapi complex, and the elimination of some of the burrows, but it would ever remain an awesome experience to ride through the Tehachapi Loop and realize what Bill Hood and the Chinamen had accomplished in the name of railroading.

The Tehachapi Loop was a master stroke of railroad engineering. By swerving the tracks in serpentine fashion around gradual curves on a 2.2 percent grade through eighteen tunnels the SP was able to raise the rails 2,734 feet in 28 miles. Southern Pacific Collection

By now it was wholly evident that the growing railroad combine, made up of Central Pacific, Southern Pacific, and California & Oregon, was becoming an ever sharper political and industrial tool of the four ambitious merchants who so energetically managed it. Any attempt to lay a line in parallel, or that might penetrate the sacrosanct ground of California, brought the Big Four down upon them with ruthless and crushing weight.

Senator J. P. Jones from Nevada who, in Congress had openly done battle with Collis Huntington over the immensity of the land grants the Big Four were gaining out of Washington, had the pugnacity not only to challenge the right-of-way monopoly of CP-SP up, down, and through California, but had the temerity to demand that Nevada lay tax to the 7,000,000 acres the railroad now owned in that state. Worse, Jones had built a narrow-gauge railroad from Santa Monica into Los Angeles, which he called the Los Angeles & Independence, and had publicly announced his intention of linking Los Angeles with Salt Lake City, by way of Cajon Pass.

Realizing that whoever controlled Cajon Pass held also natural entry to transcontinental service linking Union Pacific in Utah, the Southern Pacific arrayed itself for battle against Jones and his ambitious little LA&I. At the very time SP was wrestling with its Tehachapi Loop, one hundred miles to the northwest, SP sent a surveying crew into Cajon Pass, to physically grab off this essential gateway to Southern California ahead of its would-be competitor. They arrived in December 1874, only to find that a young civil engineer by the name of James U. Crawford, whom Jones had hired from Texas & Pacific, already had his grading and tunneling crews hard at work in the Cajon. Right-of-way was being blasted out and leveled, trestle footings already were set, Crawford's men had burrowed 300 feet into solid rock on a projected 1,800 foot tunnel. Worse, they had built permanent work camps, and were firmly entrenched in the Cajon.

The Southern Pacific surveyors went pugnaciously to work in the belated struggle for control of Cajon Pass. Unfortunately, both factions were caught in one of the worst blizzards on record. Crawford's men had the advantage, in that they could find shelter in their mountain camp. The Southern Pacific crews were forced to abandon all, and retreat to the more salubrious climate of San Bernardino, down the hill.

All evidence indicated that Jones and his little LA&I had won out against the land-grabbing SP. The city of Los Angeles, whose people had wholeheartedly backed Jones, was jubilant. Such reaction was indicative of the suspicion and hatred already surfacing in California against the ruthless and monopolistic transportation pattern that the Big Four had set upon the Pacific Coast.

Jones might have victoriously completed his dream of linking Southern

California to the East by rail, via Salt Lake City, had not Black Friday—August 27, 1876—wiped him out in the collapse of the Nevada Comstock. He and many another millionaire were victims of the financial debacle which idled the mines and snuffed out the Big Bonanza. When Virginia City was finally destroyed by fire, Jones and his railroad were finished.

Work ceased in Cajon Pass. Freed of this competitive threat and worry, Southern Pacific now frantically pushed rails toward Yuma in a new war—to grab off the southern transcontinental route ahead of the Texas rivals who were deliberately headed westward toward the Pacific Coast. Santa Fe would later scoop Southern Pacific in laying rails through Cajon Pass, and both Union Pacific and Santa Fe would battle SP for California markets through this gateway—but for now, at least, the Big Four had won.

Charley Crocker's rail-layers were a superb team. Southern Pacific after linking hostile Los Angeles to its chain of steel, pushed out to the desert by way of San Gorgonio Pass. And the race was on for Yuma. Tom Scott's Texas & Pacific, snaking its way westward, had already leapfrogged its construction camps a thousand miles ahead—intending to be first to bridge the Colorado, and thereby gain the Pacific prize. The problem facing both railroads was the necessity of crossing Indian reservation lands on the east side of the river. All of this area, a substantial part of Arizona Territory, was under military control. Permission from the Army remained an absolute requisite.

Tom Scott, determined to stop Southern Pacific's aspirations at the very banks of the Colorado, talked the Yuma commander, General Irvin McDowell, into permitting T&P to lay rails across Indian lands. Then McDowell changed his mind. The request was turned over to the Secretary of War James Cameron. Result was to bring both Tom Scott and Collis Huntington to the War Department office in Washington, each of the aspirants pressuring for the all-important decision. The War Department proved as vacillating and indecisive as McDowell had been. First SP was granted the right to lay its rails, then T&P received the nod. In the end, both petitions were revoked. The southern route was stalled by the Army, at Yuma.

The U. S. Cavalry, stationed at Fort Yuma on the east bank of the river, had a double chore—keeping watch on the Indians, on their side of the river, and the railroaders on the opposite shore. But Crocker's men were resolute and enterprising. Loading a boat with liquor and good food, the railroad delegation paid warm and cordial respects to the lonely and weary cavalry garrison at the fort. When the soldiers eagerly accepted their gifts, the railroaders proposed a monumental party. They possessed unlimited supplies of liquor and food. A good feast and whiskey-bust would help lonely men forget their homesickness and the heat and dust of Arizona.

Yuma's party lasted five days—an unforgettable one. When the officers sobered up enough to see clearly, they rubbed their eyes. Crocker's men had thrown a cantilever bridge across the Colorado. The wham of sledges on steel spikes was no dream. Southern Pacific rails were going down. When, a few weeks later, locomotives steamed across the bridge into the first penetration of Indian country, the troops of Fort Yuma were forced by law to stop them. In spite of the bold act, SP was again stalled.

This time Arizona citizenry moved into the act. Their howls of protest over the halting of railroad construction reached Washington. The harassed Secretary of War outdid himself in contradictory edicts. But one fact remained, for all to see—Southern Pacific had spanned the Colorado. Its trains and work crews were at Yuma.

Smugly the SP rested on its gains while congressional voices argued the matter. Meanwhile the indefatigable Collis Huntington got the ear of William Tecumseh Sherman, General of the Army. When Sherman, himself a national hero born out of pugnacity and recklessness, publicly praised the enterprising SP for having bridged the Colorado, and reminded America that a railroad spanning Arizona was "a great civilizer, and will enable the

This beautiful American type locomotive (4-4-0) on the Southern Pacific of Arizona is admired by Indian youths standing by the tender at the Yuma roundhouse, Arizona Territory. Golden West Collection

military authorities to maintain peace and order among the Indians," all opposition collapsed.

Huntington was equally successful in wooing President Rutherford B. Hayes and his cabinet. Pressure was put on the territorial legislatures of Arizona and New Mexico for railroad charters favorable to Southern Pacific. On October 9, 1877, Huntington won an executive order from the President authorizing the operation of trains across the forbidden lands.

Scott was whipped. He abandoned his Pacific hopes in favor of the Big Four. After the Texas & Pacific later came under Southern Pacific's wide umbrella, it was a case of gathering in the southern railroad entrepreneurs, one by one. With acquirance of the old Buffalo Bayou, and the Opelousas, Southern Pacific finally succeeded in linking San Francisco to New Orleans. When the Morgan Steamship Lines were acquired, Southern Pacific possessed rail and sea monopoly all the way to New York. The Big Four had grown considerably bigger during this feverish decade.

With pugnacity and determination Huntington, Stanford, Crocker, and Hopkins gathered in scores of tiny, struggling southern railroads, and lined them across the wide spaces into one straight and direct line. After the stock manipulator, Jay Gould, had acquired the bankrupt Union Pacific, Texas & Pacific, and other vital lines and interests, Huntington battled him through another decade to hold the southern route, to build into Mexico, and to link El Paso with the Union Pacific by way of Kansas City and Chicago. Eventually, through historic struggle and effort, Southern Pacific trains moved northward across America—from El Paso (the Golden State Route)—from San Antonio to St. Louis (the Cotton Belt Route)—and from New Orleans to Washington (the Washington Sunset Route). The once tiny Central Pacific had truly grown up.

Simultaneous with their merciless struggle to gain transcontinental status, the Big Four were looping the Pacific Coast with bands of steel. At first, and so as not to too publicly reveal monopolistic control, they operated under the shelter of half a dozen corporate entities, including Central Pacific, Southern Pacific, and California & Oregon. In 1884 the masquerade ended with a reorganization. By special act of the legislature of Kentucky, all the railroad lines, steamship lines, millions of acres of land, and other holdings were brought under the single banner of Southern Pacific Company.

In choosing Kentucky as its corporate headquarters, the combine of Southern Pacific was endeavoring to remove its operations from under the direct thumb of hostile California legislators, and equally hostile California citizenry. Kentucky offered almost no tax bite. In 1884 the Big Four were as astute and enterprising in gaining corporate shelters for themselves as are

A transcontinental passenger train bound for California pulls into the Yuma station alongside the Colorado River. Donald Duke Collection

today's industrial tycoons in seeking haven in lenient states or foreign countries. Southern Pacific's California monopoly of every avenue of shipping —railroad, ferries, and steamships—and the high freight rates which everlastingly bled the economy—were not expected to make and hold friends. In those last days of the Big Four, their company was no candidate for a popularity contest.

Long before reorganization and renaming, the California & Oregon had pushed north to Portland. Now, as Southern Pacific all the way, this famed portion, known as the Shasta Route, linked the Pacific northwest solidly with California and its lengthy valley and coast runs. In building their monopoly, the Big Four acquired steamboat lines, which gave them control of the Sacramento and San Joaquin river traffic. Jointly with Union Pacific they set up Occidental & Oriental Steamship Company, to compete with Pacific Mail. This, with the already acquired Morgan Lines out of New Orleans and New York, gave Southern Pacific tight grasp on sea freight. Rates were hiked to all that the traffic would bear.

Through ruthless suppression of competition, the big stick of economic supremacy, and the masterful political manipulation of Huntington and Stanford, the Southern Pacific maintained tight and unyielding control of the Pacific west. Not until Santa Fe and Union Pacific lanced California by way of Cajon Pass, was any of this rich meal shared with others. It is significant that during the wholesale bankruptcies of American railroads through various eras of stress, Southern Pacific never once went into receivership.

This was the time of the Goulds, the Drews, the Grant Administration, and the Boss Tweeds. Greed was the creed of every successful business, and Southern Pacific was no exception. Politicians could be bought, courts could be influenced for favor, newspaper publishers, legislators, mayors and city councilmen could be kept pro-railroad by discreetly cutting them into the pie. In California, at least, the general public was helpless before the monopolistic grip of the Big Four. Citizens didn't like it. They were fanatically anti-Southern Pacific. And so were the smaller newspapers and their editors.

A source of irritation equal in malignancy to prohibitive freight rates and political manipulation, was Southern Pacific's vast land holdings—millions of acres of public domain deeded by the state and national governments, which they were free to sell for the funds so endlessly necessary for construction and expansion. Townsites were laid out along the railroad rights-of-way. City lots and ranches were peddled up and down the lush valleys of California and Oregon. Not only did Southern Pacific hold valid mortgages on settlements and farms, but tightly controlled all transportation and freighting of their tenants. Highways were few and inadequate. There were no motor trucks in those days. The railroad was the umbilical cord which supplied and nourished the population structure. Control went to the big and apparently soulless parent.

Politicans at every level ran for office and were elected on anti-Southern Pacific tickets. For decades "the railroad" was the dragon for every office-seeker to flay and fight. Once elected, however, all it took was an annual railroad pass for the public servant and his family, the cajolery of special favors, or the promise of good jobs for friends and supporters, to soften his political stance.

In the haulage and treatment of passengers, Southern Pacific was above fault. In its compulsion to populate California's long and promising valleys, it was double gain to the railroad to induce prospective settlers out of the East. The "Zulu Trains" became a phenomenon of Southern Pacific. At low family rates the passengers moved westward in rail coaches on a train which carried free freight cars for their household furnishings, agricultural equipment, horses and cows. No railroad could do more. And a town lot or trackside farm could be purchased from the railroad for low down payment and extended credit.

It is difficult to estimate the number of settlers brought into California "Zulu" style, or by bargain excursion. Just as the SP-Santa Fe rate war filled up the cities by a railroad tour across America for a few dollars, the immense San Joaquin Valley of California was populated by trainloads of settlers, induced by Southern Pacific to fill up its vacant land. Thousands of them stepped off the train into towns that were merely railside sheds, to face a flat and endless plain. The task was to make it blossom, and to turn vacant grant land into dollars for the sponsor.

The California soil was rich and productive—providing water could be put upon it. The imported farmers, many of them from the East where lands were watered with dependable rainfall, had to learn, in the harshest possible way, the western necessity of building dams and tapping the streams. Only the surprising crops that came from the rich soil could compensate for the misery and distress of getting a start. But the pioneering phase was only one trouble. The railroad that had hauled them to this vast and vacant land, and had promised so much, turned out to be more the relentless taskmaster than the benign partner. In many cases, after the tenants had endlessly sacrificed to improve their acres, they were faced with legal battles to gain clear title to their lands. In many areas of Southern Pacific's promised Edens, there were protests, open revolt, and bloodshed.

Conversely, SP lands were often plagued by tenants who, with only rudimentary knowledge of homestead law, moved in, unbidden and uninvited. When their hopes of "proving up" title to their acres and improvements faced inevitable contest with the railroad land companies, the legal battles and evictions were usually harsh and bitter. The SP recognized no "squatter's rights."

In 1876, on Southern Pacific's land grant of 146 miles between Hollister and Goshen, in the San Joaquin—a finger into the two counties of San Benito and Tulare—six hundred settlers went to war against the railroad. They had petitioned the Federal government to restore to public entry this portion of Southern Pacific land. Their claim was that they had settled the area on the supposition that it was public land; had laid 50 miles of irrigation canals; were farming their supposed homesteads; and had built their houses. After all the labor and improvements were in, and the tenants established, the railroad, which had never laid a mile of track in the area, announced their own title to the land.

At a mass meeting in Hanford, in 1878, the settlers offered to buy the farms they had developed—but from the U. S. Government only—at $2.50 an acre. Southern Pacific was demanding much higher prices, and the settlers stubbornly refused to do business with the railroad. Suits of ejection by SP were as easily won in the courts against these San Joaquin farmers as they had been in other areas of disputed land. With the beginning of eviction, masked men, well armed, began patrolling the acres.

In 1880 the Mussel Slough War erupted, when a United States marshal attempted to place purchasers of SP land on tracts already in possession of these irate farmers. Two railroad land purchasers were killed, and six settlers were wounded. A coroner's jury, locally impaneled, declared that "the responsibility of the shedding of innocent blood rests upon the Southern Pacific Railroad Company." Throughout California there was public outcry against SP. The five settlers convicted for resisting the marshal were publicly acclaimed and later, upon their release from prison, were honored with a community-wide celebration at Hanford.

The hurry to fill up California's vacancy with settlers, and the uncertainty of land titles, were root causes of the bloody explosions such as the Mussel Slough War. In the case of the railroads, their lands had been politically issued along proposed routes. Many times the rail-laying never came within miles of the lands pre-empted, and there were plenty of areas that had never seen a mile of track. Settlers came—many of them without railroad inducement. They broke the fruitful soil, without waiting out the long years for adjudication of title.

Southern Pacific fought the squatters. They fought even their own delinquent tenants. They fought the "little man" as savagely as they had fought everyone and anything that stood in their way. Stanford and Huntington were callous and hard in their attitude toward the humble and ordinary Johns upon whom they must eventually depend for their revenues. But so were their power-blinded executives—land sales managers—down to the station masters and the local politicians who could be intimidated or coerced. The railroad had the beef and muscle. Its staff, from top to bottom, was blinded by it.

When a young novelist by the name of Frank Norris gathered the harsh story of the evicted and oppressed San Joaquin farmers into his novel, *The Octopus,* the anger of the people of California against SP reached its absolute nadir. The book's title stuck in the craw. And, though the novel is seldom read today, the railroad, even though back in public esteem, is still edgy and sensitive about it.

Public revolt against the railroads was not a thing solely germane to SP. It was happening throughout the West. Up until the Federal Interstate Commerce Act of 1887 went into effect, the common man had little redress against business malpractice, freight rate kiting, pooling agreements between railroads, and changes in service-pricing without notice. California's wrath finally erupted when, in 1879, its citizens marched to the polls and voted in a new state constitution with enough teeth supposedly in it to bite Southern Pacific where it would hurt and hinder. It named a board of Railroad Commissioners. They would control the regulation of freight and fare schedules, and land sales. When citizens later awoke to the fact that the commissioners were automatically railroad people, they fought for new and better legislation.

New York firms were discovering that shipments could be dispatched to

San Francisco by way of European ports, four dollars a ton cheaper than the coastwise rates charged by SP's sea-rail monopoly. But time, and the inevitable penetration of competitors such as Santa Fe and Union Pacific, weighted things more in favor of the public. The very people whom SP had imported with such avidity, eventually decided against the railroads, in favor of themselves.

The passing of the Big Four, and removal of management into the hands of men more anxious to change the octopodal public image of the vast corporation, moved the railroad to the bright and appreciative image it enjoys today. The huge and ornate mansions of Stanford, Crocker, and Hopkins, atop San Francisco's Nob Hill, were indicative of their appreciation of the good life the railroad had provided. Huntington, who remained in the East, was less ostentatious about his public glitter.

Of the Big Four, the first to die was Mark Hopkins, in 1887. He had gone to Yuma, Arizona, to inspect the progress of rail-laying along the Sunset Route. On a couch in his ornate private car, pulled into a Yuma siding, he laid himself down to an afternoon nap. He never awakened to return to his San Francisco mansion, then in the process of completion. His foster son, Timothy, henceforth managed the Hopkins fortune left to Mark's fashionable widow.

Death took the compulsive hard-driver Charles Crocker in 1888. He died in style, rather than in the more familiar circles of gandy dancers and bridge monkeys, in the plush Del Monte Hotel he and his associates had built on the beautiful Monterey peninsula. His son, Charles Frederick Crocker, was to capably carry on in the name of his father.

A fast moving Southern Pacific passenger train crosses the Rio Grande River at El Paso, the border between New Mexico and Texas with Mexico just to the south. Donald Duke Collection

In 1884 Leland Stanford had lost his own beloved son and heir in death. And, in the final years, Stanford's interests were more deeply engrossed in establishing a university as memorial to the boy, and in personally remaining in the political limelight, than in managing a railroad. The university he had endowed would be on the site of his model farm at Palo Alto. He was serving his second term as United States Senator from California at the time of his death in 1893. He outlived Crocker by five years.

The last of the Big Four, Collis Potter Huntington, lived until 1900. A tough-minded, lonely and dour old man, operating out of his drab Broad Street office in New York, he went on amassing power and piling up wealth to the end of his days. At the time of his death, the Southern Pacific was operating 8,000 miles of railroad—from Portland, Oregon to Guaymas, Mexico—from San Francisco to Ogden, to New Orleans, to St. Louis—with steamships linking New Orleans to Havana and New York. The little Central Pacific had grown into the widest flung transportation system in America.

Huntington, at his death, owned many other holdings besides those of SP—steamship lines, additional railroads, shipbuilding facilities, real estate of every imaginable kind. Two-thirds of his immense fortune went to his widow, one-third of it to his nephew, Henry E. Huntington. The estate was put back together again when the widow and the nephew married. Eventually the Huntington fortune found beneficial use to the people of California—in the perpetually endowed Huntington Library and Art Gallery in San Marino.

No railroad was ever operated more profitably. Unlike many lines, SP kept solvent throughout its lifetime, and paid its bills. With its expungement from California and Federal politics, and with the passing of the hard-nosed leadership of the Big Four, Southern Pacific's image grew ever brighter through the years. Its locomotives and rolling stock had, from the beginning, been of high quality. Improvement in its trackage and safety equipment became constant, especially after Edward Henry Harriman's entry into the management picture. When its superlative engineer, Bill Hood, built SP's Lucin Cutoff, across the northern portion of Great Salt Lake, the site at Promontory, where in 1869, the Golden Spike had linked East and West, became an abandoned and isolated marker in the sagebrush. A more important historical reminder was that a great railroad had come of age.

California's smoldering hate toward SP slowly turned to admiration and pride when it began to realize historically what this transportation system had accomplished in its behalf. When the Colorado River, supposedly harnessed to the peaceful irrigation canals of Imperial Valley reclamation project, suddenly broke through its ancient channel and re-created the Salton Sea, all efforts of man seemed powerless to stem the rampaging tide. Southern Pacific's first efforts, in face of the disaster, was to frantically relocate its own trackage on higher ground. To travel the old route, laid out in 1871, would have sped coaches and travelers to the bottom of the newly formed inland sea.

But that was only the beginning. The breach had to be closed. The river must be turned back to its normal course, out again to its Gulf of California mouth, instead of the wide below-sea-level basin in California's southern desert. The frightened and frantic settlers of Imperial Valley, and California citizens in general, petitioned Washington for help in the crisis. In this, the government failed the people. Washington's apathy was further compounded by the fact that the river breach had occurred just over the Mexico boundary line. Were it not for the unselfish and heroic efforts of the once-hated Southern Pacific, the battle would have been irretrievably lost, Imperial Valley would have been inundated, and the geography of the Gulf of California area would forever have been changed.

At first Southern Pacific's efforts to close the breach were futile and useless. When the magnitude of the task was fully realized, everything the railroad possessed was thrown into the fantastic struggle. In fifteen days alone, eighty thousand cubic feet of rock fill were dumped by SP into the surging flood.

Never in railroad history had rock been quarried and transported in such volume. Every quarry along the SP, from Nogales in Mexico, to Los Angeles on the Pacific, was drawn upon. Every one of the 50-cubic-yard dumpers, built by SP for the Lucin Cutoff, were shuttled into service for the herculean battle the railroad had assumed. Work trains were handled so efficiently that for days a carload was dumped into the flood every five minutes, day and night. Southern Pacific alone saved Imperial Valley—but at a monetary cost of $4,000,000.

The next novel written about the Southern Pacific was far more complimentary than Norris's *The Octopus* had been. Harold Bell Wright's amazing best-seller, *The Winning of Barbara Worth,* immortalized SP's classic struggle with the Colorado River. And that was only the first of many books to report the story.

Close on the heels of this humanitarian epic came the San Francisco earthquake and fire of 1906. Again Southern Pacific acted solely for the public it served. All along the railroad route—coast line and valley line—relief supplies of food, clothing, and medicines were gathered, and hauled with utmost speed to the stricken area. All movements of supplies and evacuees were done freely and without charge. In one day alone, 1,073 carloads of refugees were transported.

Southern Pacific's main office building, at Fourth and Townsend, had been totally destroyed in the holocaust, but its Bay shed facilities became marshaling places for the homeless. The company's stores of gasoline, oil, and explosives were issued free to San Francisco's authorities. More than 250 desperately injured people were given free care in Southern Pacific's battered San Francisco hospital. The railroad donated $200,000 for relief work, and in thirty-five days, moved 1,600 carloads of relief supplies, and more than 224,000 passengers, without charge. This could scarcely be called the picture of a railway without a soul.

Southern Pacific's streamlined Coast Daylight *was one of the most beautiful trains in the West. Speeding over the Coast Line between Los Angeles and San Francisco, the colorful red and orange* Daylight *was as vivid as California's setting sun.* Donald Duke Collection

From the days of the Sierra-piercing CP—through the era of Silver Palace Cars and Zulu Trains—Southern Pacific favored its passengers, and courted them. It was assumed that a percentage of the American citizens hauled west to California and the Pacific slope would remain on SP's side of the world—to fill up the older cities, build new ones, and populate the vacant lands in between. A busy and prosperous West meant a busy and prosperous railroad. Any form of transportation so directly responsible for populating the Pacific States could not be all bad. In spite of the dogmatic control of the Big Four, the Mussel Slough War, and *The Octopus,* SP had enriched the citizenry, while doing quite well for itself.

With superb equipment, gigantic and modern locomotives, every innovation for safety and comfort, Southern Pacific forged itself into a tool of wonder and efficiency. Its passenger trains, coastwise and transcontinental, were fast, frequent, luxurious. Such innovations as the Pacific Fruit Express, which moved the perishable produce of California and Oregon from harvest fields to eastern markets by highballing trains of refrigerated cars, brought the once disgruntled shippers to join the happy and satisfied passengers in voicing pride and praise for the big railroad with the new and young heart.

The autocrat grew more benevolent and mellow through the years, and the dissent faded to silence. No one today disputes the role Southern Pacific played in building and enriching America's Pacific States. The Chinese, whom Charley Crocker imported by the thousands to carve and lay the roadbeds of CP and SP—and of whom a substantial percentage remained in California—are no longer disgracefully maligned by politicians and labor leaders. Their children and their grandchildren have, as merchants and businessmen, achieved a plateau of success and prosperity unequalled by even their once intolerant fellow Americans. Their grandchildren are highly educated leaders in every field of endeavor. They are loyal, law-abiding Americans, and the pride of California.

Today they share the same kernel of discontent with other Americans whom Southern Pacific has, for a century, gathered to the Far West. What has happened to the big, fast, beautiful passenger trains that once made a travel wonder of the railroad their grandfathers built with such pain and toil?

But this question is another story—to be shared and answered by every railroad in America—including Southern Pacific.

Today's nostalgia stems from the fact that the Iron Horse once hauled people. Zulu Trains and Silver Palace Cars, rather than freight gondolas and boxcars, are the relics of America's remembrance. Where now are SP's *Sunset Limited, City of San Francisco,* and its coastwise *Lark,* and *Daylight?*

12

The Old Santa Fe Trail Becomes a Steel Highway

DONALD DUKE

For nearly three centuries, Santa Fe has been a magic name in the world of travel. Its fame began with the early history of the Southwest, grew with the flow of commerce that followed the old Santa Fe Trail, and has been popularized into a household term by the Santa Fe Railway. During this past century, more than ever before, it has been associated with the thought of places to go and precision passenger and freight transportation.

To readily understand the romance attached to the word Santa Fe, and why it will always linger, it is necessary to return to the time when the Southwest furnished the background for one of the most thrilling chapters in early American history, a wild West, inhabited only by Indians, all unfriendly to the progress of civilization which the railroad fostered.

The city of Santa Fe (Royal City of the Holy Faith) was founded by Don Pedro de Peralta, third governor of New Mexico, sometime between 1606 and 1610. Nearly a century elapsed before Don Diego de Vargas and his followers captured the city and built the Santa Fe Trail quite a distance toward the east. Records show that in 1716, a trip over the trail was undertaken by a group of 1,500 Spanish men, women, and children, traveling eastward en route to the rich upper Mississippi Valley where they expected to found a colony. After the party was massacred by the Indians in what now is eastern Kansas, dust would blow over the trail for nearly a hundred years.

Captain Zebulon M. Pike crossed the trail in many places in 1806, but did not follow it any great distance. Traders began to make the trip from the Missouri River to Santa Fe in 1812. Then came the days when the Santa Fe Trail developed into a well-trod path for large caravans from Independence, Missouri, to Santa Fe. Following the Mexican War, the Santa Fe Trail became a busy trade route between vast undeveloped empires, and opened the way for the colonization of the entire Southwest.

Thus the stage was set for Cyrus K. Holliday, a young Pennsylvania lawyer, who in 1854, had gone West to seek his fortune and add the next exciting chapter to the life and romance of the word Santa Fe. He planned to build a railroad from the Missouri River to Santa Fe, capture the rich commerce of the old trail, and eventually extend the railroad on to the Pacific. Although there were numerous delays and construction was not started until the fall of 1868, Holliday's dream proved to be a natural in every way.

The year before Holliday came to Kansas, the Congress had authorized surveys along five different routes to determine the most feasible location for a Pacific Railroad. The authorizations included surveys near the 32nd parallel, close to the 35th parallel, and one adjoining the 41st and 42nd parallels. The work was under way the year Holliday came to Kansas, and the reports were released to the public in 1855. The route bordering upon the 35th parallel became known as the Western Division of the Atlantic & Pacific Railroad, and, as we know it today, is now occupied by the Santa Fe Railway west of the Rio Grande River at Albuquerque to the Pacific.

It is interesting to recall here that the year 1855 witnessed the completion

Colonel Cyrus K. Holliday, father of the Santa Fe Railway, visualized his railway line with its extremities resting on Chicago, the Southwest, and the Pacific seaboard. Santa Fe Railway Collection

Citizens of Topeka gather around the Topeka station waiting for the daily train from the West in 1880. Fred Harvey got his start in the railroad eating house here. Santa Fe Railway Collection

of a transcontinental railroad generally forgotten. It was the first railroad to run from the waters of the Atlantic to the Pacific. It was less than 45 miles long, and ran across the Isthmus of Panama. The Panama Railroad was used quite extensively in the movement of traffic to and from California prior to the completion of the all-American transcontinental rail route of the Central Pacific–Union Pacific.

Holliday was among the first to conceive a railroad in the West despite the fact there were no railroads at all west of the Missouri and only the bare beginnings of one west of the Mississippi. The year of his arrival in Kansas he organized a Town Company and suggested the name Webster, after Daniel Webster, but the name Topeka prevailed. He was active in the incorporation of the town in 1857. In 1859 Cyrus K. Holliday drew up a charter for the Atchison & Topeka Railway Company. The approval of the Territorial Legislature and the governor were obtained the same year. The new Company was incorporated for $1,500,000 and organized with dreams and a handful of promises.

The new railroad, which in 1863 had been renamed The Atchison, Topeka & Santa Fe Railroad, found it difficult to convince anyone in the East that the great Kansas prairies and those farther west were suitable for anything but snakes and Indians. But the courage of Cyrus K. Holliday was dauntless. Obstacle after obstacle was surmounted until the needed capital was raised. It was October 30, 1868, that saw the real beginning of the railroad—the turning of the first shovelful of earth at Topeka. Holliday took this occasion to forecast that the railroad would be built all the way to Santa Fe and California. Laughter greeted his remarks, and many exclaimed, "The darn old fool!"

While the railroad was in organization, the Federal government passed an Act granting them three million acres of land along its proposed route. The one proviso was the completion of the Santa Fe Route to the Colorado border by December 31, 1872. Holliday and the officers of the new Atchison, Topeka & Santa Fe Railway felt they should make every effort to take advantage of this land grant. The railroad took a course south and west from Topeka. The route south led through some good coal deposits which gave the line a plentiful supply of fuel for the locomotives. By December 1869, the rails had been laid some 21 miles and the rolling stock at the time consisted of a single secondhand steam locomotive, a coach, and twelve flatcars.

Most of the towns west of Emporia did not exist prior to the coming of the Santa Fe Railroad and were laid out by the company. The only inhabitants were roving bands of marauding Indians and huge herds of buffalo. To reach the Kansas-Colorado line by March 3, 1873, as later specified in a revised charter, the Santa Fe built more than 360 miles of road in less than nine months, including the Topeka to Atchison link. The state of Kansas had been crossed and the line to Granada, Colorado, just across the border was opened to traffic May 10, 1873. With the land grant easily secured, all apprehensions concerning the future of the road vanished. Leisurely the Santa Fe Railroad considered extensions toward the Rocky Mountains, the city of Santa Fe, and to Kansas City to the east.

Building the Santa Fe Route across Kansas made possible rapid development of the northern Texas cattle business; and it lead to the rapid extinction of the buffalo herd by the sale of buffalo meat, hides, and bones. While the rich pastures of the Texas Panhandle were capable of sustaining vast herds of cattle just as they had for centuries supported countless herds of buffalo, the raising of cattle in this region never could be attempted on a large scale so long as they had to be driven to Missouri River points overland. The cattlemen welcomed the Santa Fe Route, and the so-called western "cattle towns" such as Ellsworth and Dodge City sprang up at "end of track."

By 1873 the Santa Fe Route had a main line of 469 miles and a branch line, 28 miles long, from Newton to Wichita. But bitter came with the sweet. There were few people along the new rails and little freight was to be carried other than seasonal cattle shipments. The young railroad needed traffic badly to survive and without settlers the road would die a slow death. Agents were appointed in the new towns, the East, and even in Europe, to push the wonders of Kansas and the sale of land. Tons of literature, maps, and articles were printed and released all over the world. All land-seekers were offered land at bargain prices and special rates over the railroad. The colonization of the West drew many from Europe, especially those whose ground was growing stale from overproduction. From Russia came 15,000 thrifty, stout-hearted Mennonite farmers and their families. Farmers from Prussia and southern Germany soon followed.

The land along the Santa Fe was soon bustling with activity. From bare range land ranches grew and beautiful farms developed. The wild prairies were rapidly transformed into rich farmlands by the new settlers who rushed in to obtain the choice land close to transportation. Throughout Kansas, fertile acres began to bloom and yield a harvest of grain and foodstuffs. Santa Fe Railroad agricultural agents brought in experts to show the new settlers how to take the best from their land. Kansas was on its way to wealth and prosperity.

In the first years of the cattle trade in Kansas towns like Ellsworth, Abilene, Dodge, Hays, and Newton sprang up along the rails of the Santa Fe or Kansas Pacific. Here Ellsworth is no longer the Wild West cowboy town. Santa Fe Railway Collection

As early as 1874 the directors of the Santa Fe Route wisely proposed to build far into Colorado. There were good reasons for this plan. At Canon City, and at Trinidad, were large deposits of quality coal which was far superior to any in Kansas. There was much timber to harvest and the ranches of the region would soon ship large and increasing volumes of freight in cattle, sheep, hides, wool, and all over the new line. Colorado was already famed for its precious metals, and the mining industry was bound to develop fast with an improved means of transportation to the east. The road would make it easier to bring in new mining equipment to produce rich ores with the utmost of speed.

Santa Fe's gateway to the interior of Colorado was by way of a branch line running north and west from La Junta, Colorado, on the main line to the city of Pueblo. Here a connection would be made with General William J. Palmer's narrow-gauge Denver & Rio Grande Railway. The main line continued west through Trinidad and would approach the New Mexico border where much of the overland wagon traffic could be transferred to the steam railroad. These extensions proved successful and the Santa Fe Route prospered, while troubled waters lay ahead.

Reference has been made to the Denver & Rio Grande Railway. This rival company in Colorado was projected 850 miles, from Denver, Colorado, to El Paso, Texas, and eventually on to Mexico City. By 1872 the Palmer line had been constructed between Denver and Pueblo, a distance of some 118 miles, with a branch to the Canon City coal mines 37 miles west of Pueblo. It was this branch that brought the Santa Fe Route its eastbound shipments of coal. While the D&RG sought a route to the south, it also looked upon the mines of central and western Colorado as ripe fruit available for the picking. The big problem for the Santa Fe was the transfer from narrow gauge to standard gauge cars, the time delay and the cost to the customer. The Santa Fe built its own line to Canon City, and nearly killed the local traffic of the D&RG. With Leadville and the other mines working around the clock, the Santa Fe decided to extend their tracks through the Grand Canyon of the Arkansas, popularly known as the Royal Gorge, and tap the mining traffic. The Denver & Rio Grande Railway had the same idea and both roads built to the mouth of the gorge. War was declared between the two rival railroads and only after a long legal battle in court was the D&RG able to keep the Santa Fe out of the rich Colorado Rockies. Winning the battle for Royal Gorge was a victory for the baby Colorado road.

"On to Santa Fe" was echoed up and down the Santa Fe grade. In 1877, the Santa Fe surveyed a route between Trinidad, Colorado, and the country south of Raton Mountain via Raton Pass. The Denver & Rio Grande Railway was already in the area and was thought to be ready to appropriate

Canyon Diablo, located between Holbrook and Flagstaff, Arizona Territory, was spanned by this spidery viaduct erected by the Atlantic & Pacific. Santa Fe Railway Collection

the pass for its own line into Texas. A race for Raton Pass resulted and the Santa Fe's grading crews reached the summit of the pass only minutes ahead of the rival Denver & Rio Grande men. The D&RG contested the rights of the Santa Fe in court, but in that era, possession was nine-tenths of the law. The Santa Fe had won a far greater victory than the rights to the Colorado mining districts, for had the Santa Fe lost Raton, it would have ended up a local railroad.

After crossing Raton Pass, work was continued into New Mexico Territory. Las Vegas was reached in July 1879. But as the capital was approached the engineers found the terrain extremely broken country, through which it was found physically impossible to carry a railroad to the frontier town. Santa Fe could not be planted on the main line to vindicate the title, so the engineers doubled back to Lamy and from that point a branch 18 miles in length was built to Santa Fe. By this time the city of Santa Fe was no longer the trade center of the new American West. Besides, the new ultimate destination of the Atchison, Topeka & Santa Fe Railroad was California, the Golden State. Continuing its western progress, the Santa Fe Route reached Albuquerque, New Mexico.

The way to the Pacific began to open with the acquisition of the franchise of the Atlantic & Pacific Railroad, created by Act of Congress during July 1866. The legislators had authorized a line of railway from Springfield, Missouri, to the western boundary of Missouri; then by the most eligible route to the Canadian River in Indian Territory; then to Albuquerque on the Rio Grande River; then along the 35th parallel of latitude to the Colorado River at such points suitable for crossing; then by the most practicable route to the Pacific. This act granted a right-of-way through public land to the extent of one hundred feet on each side of the roadbed.

Prior to 1876, the Atlantic & Pacific Company had built only 293 miles of line in the state of Missouri and during November of that year all rights were conveyed to the St. Louis & San Francisco Railway Company. In 1879, negotiations were begun with the Santa Fe and the completion of the railroad under the charter to the Pacific. Since the Frisco Road had run out of funds, the officers of the company were looking for another railroad to take over a part of its obligations. By an accord known as the "Tripartite Agreement" which was dated January 1, 1880, one half of the capital stock of the Atlantic & Pacific Company was transferred to the Atchison, Topeka & Santa Fe Railway. Construction of the Santa Fe Route westward under the banner of the Atlantic & Pacific Railroad was assured and rails were soon pushed across New Mexico Territory.

The conquest of the Great American Desert was no easy task. There were no towns, very little water, broiling heat during the summer, sandstorms, and tribes of Indians. While not hostile, they nevertheless failed to put out the welcome mat for the iron horse. There were canyons and rivers to be crossed, heavy grading through the mountain territory, and heavy construction which taxed to the utmost the engineering ability of man. As the Santa Fe rails pushed further west, tracks were also being laid south and west toward a connection with the Southern Pacific at Deming, New Mexico. The Southern Pacific was building south and east from California, and the new link provided the nation its second transcontinental line.

Not all the action was in the West. Expansion of the Santa Fe Route to the east began in 1875. Kansas City was emerging as an important cattle and grain market of the Southwest. Due to the fact that cattle and grain were Santa Fe's prime eastbound traffic and Kansas City lay a mere 67 miles east of Topeka, it became essential the Santa Fe have an eastern gateway. Access to Kansas City was obtained October 1, 1875, when the Santa Fe leased the Kansas City, Topeka & Western Railroad, an existing road running between Kansas City and Topeka.

Late in 1881, the officers of the Santa Fe were astonished to discover that Jay Gould and Collis P. Huntington had secretly purchased a controlling interest in the St. Louis & San Francisco Railway and were in a strategic position to prevent the Atlantic & Pacific Railroad from ever reaching California. Huntington wished to preserve his exclusive California empire by delaying or stopping the building of the Atlantic & Pacific beyond Needles on the California border. To do this, the Southern Pacific vigorously began the construction of tracks eastward across the desert from Mojave toward Needles on the Colorado River. The Santa Fe was obliged to accept the

Santa Fe's conquest of the desert was no easy task. Boiling heat, blowing sand and unfriendly Indians were the welcome mat to the West. Golden West Collection

situation and continued to push its tracks across Arizona with the hopes some kind of agreement could be worked out with Huntington. The directors of the Santa Fe Railway failed to realize that Collis P. Huntington was one of the most clever and ruthless men in America. Gould's interest in halting the Atlantic & Pacific Railroad was purely a financial one.

Tracks of the Atlantic & Pacific Railroad reached the Colorado River near Needles on July 12, 1883. As the bridge across the Colorado River neared completion, disagreements developed between Southern Pacific and Santa Fe officials. All transfer of freight and passengers traffic favored the Southern Pacific for they already had a southern transcontinental connection by way of Deming, although it was 232 miles longer than the Atlantic & Pacific

Route. Huntington demanded all shippers transport via Southern Pacific to and from California points and that traffic be routed directly over the Deming line or the Ogden gateway with the Union Pacific. Santa Fe's dream of empire was cut off right in the middle of a desert wasteland.

Various courses of action were open to the Santa Fe Route. One was to endure the existing state of things and retain the property by keeping the road solvent and pocketing the loss, hoping the Southern Pacific would give in. Another possibility was to give up the enterprise, abandon the Atlantic & Pacific Railroad to its creditors and eventual purchase by the Southern Pacific, and renounce the idea of ever reaching a Pacific port. Another possibility was to combat the Southern Pacific on their home ground. This meant building an entirely new line from Needles to San Francisco, a distance of 600 miles. Such a plan, while physically possible, was financially impractical. The remaining course, and the only one available, was to purchase the Southern Pacific line between Needles and Mojave on such terms as to secure the Atlantic & Pacific Railroad a practical and independent right-of-way beyond Mojave to San Francisco or another Pacific port.

Santa Fe officials proved to be just as foxy as old Collis P. Huntington. Several years earlier the Santa Fe had extended its Deming line to the Mexican border. By means of the Sonora Railway the Santa Fe reached Guaymas, Mexico, on the Gulf of California. At this time Mexican law provided only

The name California Limited *is only slightly less old and romantic in railroad legend than the name Santa Fe itself. In this view the* California Limited *streaks across the California desert.* Donald Duke Collection

one American railroad access to Mexico, and the Santa Fe held that card. It was apparent to many that Mexico would soon be the new frontier just like the opening of the American West. The Santa Fe held the trump card and waved the stacked deck in front of Huntington. Would he bite? The Santa Fe was willing to trade the Sonora Railway for access to California. Huntington took a closer look at the situation. He feared any extensions of the Santa Fe in the Southwest or in Mexico could destroy his Southern Pacific in the same territory. Besides Mexico looked like the new promised land. Before long Huntington had taken the bait and surrendered Southern Pacific's stranglehold on California. Huntington thought little harm could be done by the Santa Fe to the Southern Pacific which was already so firmly entrenched everywhere in California.

The goal of Cyrus K. Holliday had been won. One by one the obstacles were overcome, and by 1885 the Santa Fe Route had reached a long desired California seaport at San Diego and had also secured trackage rights into Los Angeles over the Southern Pacific until the Santa Fe could construct its own line. No longer dependent on the good will of its competitors, the Santa Fe expanded its own California trackage through extension, mergers, and the direct purchase of local short line railroads. At the same time an agreement was also negotiated providing direct access to the San Francisco region with trackage rights over the Southern Pacific's Tehachapi Pass and passage over the San Francisco & San Joaquin Valley Railroad, then under construction.

During the 1880s the Santa Fe built or acquired many railroad lines in Texas and gained access to Amarillo, Fort Worth, Dallas, Houston, and Galveston. The next big step was to cross the Missouri and advance eastward to the traffic center of the nation—Chicago. The project engineer drew a straight line between Kansas City and Chicago as the desired route. By the purchase of small railroads and by new construction this ambitious plan became a reality in 1887. With Chicago added to the system, the Santa Fe had and still has today, the only direct transcontinental route over its own rails between Chicago and California.

The problems of the Santa Fe Railway were not solved with the completion of its transcontinental route or with the completion of a network of branch lines. There never has been a time when it could pause for an idle period of indulgent reflections upon things already done. To survive, the Santa Fe has nearly always continued to improve both in property and service; all the more so because of the untold business conditions which it faces.

For nearly three-quarters of a century the only way to travel was by rail, for the speed and economy of the iron horse had swept aside the stagecoach and the steam packet. The Santa Fe Railway responded to its calling with a

Santa Fe's Moorish style passenger terminal in Los Angeles was called "La Grande" station. In this scene a passenger train departs for the East. Golden West Collection

profusion of service ranging from local trains and the typical "drummer's" accommodation to a culmination of transcontinental express trains. By the turn of the century the passenger train became the rolling symbol of a carrier's size and strength. However, the Santa Fe was ill-equipped at this time to become a purveyor of luxury on wheels. The lean years following the completion of the system had shaken the trunk and its many branches. Express train equipment had not been maintained and was obsolete. Locomotives were light and the passenger rolling stock lacked the fancy modern appliances for safety and protection. The famous *California Limited* which first began to run between Chicago and Los Angeles on November 27, 1892, was withdrawn from service during May 1896.

Under the presidency of Edward Payson Ripley, a strong man of quick decision, the Santa Fe Railway received a shot in the arm. The new Ripley administration, though anxious to preserve a strong liquid position, aggressively embarked on a plan to modernize the railroad's transcontinental passenger service.

The new *California Limited* of 1897 was a wonder of the world. An old advertising folder featuring the train stated, "Our train of luxury is limited to seven through cars. It is brilliantly lighted by electricity, generated from the axles of the moving cars. It is evenly heated throughout in cool weather, and ventilated by a new process which renews the air inside several times every hour. It should also be noted that the train has a car for nearly every travel need—sightseeing, sleeping, dining, reading, writing, smoking and social gatherings." The *California Limited* became the backbone of Santa Fe travel until the advent of the stainless steel streamliners.

As locomotives and cars improved, so did the speed of Santa Fe trains. The great reputation for Santa Fe performance came from a series of special trains, run between California points and Chicago in record time. The first of these trains was the *Nellie Bly Special* of 1890 which ran from San Francisco to Chicago in 69 hours. Nellie Bly, a reporter for the New York *World,* was attempting to beat the time of Jules Verne's hero in the book *Around the World in 80 Days.* Nellie completed her around the world adventure in 72 days with the help of the Santa Fe special train. The next fast run took place in 1900 and became known as the *Peacock Special.* An A. R. Peacock ordered a special train to keep an important business engagement in Pittsburgh. The Santa Fe took him from Los Angeles to Chicago in a record time of 57 hours and 56 minutes.

One might say it was Death Valley Scotty who blazed the trail for future Santa Fe fast trains. Scotty, who claimed a fortune from desert gold, chartered a Santa Fe special train in 1905 to whisk him from Los Angeles to Chicago in 46 hours as against the *California Limited*'s running time of 66 hours. Scotty's record remained unchallenged for many years.

The race for the transcontinental trade began with Santa Fe's illustrious *Deluxe.* This train carried only sixty passengers in style and comfort, plus a $25 extra fare charge. The *Deluxe* ran only once a week, but it was plush all the way. The club-baggage car carried current market reports, a tub and shower for ladies and gentlemen, and even a barber. One dined to Fred Harvey cuisine in the Vermillion Room which seated thirty passengers and relaxed with demitasse and brandy in the observation lounge as the miles clicked past. At night passengers slept in real brass beds rather than Pullman berths. Should the *Deluxe* arrive at its destination more than five minutes late, the extra fare charge was refunded. The *Deluxe* was certainly the prime train on Santa Fe rails; however it was sidetracked during World War I.

The *Chief* became the next prestige train to ride Santa Fe rails. Service began November 14, 1926, and it was described as "extra fast, extra fine, extra fare." The *Chief,* far more commodious than the *Deluxe,* sailed daily instead of weekly and cost the passenger less than half the old extra fare. While the speed of most passenger trains advanced, the *Chief* rolled along at a leisurely pace requiring 58 hours to reach California from Chicago. As

California was reached in the most comfortable manner over the Santa Fe Route. Here two young ladies dine in true Fred Harvey style en route. Library of Congress

passenger revenues continued to decline during the depression, it was obvious to Santa Fe officials that something had to be done to stem the tide. The rival Union Pacific, in 1934, came out with a new streamliner on a fast schedule in the Midwest behind a new breed of locomotive called the diesel. This streamliner of articulated cars constructed as a train that could not be broken or added to due to increased patronage was the hit of the decade.

The Union Pacific had on its drawing boards a super streamliner to be called the *City of Los Angeles* that would operate every day from Los Angeles to Chicago on a fast timetable. Such a train would certainly undermine any train that the Santa Fe had in service.

President Strong of the Santa Fe said, way back in 1874, "A railroad to be successful must also be a progressive institution. It cannot stand still if it would. If it fails to advance, it must go backward and lose ground already occupied." As if guided by these words, the Santa Fe secured a two-unit diesel locomotive in 1935 and conducted experimental test runs with the *Chief*. The results were impressive, and in May 1936, the Santa Fe announced a new passenger train of non-articulated type stainless steel cars called the *Super Chief* would run from Los Angeles to Chicago. The luxurious all-Pullman train carried a scheduled time of 39 hours and 45 minutes, requiring an average speed of 57.3 miles per hour including all stops. Chicago and California were in effect rushed together overnight.

The *Super Chief* was without question the most palatial train to ride on rails in the entire United States during the decade. The equipment was modern in design with pleasing colors to match the Indian motif, but the selling point was the service comparable to a grand European hotel. Air conditioning was also the frosting on the cake. No longer was the transcontinental passenger required to suffer the desert heat on a portion of Santa Fe's route. All during the years of passenger service, the *Super Chief* remained the premier all-Pullman train of the American West. Even today under the aegis of Amtrak, the service and comfort aboard the *Super Chief* is excellent.

For the experienced traveler, eating in the dining car as the train rolls across the countryside is one of the prime attractions of rail travel. It wasn't always that way!

In the early days the traveling public carried their own larder in a picnic basket. A passenger would otherwise starve to death before he reached his destination, since the dining car was a long way in the future. Eating houses were set up in connection with large railway stations along the line. As the passenger train pulled into the depot, all the doors were thrown open, and a stampede for the dining room ensued. The crowd gathered around tables to solace themselves with pies, cakes, hard-boiled eggs, ham, and a variety of breads. Before the traveler had two gulps of boiling coffee and a bite of pie, a gong announced the train's departure. Passengers hurried back to their steam cars with mouths full and hands carrying the balance of their meal.

With the increase in speed of through trains and the demand for quicker stops at stations, George M. Pullman equipped a sleeping car with a kitchen to provide berth passengers with snacks. In 1868, Pullman built the *Delmonico,* the nation's first real dining car, but it was some years before every express train carried such a complete dining facility.

A traveling freight agent's queasy stomach deserves the credit for the high standard of dining along the Santa Fe Railway. Fred Harvey, western freight agent for the Chicago, Burlington & Quincy Railroad, developed an ulcer from eating in flyblown depot beaneries. Disgusted with such fare, Harvey asked his own line for permission to open a restaurant of his own in the local station. He was turned down by the division superintendent, who thought Harvey must be daft. Fred Harvey did not give up. He approached the Santa Fe Railway's division superintendent at Topeka and received a hearty response to his novel idea to install a small restaurant serving quality

Ready for its 39¾-hour trip to Chicago, the Super Chief, *flagship of the Santa Fe Railway, is shown leaving Los Angeles Union Passenger Terminal at 8 o'clock.* Santa Fe Railway Collection

cuisine in an unused end of the freight station. This was the first of the many famous Harvey Houses and the forerunner of Harvey hotels, restaurants, and diners operated on the Santa Fe system. Never before or since have American rail travelers found such bounteous table fare, such prodigies of preparation and service, and such deluxe passenger train service as the Santa Fe offered the transcontinental passenger.

The coming of the Atchison, Topeka & Santa Fe Railway opened up the treasure trove of the Southwest—its mines, coal, copper, lead and silver; its vast oil resources; its great acres producing millions of bushels of grain, fields of cotton, and quantities of fresh lumber. It provided for the movement of vegetables, citrus, and manufactured goods. Its luxury transcontinental trains have carried millions of passengers in comfort.

Old Cyrus K. Holliday was decidedly headed in the right direction.

13

Then Came the Predators

WILLIAM R. COX

Every society produces its favorite criminal, makes of him a legend. His acts become a form of protest outside the framework of the system, thus capturing the imagination and rousing the sympathy of the down-trodden masses, the average reader of the media and the romantics who exist in all times.

The west had experienced the holdups of stagecoaches. The myth of the James boys was already burgeoning when the rails came. Enterprising newspaper reporters were ever eager to spread the tales of the adventurers who ingeniously preyed upon the traveler. The country was split by the Civil War. Civilians went armed. It was the time of the wild bunches, the hoot-owl trail, all the paraphernalia of billions of words of fiction and non-fiction.

Contrary to common belief the robbing of trains was not invented by Jesse James and his gang. It was in October of 1866 that the Reno brothers (Frank, John, Simeon, Clinton, and William) held up an Ohio and Mississippi train near Seymour, Indiana. They took $10,000 from the Adams Express car, a nice haul for those days. So far as is known they were innovators. They had many imitators.

It was not until July 21, 1873, that the James gang entered the field. They had been robbing banks and murdering people since 1866 but some-

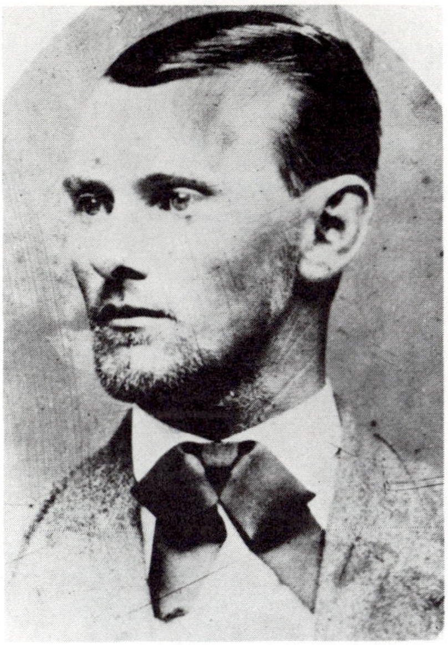

Jesse James. The Kansas State Historical Society

Frank James. The Kansas State Historical Society

how or other the news of the success of the Reno brothers seems not to have reached them.

At this time the gang was comprised of Jesse and Frank James; Cole, Bill, and Bob Younger; Clell Miller, and Bill Chadwick, also known as William Stiles. They were Missourians, out of the Border State troubles, believing or at least romanticizing that they had been ill treated by the world and all who dwelt in it.

As near as can be ascertained they conceived the plan of their first train robbery while headquartering at Council Bluffs, Iowa. Frank James and Cole Younger were dispatched to learn when and where a large gold shipment was due to be toted on the Chicago, Rock Island & Pacific Railroad, famed in song and story as "The Old Rock Island Line." The two messengers returned with what they believed to be confidential information.

Even Robertus Love, author of *The Life and Times of Jesse James,* is a bit vague about who conceived the actual plan but eyewitnesses reported what actually happened. The spot of the operation was a curve in the rails 6 miles west of Adair, Iowa. There the seven outlaws ripped loose a rail, tied a rope around it, replaced it, carried an end of the rope to a thicket where they lay in wait.

In the cab of the locomotive was John Rafferty and a fireman whose name

Jim Younger. National Center for Outlaw-Lawman History

John Younger. National Center for Outlaw-Lawman History

is lost to history. These were honest, skillful workingmen doing their job. It is useless to speculate upon the thoughts of the heroes on the business end of the rope attached to the loose rail. It is certain they were not thinking of the welfare of John Rafferty nor the fireman nor the passengers in the two Pullmans and five coaches of the train.

When the train came around the curve at 8:30 in the evening, they yanked on the rope. Rafferty, slowing down, saw what was happening. He went into reverse. Steel screeched upon steel.

And the engine turned over on its side.

Rafferty was crushed to death. The fireman was rendered unconscious but not fatally injured.

The seven bandits ran toward the train, firing their weapons. The conductor and passengers scarcely realized what was happening. They were scared out of their wits, of course. Several of the passengers were shaken up and bruised by the sudden stop. They were promptly lined up and robbed of their possessions.

Meantime Jesse and friends were busy at the express train. They looked and looked but all they found was $3,000. The take from the passengers amounted to only a couple of hundred dollars. Twelve hours later a gold shipment of $75,000 sped swiftly over the repaired rail to its destination.

Meantime John Rafferty was dead.

The James gang robbed trains thereafter and were rather more successful upon occasion. But their first job was botched. Oddly, for every train successfully looted of a large amount of money it appears that there were dozens which produced scarcely enough gain to pay for the trouble involved. Even as in this day it was safer and more profitable to step into a bank and pick up the loose cash laying around.

Sam Bass, the Hoosier farm boy turned horse race entrepreneur, then unsuccessful gambler, then a Black Hills outlaw, made a strike on his first attempt at train robbery. He was not the leader of the gang but he came in for a goodly portion of the take.

Sam Bass at the beginning of his career. Kerry Ross Boren Collection

It happened on September 18, 1877. The boss was one Joel Collins. There were four other participants. A Union Pacific train stopped at Big Springs, Nebraska, for water. The boys, disguised in red bandanna kerchiefs, moved in with drawn guns.

The Wells Fargo agent was tough. He said there was a time lock on the safe which had been set at San Francisco and would not open until it reached Omaha. Sam attacked the safe with an ax. This produced only sparks.

Then someone espied three little boxes in the car. The agent dissimulated but Sam swung the ax and this time it was open sesame.

The boxes were jampacked with twenty dollar gold pieces, $60,000 in all, consigned to Wells Fargo and the National Bank of Commerce in New York.

The passengers coughed up about $1,300 and petty cash amounting to $458 was found in another, smaller safe in the express car. Not Jesse James, not anyone so far as is known, had ever made a better haul from a train.

It seemed like a fine racket to good-natured Sam, a youngster always well liked, and inspiration for the famous ballad. He went back to Texas and continued his career. Alas, his next best score was $1,280 from a Houston & Texas Central express at Allen and that had to be split four ways with his good ole boy companions. It is estimated that after the first great job several attempts netted the paltry sum of $1,991.

Sam went on to other pursuits but oddly, in the end, it was the railways which did him in. Weary of being attacked, they put the heat on Texas Governor Hubbard, who enlisted the famed Major John B. Jones of the Frontier Battalion. Jones, a fine officer and a decent man, hated to work through a Judas but found it was the only way to get to Sam.

Jim Murphy was the traitor. A trusted friend, he learned through association with the gang that Bass was headed for Round Rock to rob a bank. He wired the office of Major Jones. There was a shootout in ambush, and Sam Bass went down and into history, dying game to add to the legend of the outlaw of the west. Thus, ultimately, the railroads won again.

Still the outlaws eyed the trains. By 1892 innumerable holdups had been accomplished with more or less success, mainly less, as noted. The Daltons were now in operation.

Bob Dalton was the leader, then there were Grat and Emmett and several others coming and going, notably the rebellious Bill Doolin, himself a leader of men and jealous ever of Bob. They were in many ways a feckless crew. They drank too much, they womanized too much, they talked too much. Bob was ambitious; he played the harmonica and his favorite tune was "The Ballad of Jesse James" with its dour refrain, "And the dirty little coward, Who shot Mr. Howard, He laid poor Jesse in his grave." Reared in the border states, young Robert Dalton yearned to emulate the maestro whom he revered.

The Daltons were not very successful. Their escapade at Red Rock, on the Otoe Indian Reservation in June of '92 was typical. The three Daltons, Doolin, Dick Broadwell, Bitter Creek Newcomb, Charlie Pierce and Bill Powers, eight of them, held up a train of the Santa Fe Railroad. When the confusion had died down the bunch had stolen a total estimated by Wells Fargo as $16,000 or $2,000 per head. Since express companies tried to hold down the extent of their losses from the public, a conservative estimate of the

From left to right: Dick Broadwell, Grat Dalton, Bob Dalton and Tim Evans, all line up for the undertaker. The Kansas State Historical Society

sum might go as high as $4,000—which would come to $500 apiece for the hard-working thieves.

Coincidentally it was at another Adair—Adair, Oklahoma—that the Daltons perpetrated their final train robbery. This was in July 1892, a month after the Red Rock caper. The line was the Missouri, Kansas & Texas, known as "The Katy Line." The spot originally chosen for the deed was Pryor, Oklahoma, but a wandering farmer walked into the campground of the gang and they feared he might get word to the authorities that they were in the neighborhood. Marshal Chris Madsen was closing in upon them at this time and the boys were a bit nervous. Under cover of night they headed down the Neosho River to Adair, a town of a couple of thousand inhabitants. The same eight men made up the gang.

Passenger Train Number Two pulled in at exactly 9:42 P.M. The outlaws took over. They captured the station agent, neutralized the engineer, fireman and conductor. But the express messenger, George P. Williams, locked himself in the car and refused to open up.

Somehow or other four men escaped from the passenger cars. They ran to a coal shed beside the tracks. The outlaws thought they were frightened escapees and ignored them. The men were officers, Federal Marshal Sid Johnson, Captain J. J. Kinney of the MK&T's special force and Captain Charles Le Flore, head of the Cherokee National Police. The fourth man was a railway guard named Ward.

Meantime several deputy officers appeared on the back platform of the last car and waved weapons, firing into ozone. It later developed that this crew had been wassailing among themselves to such an extent that their wits were not about them. Their Dutch courage soon evaporated under the fire of the Dalton outfit.

Not so the lawmen in the shed. They opened direct fire. The startled Daltons flung themselves down and engaged in battle. It was a short, hot fight and the Dalton luck was good. Johnson was seriously injured. Kinney and Ward were hit. Le Flore was rendered hors de combat by a bullet through the arm.

But as so often happens, the worst casualties were suffered by innocent bystanders. Adair had but two physicians, Drs. Youngblood and Goff. They were seated in a nearby drug store together when the shooting began. Before they could seek shelter both were victims of wild shots. Goff died a few days later, Youngblood recovered after many weeks.

Bob was still threatening to blow up the express car. Williams was still holding out. The always impatient Grat Dalton began firing into the car. The others followed suit. A volley barely missed the head of the messenger. He decided that discretion was the better part of valor. He unlocked the door.

The safe looted, the outlaws mounted and rode off. When the money was counted it again came to a measly sum, probably no more than $800 or $900 apiece. Even the far from bright Daltons realized that the business of preying on trains was not worth the risk.

It is not recorded whether or not they were aware that they had snuffed out the life of the one useful citizen in the drug store and incapacitated the other, leaving the town of Adair without medical skills and harming thereby the sick and injured among the populace.

Not long thereafter, in October 1892, Bob Dalton attempted to "See Jesse and raise him one," by robbing two banks at the same time in Coffeyville, Kansas, thereby precipitating a blood bath unequalled in the history of western outlawry. More people died there than in the Northfield Raid of the James boys and their gang—but Bob, Grat, Bill Powers, and Dick Broadwell had to die to prove the point. Truly, the point is that the Daltons were an inept bunch of bumblers.

A far more efficient gang later strode the west, emanating from the Hole in the Wall, led by Butch Cassidy and the Sundance Kid. A rollicking, beautifully made motion picture stayed fairly close to the truth about this bunch and made a fortune for the producers. However, the limitations of film dictated that they hit the highlights, romanticize several of the characters and take certain licenses. Although Butch and The Kid seem to have been likable rogues as depicted by Paul Newman and Robert Redford, there were levels of their characters and performances left untold on the screen.

The same is true of Etta Place. We do have a photograph of Etta with

Sundance taken in New York on one of their imaginative sprees and she is handsome. But a lady of noble character she probably was not. She was a gunman's girl—in a later day she would have been deemed a "moll." The movie had the courage to hint that she shared her favors with both Butch and Sundance, which was a step in the right direction.

Etta had company, including Laura Bullion alias Della Rose. This lady was a known prostitute. She became the girl friend of the Tall Texan, Ben Kilpatrick. Then there was Annie Rogers, who came out of Fanny Porter's

A formal portrait of the Wild Bunch. From right to left: Harry Longbaugh (the Sundance Kid), Bill Carver, Ben Kilpatrick (the Tall Texan), Harvey Logan (Kid Curry), and Robert Leroy Parker (Butch Cassidy). Kerry Ross Boren Collection

brothel in Fort Worth. Annie took up with Kid Curry, alias of Harvey Logan, and here is where the inevitable violence enters the story. Cassidy and the Sundance Kid may have been happy, roistering bandits but Kid Curry was "The Mad Dog of the Wild Bunch." The Kid was a snarling bully, a killer.

Altogether the Wild Bunch and their associate gangs were, like the Daltons and unlike the curiously moralistic (or asexual perhaps?) James brothers, a dissipated crew of hard-riding whoremongers, brave enough and tough enough but with only a rudimentary knowledge of the knack of survival. Unless we credit the story that Butch Cassidy was not killed in Bolivia but returned to the United States in the '30s, all came to a violent end, in or out of a penitentiary.

They rustled cattle and robbed banks but their chief claim to infamy was the holdups of trains, mainly of Union Pacific trains. The Hole in the Wall was in central Wyoming. It permitted egress to the north and east but had a narrow adit on the south. It was not until the late '90s that "Robert" or "George Leroy" Parker, the Butch Cassidy now so well known, took over the gangs and organized them. With the Sundance Kid, Harry Longbaugh, and Kid Curry and some others he put together what was known both facetiously among themselves and seriously to the ever pursuing Pinkerton Detective Agency as "The Train Robbers Syndicate."

What with notes left in hollow trees and rock crannies, speedy messengers a-horseback, telegrams and go-betweens among secret sympathizers, the Bunch seemed always to know who was where and what was about to happen. There were a few gun battles, mainly due to betrayals, otherwise they rode high, wide and handsome throughout the west from Canada to Mexico—and generally to Fanny Porter's house in Fort Worth.

A typical example of their method of operation occurred on June 2, 1899, at the peak of their success in robbing trains. It was the UP again, at Wilcox Station. The engineer obeyed the danger signal of a red lantern and slowed down, stopped. Butch and friends ordered him to cut the express car and the baggage car loose from the rest of the train and pull over a bridge a couple of miles ahead.

They then dynamited the bridge to foil pursuit by the second section of the train. It was here they first encountered Woodcock, the stubborn express agent. They handled him without hurting him despite Kid Curry's threats. They blew up the car and scattered bank notes around the countryside. They harvested the notes to the tune of $60,000 and vamoosed.

The town of Baggs saw them next. They shot up the place just for fun, then spent the loot. People in the small, outlying towns could grin at their high spirits—and take their money.

There was an aftermath to Woodcock. A posse got on the trail of the

Bunch. There was a skirmish and young Sheriff Joseph Hazen was shot to death. Kid Curry claimed the kill. Since Butch and the Sundance Kid were known to deplore murder it is quite possible that Curry's claim is valid. The catch here is: Why did such nice young men as Cassidy and Longbaugh consort with Curry? Long Nose George Curry from whom Kid took his nom de plume? Harry Tracy of the long chase and tragic end? Could it be that, like all gang lords even until now, they welcomed hatchet men?

It was August 29, 1900, when the Wild Bunch surfaced with another successful train robbery. Again it was the Union Pacific—and again, amazingly, the express messenger was Woodcock. Again the procedure at Wilcox was repeated—this time they nearly blew Woodcock apart. But this time the word went out, "get the Wild Bunch." Rewards of $1,000 per man and up were proffered. Railroad police, the Pinkertons, every local sheriff and town marshal were alerted. There was an actual photograph of several of the Bunch, stupidly posed for, eagerly grabbed by the Pinkertons. The net was being woven. The time of the wild riders was coming to an end. Frank H. Spearman, a railroad man, was actually writing fiction about the Bunch—it became a classic under the title *Whispering Smith.* The media was expanding, newspaper reporters and magazine men were everywhere, nosing about, asking questions, sending in fanciful stories, sometimes managing to get at some part of the truth.

Butch and Longbaugh evidently wanted to quit. They had somehow saved some of the money they had stolen. They had been to New York where the photo of Etta and Sundance was taken, they had realized there was another world outside the mountains and ravines—and rails—of the West. The frontier was shrinking, the old laws were being supplanted by strict supervision of the population. As property became more valuable, property was better protected.

Still Kid Curry urged one more job. The others capitulated. The scene was Malta, Montana, and for a change the road was the Great Northern.

The Bunch knew a good thing when they had it. They repeated their safe and sane m.o. They grabbed $40,000 in unsigned bank notes. They rode off to Fanny's place, Kid Curry, Laura, Butch, Sundance and Etta, Texas being the farthest piece of the west from Montana.

They forged signatures on the notes. A bank clerk caught the deception.

Etta, Cassidy, and Longbaugh took off. They fled the United States for Bolivia. From there on all is confusing, true story against myth building the legend as it always must. The greatest gang of train robbers were finished, an era had ended.

There were, however, footnotes to the story of the train robbers. Black Jack Ketchum operated in New Mexico about the same time as the Wild Bunch was working the northern states. In 1899 his gang hit a train at Twin

Mountains and his brother Sam was shot by conductor Frank Harrington. Before his demise Sam boasted of being brother to Black Jack—whose real name seems to have been Tom Ketchum—or "Ketchem."

They caught Tom, tried him and convicted him of murder. They built a scaffold. Ketchum was a tall, heavy, handsome man with a thick mustache. They played him out, at his request, to soft fiddle music. They dropped him.

Someone had bungled. The rope tightened with a jerk. Ketchum's head separated from his body. There is a gruesome photograph of the happening in existence, not recommended for those with weak stomachs.

On the other hand there was the comedy of the "Jennings Gang." For utter futility they took the cake.

There were three Jennings boys, sons of a respectable judge dwelling in Enid, Oklahoma. One of them seemed to have brains, at least he was able to hang out a shingle and practice at law. Unfortunately he got into an argument with Temple Houston, grandson of Samuel, and foolishly threatened to gun down the flamboyant legal light. Temple killed him in self-defense.

The other pair toiled not, neither did they spin but they drank a lot and hung around with the good ole boys including one Little Dick West, a scroungy offcast of the Wild Bunch. When the judge threw them out they determined to hit the owlhoot trail and emulate the great train robbers. For this they were hardly prepared.

Their first attempt was at Edmond, Oklahoma. They were run off by a sixty-five-year-old conductor who waved a red lantern at them. It seems they were afraid of things that go bump in the night.

Around the first of the following month they tried the MK&T south of Muskogee at Bond Switch. This time they piled ties on the track to stop the train.

The engineer saw the ties, increased his speed and ran through the obstruction, scattering kindling wood in all directions.

The gang sulked. They added two clodhopper farm boys. They decided night was not their time and on the first of October they approached a road gang working the rails of the Rock Island Railroad eight miles north of Chickasha and forced them at gunpoint to flag down the passenger train.

They lined up the passengers, wearing the obligatory bandanna handkerchief masks. They collected $300 and the watch of conductor Dacy.

Then they went for the express car. The messenger informed them that the safes were locked, could not be opened until they reached Fort Worth, showed them all the keys he had. He was probably telling the truth.

At any rate, news stories of the Wild Bunch had told the world that all good train robbers must carry dynamite for emergencies such as this. They piled the stuff atop two safes, a little one and a big one. They lit the fuses and ducked. The explosion blew out the side of the car and tumbled the safes to ground.

Safes were made of sturdy stuff in that day—they did not burst open. Worse, the explosion blew off the bandanna mask of Al Jennings. Little Dick was already well known by his picture on dodgers hung in public places. Now Dacy recognized Al.

The gang took off with the $300 and Dacy's watch. The train went on and news of the holdup and identification of Little Dick and Al Jennings given Marshal Bud Ledbetter, one of the most efficient of the many Oklahoma law officers.

Ledbetter did not bother to form a posse. He waited until an informer assured him that the trio—the farm boys having vanished with their ill-gotten gains—were traveling south from Muskogee in a wagon. He rode down to Rock Creek and felled a tree across the trail.

When the wagon stopped, Ledbetter arrested them. They meekly surrendered. He made them drive back to Muskogee. He wanted to collect a bet he had made, twenty dollars to ten that he'd bring them in single-handed without a fuss. He knew his quarry.

Frank and Al both served five years in the penitentiary. Frank came out and settled down. Al came out, got his citizenship restored in 1907, sold a terrific pack of lies to *The Saturday Evening Post,* became nationally famous and ran for Governor of Oklahoma.

He was overwhelmingly defeated. As Burton Rascoe remarked, "Oklahomans have commonly preferred, in the matter of governors, bandits who have *not* reformed."

But then the late critic, Mr. R., was known as "Irascible Rascoe."

These, then, were the fabled train robbers. There were others. They did not have the charisma of the James Boys, Sam Bass, the Wild Bunch, they left faint footprints in the sands of time. They were a nuisance to the railroads, they caused loss of life, loss of property. They were criminals. They were bred in violent days on a violent frontier. They found ready historians beginning with Ned Buntline and continuing to the days of yellow journalism when the New York *World* had not yet found its proper niche in newspaper history, when *Police Gazette* and the dime novel and young Willie Hearst were catching the imagination of a public rapidly learning to engorge sensationalism in the daily and weekly and monthly print.

The true romance was in the singing rails, the mournful hoot of a whistle at night, the conquest of time and space which so swiftly changed the theme of empire westward. It is sad that the airplane managed to accomplish what ten thousand robbers could never have managed—to destroy the passenger train.

14

Railroad Tragedies in the Old West

ELMER KELTON

It was August 7, 1904, and a couple from Pueblo, Colorado, were heading home in a buggy after a Sunday outing 14 miles up the railroad track to Pinon. Darkness had caught them only halfway to their destination. Thunder rumbled and lightning flashed to the west, a lingering reminder of showers which had fallen since late in the afternoon. Heavy clouds made the night very dark, and Walter Hart trusted the horse to pick its way along the county-maintained wagon road.

The horse stopped, and no urging could make it move forward. Climbing down, Hart walked around in front of the buggy and found to his astonishment that a normally dry arroyo known locally as Hogan's Gulch was running full, and the old wooden bridge which spanned it on the county road had been swept away.

Hart knew it hadn't rained that much here; there must have been a cloudburst farther up toward the mountains. He also knew he and his wife wouldn't get home tonight. He turned the horse around and started back.

From the north, on the Denver & Rio Grande railroad tracks that paralleled the county road, the Harts saw the lights of Train No. 11, heading south from Denver for Pueblo and points east. Wishing they were on the train so they could get home, the Harts watched the train pass, and they turned their heads to keep watching as it moved on south, toward the railroad bridge which spanned the gulch now bankful of rushing water.

The scene in this unidentified photograph was repeated countless times in the early West as crowds of the curious flocked to see results of derailments, collisions, and other tragedies of the rails. Southwest Collection, Texas Tech University

Suddenly they heard a crash and the splintering of wood. The acetylene headlight of the engine turned upward a moment, reaching for the low-lying stormclouds. Then there were more crashing sounds. The train's lights blinked out. Finally, except for the rolling water there was total silence, and total darkness.

The train had disappeared.

The Harts had been the only eyewitnesses—except for the surviving victims—to the most disastrous train wreck in the history of the West. They had been within a hundred yards when the weight of No. 11's engine collapsed the flood-weakened Bridge 110-B, plunging Engine 1009, its tender, a baggage car, smoker, and chair car into the angry waters of Hogan's Gulch.

At least ninety-six men, women, and children died in a matter of moments.

Railroading began on a local or regional basis in scattered parts of the West and Southwest before the Civil War, but it did not start its major expansions until late in the 1860s. By then, railroad pioneers in the East had learned much about disaster on the rails and, perhaps, some lessons in avoiding them—provided such avoidance was not expensive.

Starting with the derailment of a Camden & Amboy train in New Jersey in 1833, the list of railroad accidents in the East grew more and more frightful with the passing years, capped perhaps in 1867 at Angola, New York, and in 1876 at Ashtabula, Ohio. At Angola, two rear cars of the New York Express ran off of a truss bridge and fell 40 feet into the water. Wood-burning stoves set the wreckage afire, and fifty people died. At Ashtabula, the collapse of an untrustworthy Howe truss bridge beneath the Pacific Express plunged a locomotive and ten cars 150 feet to a frozen creek below. Eighty-three people died instantly or were burned to death in the fire which swept the splintered cars.

In 1887 a wooden trestle burned out near Chatsworth, Ohio, and a fifteen-car excursion train bound for Niagara Falls plowed off of it, piling up in a mass of wreckage and immediately catching fire from its kerosene lamps. Eighty-two passengers died.

Although the early West had its train wrecks, some genuinely spectacular, it never was plagued to the degree that the Eastern part of the country was. Wide-open spaces were less conducive to head-on and rear-end collisions. Congestion was less, and schedules were not so crowded. Equipment had been improved. Construction was more competent than on some of the early Eastern roads.

But perfection was never attained.

The Golden Spike joining the rails of the Union Pacific and the Central Pacific was put in place with much ceremony May 10, 1869. Six months later, on November 15, the Far West had its first major train tragedy, a head-on collision between two Western Pacific passenger trains near San Francisco.

A report that day in the San Francisco *Chronicle* stated that the regular morning train for Stockton was trying to make up time and collided with a six-car passenger train which had left Haywood, bound for Alameda. Both trains were moving at full speed.

Said the *Chronicle:* "The crash was terrific. As the two trains met, wood and iron shattered like fragile splinters. Cars were heaped in one mass of wreck and ruin together. Three cars of the Haywood train and four of the Western Pacific were totally ruined in the awful crash. The carnage was horrible! Twelve corpses were counted on the spot, and how many more the ruins may contain is left to terrible surmise, as the cars were known to be full."

The engines were smashed to pieces. The engineer of the Alameda train jumped just before impact and saved his life, but his fireman and the engineer and fireman in the other cab died instantly.

A passenger by the name of S. M. B. Haley gave this statement:

"The smoking car, in front of ours, was driven directly through the one I was seated in, its side running parallel with our right. We were all forced back to the rear end of the car with the speed of lightning. Two men on the righthand side, one on the lefthand and three before me were killed outright. In the rear of the car we were packed together in a confused mass of wounded, dead, seats, wood, iron and about everything of which a car is composed."

The *Chronicle* told of two Chinese taken from the wreck, both badly mangled. "Both bore their pains with the stoicism of North American Indians and refused the assistance tendered them by the whites and were taken in charge by their countrymen."

One experienced railroader who happened to be sitting in the smoking car had the presence of mind to lower his head and raise his feet in the moment of impact. Wreckage slid over and under him but left him almost untouched.

When the dust settled and the official death count was placed at sixteen, the newspaper reported that a coroner's jury pinned the guilt on a switch tender. It appeared the railroad had given him a timetable and written instructions but had not adequately investigated his competence in handling them. He could neither read nor write.

Old West train robbers sometimes blocked the rails to stop a train, but few were so coldblooded as to wreck a train purposely and be responsible for the carnage that would have resulted.

Montana newspapers in 1892 printed a reminiscence from an unidentified railroad telegrapher which may or may not be true. The story did not specify his name nor the date on which the incident was supposed to have happened. He said he was stationed at the small hamlet of Medicine Hat on the Northern Pacific. One stormy night he was held at gunpoint and bound by outlaws.

One of these outlaws, evidently a former railroad telegrapher himself because of his knowledge of the routine, sat down at the key and began tapping out messages, trying to determine the location of two trains due from opposite directions; both had been thrown off schedule by the storm. When he had done this, he began sending false messages, arranging for a head-on collision of the trains at a point above the station.

The intention of the outlaws was to rob the wreckage.

But before the deed could be accomplished, lightning struck the telegraph wires, killed the bogus telegrapher and set the building afire. The other outlaws fled as townspeople came running. The rightful telegrapher freed himself from his bonds and ran up the track with a lantern to try to stop one of the trains.

In the blackness of the storm, the engineer failed to see him and passed him by. But the sight of the flaming railroad station made him bring the train to a stop, and a collision was averted.

This is the kind of dramatic story which prompted the late, great folklorist J. Frank Dobie to say that if it didn't happen just this way, it *should* have.

On April 26, 1886, shortly after the collapse of a bitter railroad strike, a Missouri Pacific freight was pulling into Wyandotte, later Kansas City, Kansas, when the engine and several cars suddenly left the track and rolled down an embankment, some of them landing in the river. Killed on the spot were a fireman and brakeman. The engineer died later of injuries. Only one crew member—a brakeman on the rear of the train—escaped uninjured.

Investigation showed that the tracks had been sabotaged and the train intentionally wrecked.

A noted railroad detective of the nineteenth century, Thomas Furlong, was called in on the case. He came quickly to a theory that the wreck was an act of revenge. He suspected that the Knights of Labor, very strong in that time, was somehow implicated, at least on a local level.

In his memoirs written some years later, Furlong revealed how he went about unraveling the crime. A lucky break gave him an opening, and he drove in the wedge that broke the case by some slick undercover work and more than a little play-acting.

After the so-called Wyandotte case, train crews working in the region became wary and watchful. Near Tampoo, north of the first incident, a train crew came upon several men in the act of sabotage. Stopping the train and giving chase, they managed to catch one man. He turned out to be a former switchman and a local officer of the Knights.

A Furlong operative named George Fowle studied up on the secret rites of the Knights, including passwords and handshake, which had been determined in other investigations. Posing as a representative of the national Knights headquarters, there to find out the true state of affairs, he obtained the release of the arrested suspect and spirited him away to St. Louis. There he was met by Furlong and a couple of other operatives, posing as officials in the national organization. The suspect spilled the full details of the incident to them on the assumption that they were on his side and that the full national organization was going to defend him. Having in hand the names of all accomplices in the wrecking, the railroad detectives made a complete roundup. Several offered full confessions in the hope of leniency.

One surprising piece of information was that the wrecking of the freight was an accident. The real target had been a passenger train. Had that plan succeeded, the loss of life would probably have been far heavier.

Furlong did not succeed in obtaining convictions, even though armed with signed confessions. The influence of the Knights was strong, and public bitterness against the railroads for their many wrongs and general arrogance was high. Two attempts at trial ended in hung juries. But there were no more train-wrecking incidents on that line.

A freakish accident 60 miles from Great Falls, Montana, April 7, 1898, was said to be the worst in that state during the frontier period.

Westbound freight No. 24 was pulling up to the Dry Forks bridge with five empties and sixteen loaded cars, one carrying a cargo of dynamite. For some reason the dynamite exploded, wrecking the bridge and splintering ten of the cars, blowing telegraph poles out of the ground and cutting off communications. The wreck then caught fire and burned. Dead were three crewmen—the engineer, fireman, and head brakeman.

Most of the spectacular train wrecks, being unexpected, had few eyewitnesses. An exception, because it *was* expected, drew a crowd estimated as high as 30,000 to an open stretch of country near a short-lived railroad stop appropriately known as Crush, Texas, September 15, 1896.

The occasion was a grand publicity stunt dreamed up for the Missouri, Kansas & Texas Railroad, the MK&T, better known then and now as the Katy. William George Crush, general passenger agent, had read about a staged train wreck for similar purposes near Cleveland, Ohio. Here, he thought, was a splendid opportunity not only for nationwide publicity but to sell excursion tickets by the thousands.

He had no way of knowing that his brilliant show, which drew spectators from all over Texas and many other states as well, would turn into a disaster that almost wrecked his personal career and entrapped the Katy in damage litigation that would stretch on for years.

For the location he chose a natural amphitheater between three hills on the Katy tracks between Waco and Hillsboro. A temporary station set up there was named in his honor. It was a big political year, being the time of William Jennings Bryan's first campaign for the presidency, and Crush invited any and all candidates to come and address the crowds. Many did, all day long.

Motion pictures were in their infancy, the peep-show period. Thomas Edison sent a cameraman all the way from New York, shipping with him a bulky Kinetescope camera to record the event in motion pictures. He was a forerunner of the later newsreel photographers.

Chosen for sacrifice were two Baldwin engines, still in good working condition but light in weight and becoming outmoded for the heavy work the times demanded. They were shined and painted to look their best, the

The two locomotives before the collision and at the moment of impact. Both these photos are credited to the photographer Deane of Waco, who lost an eye as a result of flying debris.

cabs a brilliant green and the tenders a shining red. The high stacks were red, the bells gaily ribboned. Six cars were placed behind each engine, the cars brightly painted and covered over with ads, not only for the railroad but for the annual state fair and other things.

The response was staggering, far beyond Crush's dreams. By noon on the day of the big wreck, an estimated 30,000 people jammed the area between the hills. Mounted on a prancing charger, Crush rode through the crowd, helping move people back beyond what was considered to be the danger zone. At five o'clock in the afternoon the two trains puffed up toward each other in a final salute, and to have their pictures made. That done, one train backed up the hill on the south, the other up the hill on the north. Smoke poured from their funnels in a great black streak. At ten minutes after five, Crush raised his hat. The trains began moving down their respective hills, gaining speed, the black smoke trailing.

The crews set the throttles and jumped off while they could. Now it was in the hands of the gods. Faster and faster moved the engines. Faster and faster beat the pulses of 30,000 hushed spectators, come to see the greatest show of their lifetime.

Experts had assured Crush there was no danger to the crowd; all the precautions known to mechanical skill had been taken to assure that the boilers would not explode. It was virtually impossible that this could happen.

But happen it did. With a tremendous roar, both boilers ruptured on impact. While the cars rushed together and telescoped into a mass of splinters and iron, the engines blew apart. The air was full of whistling, screaming missiles, some as small as a postage stamp, some as large as a driving wheel.

In the awed words of the Dallas *News* the following day, lethal pieces of iron and steel were "falling indiscriminately on the just and the unjust, the rich and the poor, the great and the small."

On the special stand built for the photographers, the Edison man quit cranking his machine and huddled behind it in terror while debris rained down around him. A Waco photographer on the stand beside him was struck in the eye by a bolt two-and-a-half inches long. He lingered on the point of death for days, then recovered, minus the eye.

Another Waco man, Ernest Darnell, was killed by a falling chain which crushed his skull. Some 375 yards from the point of impact, a woman was killed by a flying timber. Other people were injured by the rain of debris, or trampled in the sudden wild stampede.

In the wave of recriminations that followed the backfiring publicity stunt, the board of directors dismissed Crush. But the line's president later relented and put him back on the payroll. The Katy also had many good lawyers on the payroll, and it needed them.

When the dust and smoke had died down and the wounded and dying were removed, intrepid souvenir-hunters fell upon the wreckage like a plague of locusts and carried off just about everything that was not too heavy to lift.

Later, tearing into the remains of Engine 1001, a wrecking crew found a railroad watch which had purposely been left inside to mark the moment of impact. It was still running, about the only thing which escaped the wreck in one piece.

In June 1878 the *Ford County Globe* in Dodge City, Kansas, reported a Colorado wreck eerily like the one which would go down in history twenty-six years later as the worst in the West. The ingredients were all there, but the train was a freight and carried only a small crew, plus one known tramp.

The first newspaper report said the wreck occurred at a washed-out Kansas Pacific bridge on Kiowa Creek east of Denver in the middle of a stormy night. The creek, usually dry, was running full from bank to bank when the engine went off into it. The entire train—nineteen empty freight cars—followed after it. No one survived. The fireman's body was recovered 2½ miles downstream.

The freight cars were washed along the flooded creek and smashed. The engine's great mass of iron sank so far into the mud that another newspaper article the following September reported the search still on. Some believed the engine had blown up, and this was why it could not be found. Said the *Globe:*

"Another and more probable theory is that the ponderous machine sank deeper and deeper into the quicksands and has gone the Lord only knows where, but most likely straight down towards China. A large force of men are still working away with a steam power sand pump, and the trains still run around the break on a track that runs down the bank over the dry riverbed and up the opposite bank on a grade which for audacity of enterprise compares with anything in the mountains."

Colorado's spectacular 1904 disaster happened a mile north of a station ironically named Eden. Eden had a post office then, though that was later closed in 1914, and about twenty people lived in the quiet, tiny village which exploded into national fame in banner headlines across the nation the following day. It sat about 110 miles south of Denver and a little more than 6 north of Pueblo's city limits on the main line of the Denver & Rio Grande.

Train 11 was full of passengers that Sunday evening, a large number of them residents of Pueblo going home after weekend family excursions to Denver or to the resort city of Colorado Springs near Pikes Peak. There were, in addition, many through passengers being carried for the Missouri Pacific's run from Pueblo east. It was for these that two Pullman cars and a diner were hooked to the end of the train. These three would be the only cars which survived, air brakes leaving them perched on the brink as the rest of the train plunged off into flooded Hogan's Gulch.

No. 11 had made up in Denver earlier in the afternoon, pulling out of that station at 5 P.M. for the 116-mile trip south to Pueblo, where it was due at 8:15 P.M. to make connections with the Missouri Pacific. A light rain was

The crowd at the wreck. This photograph, also credited to Deane, most surely was taken by an assistant; by this time Deane had been taken away for treatment.

falling in Colorado Springs when the train pulled in two hours later to take on an unusually heavy run of passengers. Many had been to the resort city for a final pleasant outing before summer gave way to chilly fall.

Engineer Henry Hinman was given a note advising him of heavy rain to the south and warning him to be watchful. Knowing how treacherous these heavy mountain rains could be, turning dry arroyos and lazy creeks into roaring torrents, Hinman slowed as he approached each bridge and trestle. He was about fifteen minutes behind schedule as he neared Bridge 110-B spanning a normally insignificant little arroyo named for the man who owned the land.

Hinman could not see in the darkness that the gulch at this moment was running bank full, that it had swept away a wooden bridge which spanned the county road just west of the railroad, and that the debris had slammed hard against the wooden pile railroad bridge, badly weakening it. This county road crossing had stopped Walter Hart's buggy horse, causing the Harts to turn around just before they witnessed the awesome thing that was to happen.

Hinman cautiously eased into the downgrade that led to the bridge. Fireman David C. Mayfield testified later that the train was moving only fifteen to twenty miles an hour, and that the headlight of the engine revealed no sign of trouble on the 32 foot bridge, no sign of the water lapping just beneath the tracks.

But as engine and tender went upon the bridge, their 150 tons began to move the weakened timbers beneath. Feeling the sway, Hinman pushed on the throttle, trying to get up speed to reach solid ground on the far side. It was the last voluntary move he made.

The locomotive began to roll backward as the bridge collapsed. Fireman Mayfield had time only to leap out the cab window, putting himself in the hands of God. For a second the headlight seemed to be shining straight up, then the locomotive plunged into the rolling waters. One by one, the tender and three trailing cars rolled out over the brink, seemed to pause a moment, then each in turn went into the maelstrom, hurling screaming passengers to almost instant death.

Automatic air brakes saved the last three cars. A Pullman was stopped with its forward end hanging out over the precipice. Almost the only survivors of an estimated 162 people on the train were those in the two Pullmans and the dining car, which trailed at the end; it was to have been left in Pueblo.

Fireman Mayfield landed in a shallow ditch when he leaped from the falling cab. There, in horror, he half-heard, half-saw the cars follow the engine into the roaring water. He called for the engineer, but Hinman never heard him. Crawling, stumbling, scrambling in the water and mud, Mayfield managed to get up out of the arroyo. He could see nothing in the blackness, and heard nothing but the surging torrent. Stumbling, walking, running, he made his way downtrack toward the station at Eden. Partway there he met a railroad employee walking the tracks, checking for possible rain damage. From a distance the track walker had seen the headlight of the train, then had seen it wink out. He did not know what had happened; he only knew that the train should have passed him long before he came upon the injured, exhausted fireman.

The fireman's report, tapped out from the little station at Eden, was the first word to the outside world.

By first light on Monday morning, hundreds of people had gathered on the banks of the arroyo, ready to start rescue operations as soon as they could see. What they saw chilled them to the marrow.

In the bed of the arroyo, revealed by the receding waters, lay the smashed engine. The chair car and the smoker and baggage car with their cargo of drowned or drowning humanity had been carried downstream, smashing to pieces against first one bank of the arroyo and then the other, the hulks coming to rest finally at the confluence of Hogan's Gulch with much-larger Fountain Creek more than four hundred yards beyond the collapsed bridge. Wreckage was strewn along the arroyo's banks all the way from the point of the plunge to as far as spectators could see, to Fountain Creek and beyond. The first bodies were found almost as soon as the sun came up. Among them was that of engineer Hinman.

The Pueblo *Chieftain* published an extra that morning, its headline proclaiming: NEARLY ONE HUNDRED LIVES LOST IN MISSOURI PACIFIC TRAIN WRECK AT EDEN. Even at that early hour, the estimate was amazingly close. In the end the official death toll was given as ninety-six, not counting one injured survivor, Tony Fisher, who lingered nearly a month and finally died. Only two other men besides Mayfield and Fisher were known to have crawled out of the arroyo alive.

The official death count was never considered totally accurate because no one knew exactly how many people had been on the train. The chair coach had been so full that passengers were standing in the aisles. The conductor who had the figures was among the dead, and his records were destroyed. The actual toll could easily have been more than a hundred. Bodies were swept by Fountain Creek into the Arkansas River and a few were known to have drifted as far as Fowler, Colorado. How many lay forever entombed in the sands could never be known.

One bizarre postscript: long after the tragedy, a farmer living downriver found the body of a wealthy Massachusetts man known to be among the missing. He held the body, refusing to give it up without first receiving a cash reward from the family. Enraged local citizens promised him a much different type of reward, possibly a fatal one. He backed down.

Battered old Engine 1009 was lifted out of the mud, rebuilt and kept in service on the D&RG for thirty-two more years before finally being consigned for scrap.

Disaster continued to stalk the Denver & Rio Grande. Just a month after the Eden wreck, a freight broke in two and killed a brakeman near Marshall Pass. In October, a head-on collision between a passenger and a freight killed a fireman and injured sixteen people near Portland.

Then, on March 16, 1906, a telegraph operator dozed during a snowstorm, failing to give a new set of orders to a passing passenger train. The result was a head-on collision 30 miles from Royal Gorge that killed thirty-five people. Many of the injured were trapped in the wreckage and burned to death by a fire that raged through the smashed trains.

A large percentage of the dead were homeseekers, some of them newly-arrived immigrants, on their way to hunt for farming lands. A large family was wiped out except for two sons. One of these, lying in a hospital, said he had had a nightmare a few months earlier and clearly saw the death of his whole family in a train wreck.

The telegraph operator, who took all the blame on his own shoulders, said a work overload had kept him at his post for three straight days and nights, and he had been asleep when he was supposed to be out stopping a passenger train that was running an hour-and-a-half late.

15

The Western Railroads Today

DONALD DUKE

Of all the forms of surface transportation which have been developed during man's westward march across the United States, the one which has contributed most to the spread of civilization in the American West is the railroad.

Today historians and scholars of the American West consider railroads to be hopelessly out of date and near death. They place the nail in the lid of the coffin on account of the decline of the passenger train which has been precipitous in recent years, and by the bankruptcy of the giant Penn Central system which has been blasted in the press. Too many, it would seem, take the railroad for granted. It has been about for more than a century and is now getting kicked around by the government, the public and the press. Little do the critics realize the important part which the railway plays today in our everyday lives. The railroad carries the bulk of the materials which go into the production of our homes, the furniture and furnishings, the bulk of the fruit and vegetables on the table, nearly all our processed meat, the clothing we wear, and even the cars we drive. While the western railroads might look dead to some people, they are alive and still kicking up a storm. They are modern, efficient, and turn a profit for their investors.

Once upon a time they called freight trains "drags." In railroad terms this meant a train that left one terminal and reached the end of the line when it got there. Some might call this a slow freight. Not any more! Today freight

Santa Fe's Super C *is literally the fastest freight train in the world, making a daily 2,200-mile run between Chicago and Los Angeles in less than 40 hours. It was introduced in 1968 as an all piggyback and container train.* Santa Fe Railway Collection

trains whip along and the fastest of them all—Santa Fe's *Super C*—clicks off the 2,200 miles between Chicago and Los Angeles daily in less than 40 hours. That is just one half hour slower than the *Super Chief*. When you count the cars on this super train, just think how many trucks this one train takes off our overcrowded highways. Aggressive "can-do" railroading like this is of the very essence of western railroading.

Here is a perfect case in point. In Los Angeles, California, a truck-trailer loaded with electronic and aircraft parts rolls into Hobart Yard of the Santa Fe and is rolled aboard a special flat car. This flat will be coupled to the road's *Super C* which is a strictly trailer-and-container train, and it's the hottest thing on western rails. Carrying top running priority over any train on the system, even the *Super Chief,* and its developing new high-rated traffic which used to travel by air freight.

For this run to Chicago, all the complex technology of a modern rail system is brought to bear on that one car. It is pulled by three diesel locomotives with a combined strength of 10,800 horsepower; it is stopped by air brakes three times that powerful; it is whisked around slower trains in the wake of oncoming trains; and its car manifest is known at the other end of the line practically before the train leaves Hobart Yard for Chicago by the use of microwave communication. The entire cost of the journey; less than half the cost of air freight, and nearly twice as fast as direct truck dispatch, and the service is door-to-door. You say the western railroads are dead—hardly!

Much of the technology which makes this trip possible has been in existence for a long time, but not quite so refined. Automatic signals came into wide use before the turn of the century and gradually improved until now one man can control the main line of a railroad division by means of electronics, even at a hundred miles distance. Trains are no longer dispatched by the telegraph to some way station and hooped up to the onrushing train, but are sent by radio direct to the train's engineer and conductor. Computers are now employed to shuttle cars from one train to another; and some railroad men foresee fully automated trains pulled by crewless locomotives.

The story of modern western railroads really begins as World War II ends, as the motive power controversy so abruptly shelved by the needs of war starts to blossom anew. What form of motive power was there to be? First off, just what kind of railroads were there to be as a nation worked its way back to prosperity?

The names of the western railroads were just as big as before the war. There was the Santa Fe Railway, the Union Pacific Railroad, the Southern Pacific Company, the Great Northern Railway, the Northern Pacific Railway, the Denver & Rio Grande Western Railroad, the Western Pacific Railroad, and the Chicago, Burlington & Quincy Railway to name but a few of the giants. The names hadn't changed, and the lines went to the same places as before the war. Tehachapi Loop, Weber Canyon, the mighty Sierra grade, the Mojave Desert, Stevens Pass and a host of other western landmarks associated with the lore of the railroad didn't look much different as the war years passed. The only change was the look of the trains rolling by, even if ever so slowly.

The most notable change for western railroads was the transformation from steam to diesel motive power. The diesel's quick decisive defeat of steam led many to believe that the transition was inevitable, that the western railroad industry was waiting with open arms to embrace a new source of motive power. The period of transition, though brief, was fraught with drama as first the gasoline rail car and then the diesel-electric locomotive ran head-on into a variety of obstacles ranging from engineering problems to prejudice.

A substantial number of very modern steam locomotives had been delivered just prior to and during the war, and there was a considerable body of opinion within the industry that had by no means accepted the invincibility of the diesel-electric. Steam motive power in the West were big, unique, and different. Motive power rosters of western lines carried just about every type of wheel classification which rode American rails. The Union Pacific had twenty-four of the largest steam locomotives in the world. These giant 4-8-8-4 type Mallet locomotives, known to rail buffs and railroaders as "Big Boy," weighed 340 tons and could pull a freight train nearly two miles long with ease. How does a diesel salesman tell a railroad like the Union Pacific it should switch to diesels with power like that? Especially when the UP owned coal mines all along the line.

Although the diesel-electric played an increasingly significant part in the modernization of rail passenger service after the Burlington's epochal *Zephyr* in 1934, its role was a marginal one until the start of the war. The Santa Fe and Southern Pacific were looking for a new type of motive power. For years these roads were plagued with water problems on their desert lines. While there was water, it was full of alkali and hard on boilers, and firemen fought to keep up steam. The diesel-electric was a welcome sight to these two western carriers and saved the lines during the war. By war's end, the major diesel builders were producing a flood of mass-produced diesel machines and on a production line basis like automobiles. The lure to change worn out steamers for bright and shiny diesel locomotives was challenging to say the

It was the western railroads that led the nation with streamline passenger trains. The Burlington's Pioneer Zephyr *was America's first diesel-powered streamlined train.* Donald Duke Collection

least. By the end of the 1950s, most of the steam locomotives had vanished as the prime means of motive power on western railroads.

To the legion of railroad buffs and historians, the diesel-electric locomotive was an intruder, an icon-smashing, prosaic machine that drove the old Iron Horse to pasture. Sans smoke, side rods that clanked and high spinning driving wheels, the round-nose diesel looked more like a tomato bug on wheels than a locomotive. It further offended the cult by the lack of a mellow and beautiful whistle.

There was just something about a steam locomotive that warmed the heart of every man. Perhaps it was the suggestion of latent power which it signified. The steam locomotive and that whistle just sounded like what a railroad was supposed to be. With the passing of steam few stopped at the crossing any longer to watch the trains roll by. The train watcher's heart had been broken by the throb of motors and the blat of a horn. Only the clickity-clack of the rails remained to remind one of the love of railroading.

One of the outstanding developments of western railroading was the coming of the streamliner. While the first successful trains were introduced in 1934, the change from Pullman green to stainless steel came quickly in the West. All western carriers introduced new service like the *Super Chief* on the Santa Fe Railway, the *City of Los Angeles* on the Union Pacific, and the *Daylight* trains on the Southern Pacific, to name just a few. This was the time when one took the passenger train because it was the most comfortable, convenient, and rapid mode of long-distance travel, other than the family automobile. In many towns it was the only mode of public transportation, and it sort of enjoyed the status of an institution.

Railroad passenger travel began to decline much earlier than most historians tell you in books, or the outpourings of newspaper features on the death of the railroad. It began to decline when Henry Ford started to produce his famous Model-T Ford on an assembly line basis. While travel by train was still heavy, and the luxury way to go, America slowly became a nation of individuals going here and there at his own pace instead of by timetable.

Streamliners were designed and built to reduce air pressure or wind resistance as much as possible, and this together with lightweight materials, permitted greater speeds with a given amount of power. Streamliners caught on fast. Passenger train revenues really came from the businesssman who favored first class service in the Pullmans. By this means he could travel, eat well, and sleep en route. He could have his breakfast and arrive at a meeting refreshed. Things were looking up when World War II rolled around and every piece of railroad motive power and rolling stock was pressed into service. The western railroads were well equipped after the depression and held on better during the long conflict.

At war's end, the streamliner with first class service was placed back on the track. All western railroads spent millions for new coaches, dining cars, Pullmans, and lounge cars. It was a race to see who could provide the most luxurious equipment, schedule, and service. The railroads in the West were ready for the influx of tourists who longed for a vacation, and the businessman who wished a compartment instead of the upper berth he was accustomed to during the war. Many new trains were placed in service between California, Oregon and Washington points to Chicago and the Midwest. Such trains as the *California Zephyr* of the Western Pacific-Rio Grande-Burlington, the *Empire Builder* of the Great Northern Railway, and the *North Coast Limited* of the Northern Pacific. The Southern Pacific introduced a new *Sunset Limited* to New Orleans and the *Golden State* between Los Angeles and Chicago as a joint operation with the Rock Island. Things looked bright and patronage picked up at a rapid pace.

As these new streamliners sailed across the country there came a loud noise in the sky. It was a huge winged bird with four motors and seats. This giant of the air could whisk a businessman from New York to Chicago in two and one-half hours, or fly him from Los Angeles to New York in ten. When flying a businessman could take care of his affairs in a single day and return home for dinner, or finish his transactions in New York before his train had a chance to get to Kansas City. This prime traffic left the rails in droves and the trains ran half empty for lack of customers.

America's inter-city passenger trains were rapidly vanishing from the rails. If the trend continued, they could become a relic like the stagecoach and the luxury ocean liner—a victim of transportation progress. Various "Super Trains" were tried out and while experiments, they did lure some back to the rails, but it was a lost cause. In certain high density regions new modern trains worked, but the traveling public was now time and speed conscious. There was no time to relax and enjoy a good dinner as the countryside flashed by. Only the retired had time for a luxury land cruise.

With the introduction of Amtrak on May 2, 1971, the rail passenger business in the United States passed into the hands of a government agency. In time trains were upgraded and in the years of operation since most trains have been made to pay their way and there is light at the end of the tunnel. Only time will tell.

Freight remains the lifeblood of the modern western railroad. To meet the challenge of trucking, a new generation of huge freight cars have gone into service, with many especially tailored for a particular shipment. These giants are both transforming the western rail fleet and helping make lower freight rates possible for heavy shippers. The new cars include not only long flatcars hauling two truck trailers apiece and rack cars hauling fifteen new automobiles, but also whale-shaped new tank cars, house-sized box cars for auto and aircraft parts, and huge hoppers carrying 100 tons and more of grain, flour or sugar in one load.

The freight train of today is no longer just a string of box cars, but an array of specialized modern freight haulers equipped with rolled bearings on the wheels and better springing to give goods a ride like a feather. Most of the western rail fleet of cars have cushion-type underframes or what a railroad man calls "draft gears" for easier couplings, and damage free freight on arrival at its destination. In reflecting the size escalation, the average capacity of a new freight unit is nearly 80 tons—40 percent greater than a freight car at the end of World War II.

The fastest growing rail service in the West is the trailer-on-flatcar or better known as "Piggyback" service. Here trains of specially equipped flatcars are used to transport the highway trailers on fast schedules between large cities

This giant "Piggybacker" was developed by Southern Pacific to reach a truck trailer or container quickly at any part of the train. This mobile vehicle takes only 90 seconds to load or unload a 45-ton trailer. Southern Pacific Collection

in the West. Only a few minutes are required to load a trailer onto a flatcar and anchor it securely. When the flatcar arrives at its destination, the trailer is unloaded and hauled away to complete the journey. Piggybacking is faster, cheaper, and more efficient than direct highway transport. Also this service removes heavy tractor trailers from the public roads.

The refrigerator car has completely changed in the last twenty years. Huge blocks of ice have been replaced with a refrigeration system on each car that provides zero temperatures, and without servicing the whole trip. Fresh vegetables, dairy products, meats, fish, and other foods can be shipped and reach the markets garden fresh. Long trains of California citrus, Washington State apples, and Idaho potatoes move to market in blocks of refrigerator trains during the year.

Another recent innovation of western railroads is the unit train, a highly efficient means of moving great tonnages between two points at sharply reduced rates. Unit trains are used chiefly for transporting coal, ore, grain and livestock, but are adaptable to almost any bulk commodity. Long unit trains

A unit train, featuring solid trainloads of a single commodity between designated points. Santa Fe daily operates a unit train between New Mexico coal mines and Kaiser Steel in Southern California. Santa Fe Railway Collection

The "Vert-a-Pac" car is a Southern Pacific innovation that carries thirty compact cars fully enclosed by hanging them nose down from side walls which double as ramps: by this means cars arrive at the destination damage free. Southern Pacific Collection

carry coal from Utah and New Mexico mines to Fontana, California, and the furnaces of the Kaiser Steel Company on the rails of the Union Pacific and Santa Fe respectively. From California's Eagle Mountain region comes long unit trains of iron ore bound for the same destination. Empty unit trains rush back for reloading. Such trains, operating between origin and destination without going through freight yards, reduce the delivery time and cost of shipment.

Ocean shipping which used to operate via the Panama Canal is now placed in containers and transported from California ports to New York via a railroad land bridge. Almost every day the Santa Fe carries a full shipload of container freight from San Francisco-Oakland and Los Angeles-Long Beach ports to Chicago and then on to New York for transshipment to Europe. Such travel saves more than two weeks travel time by ship. In other cases frequent sailings are co-ordinated with frequent rail freight schedules, adding up to the fastest way to import and export.

A dramatic railroad success story is the expanded use of huge bi-level and tri-level frame type cars, capable of hauling twelve to fifteen automobiles

A Union Pacific employee can reach anyone anywhere on the railroad speaking over microwave radio. This microwave dish is just one antenna in a 3,400-mile network. Union Pacific Railroad Photo

or trucks. These new cars have replaced the laborious methods of loading four automobiles in a closed box car resulting in faster handling at far lower costs. Today, more than 50 percent of the automobiles sold on the West Coast have traveled from Detroit aboard one of the auto-rack trains and it takes more than nine hundred trucks off the highways each month.

The western railroads have moved into the electronic age just like any other forward looking industry. Sophisticated information gathering and processing equipment has transformed railroad operations, with electronic computers pointing the way toward both more dependable service for customers, but more efficient use of all rail facilities. These electronic gadgets keep track of freight cars, program switching moves in the yards and assist the gathering of freight trains in half the time, and deploy motive power. These machines can also locate a freight car on the line in a matter of minutes and advise an inquiring traffic manager when he will receive his car of freight.

Western railroad technology has advanced just as rapidly in the field of communications. Microwave and radio communications not only pass along general information, but data on train consists, the volume of traffic, etc. Radio communication between train dispatcher and the locomotive engineer in the cab, and the conductor in the caboose has replaced the familiar old

Tomorrow's railroad is here today at Southern Pacific's West Colton Yard, 50 miles east of downtown Los Angeles. One man in a tower above the "hump" controls 93 miles of track with a capacity for 6,800 cars in 24-group tracks. Southern Pacific Collection

station telegraph. Closely related signal improvements keep the trains rolling all the time instead of waiting on sidings to let a train pass. This was brought about by the utilization of Centralized Traffic Control. This system is almost like running an entire model railroad from one location. The only difference is the CTC operator is running an entire railroad division or hundreds of miles of railroad from a panel in front of him. Trains are simulated by moving lights on a giant board and every stretch of rail and switch is shown, as well as the color of the signal in front of an oncoming train. The operator can open and close switches, change the color indication on the signals, and make contact direct with the engineer or conductor of a train with the flick of a finger. CTC has so improved the operating efficiency of the railroad that it has boosted the capacity of a single track main line to that of double track and saved the railroads millions of dollars in track maintenance.

Railroading in the West has continued without interruption since the driving of the Golden Spike at Promontory, Utah, on that clear day in May 1869. The story of western railroads is not only filled with romance, adventure, and great achievement, but remains first class in operation, modern in physical plant, and headed by highly efficient management teams.

Index

Page numbers in *italics* refer to illustrations.